SLE

1

Roots
of Tragedy

ROOTS
OF TRAGEDY

*The United States and the
Struggle for Asia, 1945 – 1953*

LISLE A. ROSE

Contributions in American History, Number 48

GREENWOOD PRESS
WESTPORT, CONNECTICUT • LONDON, ENGLAND

Library of Congress Cataloging in Publication Data

Rose, Lisle Abbott, 1936-
    Roots of tragedy.

    (Contributions in American history ; no. 48)
    Bibliography: p.
    Includes index.
    1. United States—Foreign relations—Asia.
2. Asia—Foreign relations—United States.   I.   Title.
DS33.4.U6R65   327.73'05   75-35354
ISBN 0-8371-8592-0

Library of Congress Catalog Card Number: 75-35354
ISBN: 0-8371-8592-0

First published in 1976

Greenwood Press, a division of Williamhouse-Regency Inc.
51 Riverside Avenue, Westport, Connecticut 06880

Printed in the United States of America

In memory of Charles Crooks
of Deep Gap Farm
who graced many lives with
his friendship

Contents

Preface

The reader deserves some warning about the limits of this inquiry. I have not tried to write a history of what I term the great revolt against Western imperialism in early postwar Asia. I possess neither the linguistic nor professional competence for such a task, which in any case is sufficiently vast as to require many volumes over many years. Nor have I attempted a panoramic and detailed history of U.S. relations with the emerging nations of the Far East during the eight tumultuous years following the close of World War II. What I have attempted is a study of America's response to Asia's rebellion against Western domination in order to determine as best I can why that response was so tragically inappropriate. I have, then, written an American, not an Asian, history and one sharply limited in scope and scale. But I hope that students of the Asian scene as well as an increasingly aware and informed general public may find some value and profit in my discoveries.

A number of people have given generously of their time and talents in the shaping of this study. Richardson Dougall and John Glennon of the Historical Office, Department of State, read all or parts of the emerging manuscript as did Professors Robert Ferrell of Indiana University and Lawrence Kaplan of Kent State University, both long-valued friends and critics. If we did not always reach a meeting of the minds, my knowledge of diplomacy, the diplomatic process, and the development of America's Asian policy was greatly enhanced by their many helpful comments and suggestions. Professor Jon Wakelyn of Catholic University expressed gratifying interest in the work, and his unflagging support of an often demanding author throughout the period of writing and publication is deeply appreciated. My mother, Mildred Rose, also read the manuscript with the expertise of long years as a professional editor and saved me from a number of stylistic gaucheries. My wife, Maribeth, again assumed the major burden of typing and of editorial criticism. Without her considerable efforts the manuscript would never have been completed. Of course, I alone am responsible for errors of fact and interpretation.

LISLE A. ROSE
Falls Church, Virginia
Christmas 1975

chapter **1**

The Great Revolt

In late summer the long war ended in two blinding flashes of light and death over Japan, and then the great revolt began. It erupted in half a dozen different spots and flowed all across the plains and mountains, plateaus and rice paddies, villages and cities and jungles of Asia. By mid-autumn 1945, just three months after Hiroshima, British rule in India was being increasingly challenged, a strong, active nationalist movement was afoot in Burma, Indonesia was convulsed by civil violence, French rule over Indochina was being contested by a vibrant native movement, civil war was raging in China, and a plethora of native parties was increasingly restive under Soviet-American occupation in Korea.[1]

The sources of the great revolt were as numerous and varied as the human experience itself. There was Asia's widespread and long-standing misery, her poverty, frequent famines, and ever-present filth and disease. There was the century-old presence of the white man with his awesome privileges, his power, his wealth, his isolation from the native life around him, his grating and incessant sense and expression of racial superiority, his often gross insensitivity to the splendor and ineffable delicacy of the cultures surrounding him. There were the threats posed to native society and personal esteem in the spread of European political, economic, and cultural imperialism with its many disruptive—and for the educated handful amongst Asia's millions, alluring—influences. There were the frequent collisions of personality and temperament between the often arrogant and crass representatives of Western technology and religion and the indigenous populations of the East with their own ancient, proud, and sensitive traditions and life-styles. There was the attraction of European ideologies —nationalism, socialism, democracy, and communism—the latter peculiarly attractive to many Asian minds because it was a product of modern Western thought and yet a rejection of the exploitative, primitive, capitalistic culture from which it had sprung. Surely, too, a profound sense of personal and collective destiny animated those Asians who sought, as World War II came to a close, to free themselves and their people from imperial domination.

But, above all, there had been the powerful example of Japan, herself an Asian nation and race which had remained politically free while successfully incorporating Western industrial and military technology into an indigenous culture and had then competed successfully with the Atlantic powers for a place among the great nations of the earth. Widely feared as she was throughout much of Asia for her own predatory ways, Japan had found as early as the late 1930s that her call for a Greater East Asia Co-Prosperity Sphere that would liquidate European imperialism and reserve Asia for the Asians had acquired magnetic appeal, particularly in light of the confused and chaotic situation in China, where both the democratic and communistic dogmas of the West had evidently failed to take firm hold.[2]

World War II strengthened the appeal of the greater Asian message even as it discredited and destroyed its chief messenger. Deeply hated as Japan became for her barbarous behavior in China and her often brutal, if ephemeral, rule over wide areas of East Asia and Oceania, she nonetheless revealed to millions of Asians once and for all the essential humanity—in all its weakness and corruptability as well as nobility and strength—of the Western master. For it was Asian bayonets in the hands of Japanese soldiers that routed Westerners out of their comfortable enclaves of power and privilege all over the Far East. Englishmen were flushed from the Raffles Bar in Singapore, Americans from the Army and Navy Club in Manila, Dutchmen from their spacious plantation homes in Java and Sumatra. Amused condescension in many Western circles in Asia that the "Nips" would dare to challenge European imperialism—even while Europe itself was engaged in a ferocious civil war—swiftly turned to shocked disbelief as the Japanese tide engulfed one Western outpost after another in the gloomy early months of 1942. When at last the forlorn Western garrisons in Malaya and Hong Kong, Java and the Philippines fell, and their proud defenders began long marches to years of squalid and degrading captivity, many a Westerner shared the sense of outrage expressed by one roughed-up journalist who cried out to his Asian captors: "*You can't do this to me, I'm an American.*"

But it was all true. And by the time the first Tommies were at last able to heed Kipling's old cry to the British soldier to return to Mandalay and the Americans has reconquered the Philippines and had moved on to swarm over the island gateways to Japan, the old Asian world, like that of Europe which it had served for so long, was gone forever. Too many thousands of Asians had been recent witnesses to the humiliation of their former colonial masters to sink back into apathetic bondage. They thirsted to seize and shape their people's destinies, unburdened by any traditional influences and restraints. "The emancipation of Asia and the categorical denial of the right of one people to dominate another," an Indian writer said in 1944, "are vital to the maintenance of lasting peace."

In their implacability many of Asia's revolutionary leaders were all too willing to employ in the name of a new humanity and nationalism the most heartless and ancient methods of despotic coercion. For they had been bred in a bitter school. Their shared experiences in hardship and endurance were truly remarkable. They had all led lives of harassment and hope, comradeship and betrayal, idealism and imprisonment. Some, like Mao Tse-tung and his fellow Chinese Communists, had fought and marched for months on end through remote western provinces of China, never knowing whether the next day might not be their last; some, like the Indonesian nationalist, Sajhrir, had been exiled to the fetid, disease-ridden jungles of New Guinea; some, like the wispy little Annamese Communist, Ho Chi Minh, had wandered the earth for years as frustrated revolutionaries and watchful observers from abroad of the mounting trials of colonialism in their homeland; some, like Syngman Rhee, had led long lives of precarious fortune on the fringes of power in a foreign land, wasting the best and most productive years of their lives pleading vainly for support from unsympathetic and disinterested officials. They had—all of them—endured. The cost to good will and restraint, compassion and decency, would only become clear once they had attained the cherished goal of power. All that was certain as World War II drew to a close was that their opportunities had never seemed as bright.[3]

But at Whitehall in London, at the Quai d'Orsay in Paris, and at The Hague in Holland, the masters of a shaken and impoverished European colonialism were as determined to restore the old order in the Far East as their Asian opponents were to destroy it.

As early as March 1945 the State Department was uneasily aware of the rekindled imperialistic ambitions of the British. A memorandum prepared in the Office of British Commonwealth and North European Affairs gloomily pointed out "that British policy toward the problem of dependent territories has so hardened in the past three years that there is little prospect of British agreement to substantial modifications of the prewar *status quo* in colonial areas."[4] As for China, British reaction to American efforts to project the Kuomintang government of Chiang Kai-shek as *the* major political force in postwar East Asia bordered on outright contempt. At the Cairo Conference of 1943 and again at Yalta in February 1945 Churchill simply washed his hands of any involvement in matters relating to postwar China, including the Soviet-American agreement at the Crimea, which reintroduced Russian power and influence into key areas in north Asia in return for promised Soviet entry into the Pacific war. The British acquiesced in the arrangements concluded by Roosevelt and Stalin, but had nothing to do with the negotiations that led to them.[5] The reconstruction of European colonialism in the borderlands of China, not the revival of China as the great Asian power, was what preoccupied the policy makers of Whitehall throughout 1945.

The Gaullists of France were no less determined than their British counterparts to restore European rule to Asia. During the spring of 1945 France had suffered two humiliating setbacks as she sought to restore her power and prestige in the Middle East and tried to expand her southeasternmost borders at the expense of her recent Italian enemy. Both efforts were blunted: by the British in Syria and Lebanon with tacit backing from Washington; and by the Americans themselves in regard to the disputed Val d'Aosta frontier region in the ancient Savoyard between Italy and France.[6]

By late summer, however, the ever-resilient de Gaulle had recovered both pride and audacity. On August 1 he ordered General Beynet in Beirut to "stand firm" in the face of further possible British gestures. The Churchill government was gone now and "socialist" foreign policy promised to be more "flexible." Moreover, France was now a member of the five-power Council of Foreign Ministers established at Potsdam to conclude peace treaties in Europe. This, de Gaulle told his military chief in Lebanon, "will give us means of maneuvering the affairs of the East in general." With a bit of luck, great skill, and unremitting tenacity, France might yet regain her place among the nation states. "On the world level," the general modestly informed the Paris correspondent of the *Times* of London in early September, "Britain and France are the two major powers who act as the guides of nations whom they lead on the path of material development, political maturity, and civilization generally.''[7] Holding such attitudes as these, there was no possibility that de Gaulle would peacefully acquiesce in the dismemberment of the French empire in Asia by a ragged horde of unknown Tonkinese revolutionaries.

So the future of Asia hung in the balance as the great Pacific war came to a close in August 1945. But there was one nation in the world whose unimpaired power and enhanced prestige might well tip the Asian balance decisively toward revolution or reaction. This was the United States.

All across the land, physically untouched by the just-concluded holocaust, happy hordes celebrated the end of the war that August with as much enthusiasm and relief as any Asian or European. And yet sensitive observers noted an underlying grimness to the festivities not unlike the mood of the high war years. People seemed as utterly determined to be gay as they had earlier been to make war.[8] Millions sensed that the world had been horribly wounded—that victors and vanquished alike had contrived over the past six years to make a wasteland and had then agreed at last to call it peace. America, to be sure, stood at the pinnacle of world power, economically predominant, militarily omnipotent, politically supreme. It seemed to some that with the atomic bomb in her possession and her vast industrial plant intact and capable of unlimited production, the United States could—and should—shape the postwar world as it wished.[9]

Yet the task would be immense and immensely complex, and millions of Americans were weary of immense tasks with their attendant sacrifices, fatigue, and discipline. So power blended with anxiety and also with a dreadful naiveté concerning Asia, which was the product of three centuries of self-imposed and proud isolationism. Prior to 1941 the great bulk of Americans had not wanted to know much about the world around them, and they had quite naturally developed a cluster of symbols and myths about Europe and Asia that were compounded of an equal mixture of fear and ignorance. Europe was neatly bisected by the evils of dictatorship and follies of the imperial democracies. Asia's millions were untutored and uncivilized; but for several decades a great, romantic hope had existed in countless American hearts that with good will, religion, education, technology, and trade, at least some of these millions could in some significant measure be evangelized, democratized, Americanized. Asia's multitudes—excluding the predatory Japanese, of course—might in time become good neighbors providing good markets, thus participating to a degree in the great forward progress of mankind toward some dim goal of earthly good. Now at the close of World War II, partly by default, America held the power and seemingly bore the responsibility to fulfill her vague and generous aspirations for a better world.

But what kind of world should it be? Should the old prewar order—purged of its Nazi and Samurai elements—be restored? And if so, in what measure and to what degree? In restoring the vitality of democracy in Britain and France should the imperial systems upon which much of that democracy rested also be restored? And how should the newly won power of Soviet Russia, which had been obtained at terrible cost and suffering, be treated in both Europe and Asia? How far and in what fashion should America project her own power onto the Eurasian land mass? To what extent should the revolutionary ferment so clearly emerging in Asia be permitted to shape the immediate course of international politics? These questions had preoccupied and perplexed American policy and public opinion makers throughout World War II. They had not been resolved at the moment when the atomic bombs and the Soviet entry into the war against Japan wrote an abrupt and dramatic finish to battle.

America's approach to prewar Asia had been compounded of disinterest, vibrant idealism, and often heartless cupidity. Vast areas of the Far East had been virtually closed to American enterprise from the first: Indochina belonged to the French empire; Indonesia to the Dutch; Malaya, Singapore, and Hong Kong to the British. Traditional American antipathy to European imperialism, bred in the years before and during the American Revolution, generated the unreflective and essentially apathetic notion that the peoples of these areas suffered in colonial bondage and yearned to be "free" if they could—free to create their own systems of government basically upon the model first given the world by the thirteen revolting North American colonies in 1776. But in a world where Western imperial domination over most of Africa and Asia had become traditional, there was little disposition to contest the status quo.

China, however, was another matter. While respectable businessmen and ne'er-do-wells alike ruthlessly exploited the white man's privileges in this ostensibly sovereign land through the unequal treaty system imposed upon it by the West, and while American gunboats cruised China's rivers along with the vessels of other Western powers, the missionaries of Christianity and democracy nurtured the assumption that China's destiny was ultimately America's responsibility. China was a charge upon the American conscience. Americans thus brought to China during the last decades of the nineteenth century and the first four decades of the twentieth "a rich fare of good and evil" on a person-to-person and group-to-group basis. Some founded schools and hospitals, which served to ameliorate the degradation of daily life in a decaying social and political order. Others made use of such treaty devices as low tariffs and most-favored-nation arrangements and, above all, extraterritoriality and wittingly or unwittingly aligned themselves in the Chinese mind with those other Western "barbarians," the British and French, who had brought political and social humiliation to China in the form of the poppy seed and the opium den.[10]

The coming of World War II stimulated in countless American hearts a bewildering variety of emotions toward the Far East as well as the rest of the world. There was initial guilt that the country was not doing more to halt the spreading stain of Nazism and Japanese militarism, and this, in turn, helped to breed all sorts of romantic notions about those who were. The Russian and Chinese peoples and governments came to be viewed in many circles as incipiently or truly democratic because they were fighting the battles that American democracy refused to fight.[11] China finally became America's Poland: Here we would at last draw the line against Japan and demand in 1941 that she withdraw and admit failure in her four-year war before we would seriously consider negotiations to reduce the numerous tensions existing between the pro-Allied government in Washington and the Axis government in Tokyo.[12] And when at last American intransigence induced a sufficient sense of desperation in the minds of Japan's ruling military fanatics to send them down the road to Pearl Harbor, the easy illusion of a global crusade of good against evil was confirmed in the American mind. Now at last we were "in it" not only with the brave peoples of Britain, Russia, and China, but with all those millions in Europe and Asia who demanded freedom from foreign domination. Together we would not only win a righteous war, but make an enduring and righteous peace as well. And in the desperate yet heady days of 1942, 1943, and 1944, while the Western powers renounced their unequal treaty rights in China and the Soviet Union ostentatiously disbanded the Comintern, millions of Americans came to accept the notion that the postwar world must be new—not revolutionized, to be sure, but certainly thoroughly reformed. The prewar order could not and must not be restored. Above all, the evil of Western imperialism, which Americans convinced themselves they had embraced but faintly if at all, must be eradicated. The peoples of Europe must be spared further jealousies which the rival imperial systems had so vibrantly generated earlier in the century; the peoples of Asia must be spared further degradation which the imperial systems had continued to create throughout the century. The common man of Asia, no less than his counterparts in Europe and America, must be brought to a new day of freedom and dignity if the world was to be spared a third, and fatal, global holocaust.

Such was the facile thinking that underlay much of the wartime rhetoric and propaganda in the United States between Pearl Harbor and Hiroshima, and in a sense it was not irrelevant to the emergent mood across the Pacific. Yet Americans assumed that whatever course the reforms or even revolutions might take in postwar Asia, they would conform, specifically as well as broadly, to the contours of the American experience. Open parliamentary procedures, firm guarantees of civil rights, secret ballots, all of the paraphernalia of a true democratic order on the American model, would come eventually to all of Asia, it was hoped, and in that way, and only in that way, could the world at last be made safe for democracy. Translated into policy, these emotions seemed to bind the United States irrevocably to the Kuomintang government of China and to some kind of support for nationalist aspirations elsewhere in Asia.

By 1944, however, Asian realities began to conflict sharply with American aspirations. The result was mounting American disillusionment, especially in China. There, after seven years of war following nearly three decades of revolutionary turmoil, Chiang Kai-shek's regime seemed a shambles. Inflation was rampant, corruption was rife, daily life for the masses in Kuomintang-controlled areas was harsh and uncertain. The Nationalist capital at Chungking—persistently hot, humid, and overcast throughout the summer, its denizens waiting only the day when they could go "downriver" to Shanghai—reeked of demoralization and cynicism.[13] "To put the matter simply," one China expert would recall years later, "Pearl Harbor threw us into a formal alliance with the embattled Chinese Nationalist Government at a time when that Government had lost its vital sources of support and had become essentially one faction among several."[14]

Both Kuomintang and American officials in China were aware of the desperate seriousness of the government's plight by the final years of the war, but Asians and Westerners diverged sharply in their assessment of the situation and the remedies that should be applied. For Chiang and his colleagues the wisest—indeed the only—course that seemed open was to hold back the best and largest portion of their American trained and equipped army from the Japanese war and to use it to harass their domestic opponents until such time as Allied efforts elsewhere would lead to a

Japanese surrender. Then a final, victorious military showdown with the Communists would be within reach, and Kuomintang rule could at last be placed beyond challenge.

And yet the Communist enemy in the north was a frightening enigma. For nearly twenty years, ever since the great Kuomintang purge of its Communist element in 1927, Mao and his cohorts had refused to die or disappear. They had been pursued all over south and west China, penned up for a time in the farthest reaches of the northwest, and still they had endured, posing the constant threat of civil war and civil opposition to the Kuomintang throughout the 1930s and 1940s. The United Front forged against Japanese aggression in 1937 had been a sham for most of the war and everyone knew it. As early as January of 1941 Kuomintang forces attacked the rear guard of the Communist army and from then on "it was obvious the situation was deteriorating as the Communists got stronger and stronger" throughout north China, "and the effects of war, inflation, and attrition weakened the Kuomintang."[15] But while Chiang prepared to gamble all on one great postwar military stroke against the Communists, his increasingly uneasy and unhappy American allies were seeking out other solutions to the China tangle.

American wartime policy in China was based on two predominant considerations. First and foremost, Americans wanted to win the war against Japan as expeditiously and cheaply as possible. They had hoped to enlist Chinese arms and effort as a possibly decisive military factor against Japan. By 1944-1945 this hope was clearly chimerical. Washington had long since turned to Stalin and the Russians for aid in what was presumed to be the final stage of the Pacific war—an invasion of Manchuria and conflict with the Kwantung army there in tandem with a direct American assault upon Japan proper. Yet if China could in any way be propped up, even at this late date, it could only aid the final effort against Tokyo. Second, millions of Americans in the 1940s still felt an enormous emotional involvement with China. "I recall my own thinking during the forties when I wasn't in government," a U.S. senator recalled years later. "Everything we heard was connected to the traditional view of Americans toward China. There was desire to evangelize and somewhat patronize. Many people had deep feeling and affection for the Chinese, although in a somewhat patronizing way. The Chinese were conceived to be a massive group of simple people, but there was some respect for the high and rather special Chinese intellectual traditions. This view was terribly, terribly widespread. . . ." "We were in a great war," another American official was later to remember. "The American people were terribly concerned about that war. . . . Chiang Kai-shek since 1937 had been fighting more or less with the Japanese. He didn't give up." The moral pressure on the United States not to give up on Chiang was correspondingly great.[16]

The most poignant influence upon public thinking toward China in these days was thus religious and idealistic, not coldly political nor intellectual. "Churchgoing Americans—and that was most Americans—had grown up believing that of all the Lord's vineyards, China was perhaps the most beloved."[17] The idea that China could at once be both evangelized and democratized through strenuous, unremitting American effort died hard, as the poignant outcry of loss and betrayal in 1949 amply demonstrated. What has been said of the American approach to Vietnam in the 1960s— we "wanted the Vietnamese to be Americans," we "saw them in American terms"[18]—applied with equal if not greater force to China in the 1940s.

Between June and October of 1944, however, an ultimately fatal lesion appeared in America's China policy. In June, largely at the instigation of globe-trotting Vice-President Henry Wallace, Chiang reluctantly permitted a contingent of sixteen Americans to contact the Communist leaders in Yenan and to explore the possibility of reincorporating Communist elements in an all-Chinese army against Japan. This was part of an emerging policy in Washington to form a coalition government in China between Communists and Nationalists, which would ensure postwar Chinese political stability and power, yet would leave Chiang and his Kuomintang colleagues in control. At the same time Roosevelt asked Chiang to place General Joseph Stilwell in command of all Chinese armies, including those of the Communists. Here was a clear warning to the Kuomintang leader that the American government was becoming disenchanted with his leadership, with the chaos in China, and with the debilitating conflicts between Nationalist and Communist forces. For the impatient, ramrodlike Stilwell and the conspiratorial Generalissimo had come to cordially detest one another after a ceaseless two-and-one-half year contest of wills. Chiang temperized, agreeing in principle to Roosevelt's request that an American be placed in command of all Chinese armed forces, but asking that a special representative competent in military matters be sent to Chungking to discuss details. As a price for even this token acquiescence Chiang demanded and got the removal of the outspoken and energetic Stilwell, who had demanded for months that the Nationalist government either stand and fight the Japanese or, in effect, give way to some other Chinese group willing to wage a full-scale war against the invader.[19] Roosevelt, making one of the worst decisions of his life, sent out Major General Patrick J. Hurley,[20] a noisy, egotistical, and troublesome figure who had somehow managed to plant himself on the periphery of the Washington political scene during Herbert Hoover's presidency and who had remained on the fringes of power and decision making ever since. China was to be his biggest assignment. It was to end his political career on a note of total failure.

Hurley was a general in name only. He was in fact a rather typical product of the success-oriented business society and political culture of early twentieth-century America. An initially dirt poor, largely self-educated, and dangerously unsophisticated careerist in business, law, and politics, Hurley had risen out of oil-rich Oklahoma to become—after a strenuous personal lobbying effort—Secretary of War in the Hoover cabinet, and then, in the thirties, a good friend of Franklin Roosevelt. With the outbreak of war in 1941 FDR, apparently for no other compelling reason than to help an eager friend get into uniform and policy making, commissioned Hurley and sent him off on a series of personal missions, first to Australia and New Zealand, later to the oil kingdoms of the Middle East, and, finally, to China, where the Oklahoman's mission was swiftly transformed into an ambassadorship in November of 1944. A basically good, decent, charming, and physically attractive man with a dramatic white mane and mustache capping a six-feet two-inch frame, Hurley believed simply and deeply in the ideals of the Atlantic Charter, including the right of all peoples to freely choose their destiny by peaceful means. He also more than half-believed in the greatness and political legitimacy of Chiang Kai-shek. When the conflict between Communists and Nationalists at last reached a showdown in late 1944 and 1945, Hurley was unable to define unfolding events in terms of indigenous civil war, but interpreted Communist aspirations in terms of an illegitimate revolt by an alien force against duly constituted authority. Above all, Hurley proved to be too blustery and turbulent a personality. He became an essentially unstable troublemaker when events failed to move his way in the often polished, sophisticated, and brutal world of international diplomacy. It may be safely said that he never fully grasped the complexities and dimensions of his job in China. Roosevelt's decision to elevate him to the Chinese ambassadorship was an act of incredible folly.[21]

From the moment of his arrival in Chungking in October 1944 to the end of the Pacific war nearly ten months later, Hurley oscillated wildly between optimism and pessimism in his assessment of chances for a true coalition government in China. He enjoyed some tentative successes in getting Kuomintang and Communist officials together to discuss the question of political coalition, but his eye, like that of Washington, was primarily fixed upon the Soviet Union. He seemed more than half-convinced of the currently fashionable opinion that the Chinese Communists were but tools of the Kremlin. He was thus elated when visits to Moscow in the autumn of 1944 and again in the spring of 1945 yielded persistent assurances from Stalin and Molotov that in Russian eyes Mao and his hordes were at best "Oleomargarine Communists," not worthy of the name or the faith, and that the Soviet Union supported the American program for promoting Chinese political and military unity under Chiang. As late as June 1945, on his return to China from his second trip to the Kremlin, Hurley exuded confidence that he could shape and control the chaos in Chinese politics, describing himself as the best friend the Chinese Communists had in Chungking. But he was deeply disturbed by the Yalta Far Eastern Accords, which permitted Russian power and influence to reemerge along the northern borders of China in return for promised Soviet entry into the Pacific war. Stilwell's successor as American military commander in China, General Albert C. Wedemeyer, shared Hurley's unease, as did various State Department officials including Harriman and Kennan at the embassy in Moscow.[22] None of these men could ever free themselves from the conviction that Russian postwar expansion into Manchuria, Korea, and enclaves abutting north China was linked intimately to Mao's growing strength and popularity within China.

Such a view was most emphatically not held, however, by an able and spirited group of younger men within the Chungking embassy and Wedemeyer's headquarters. Understandably disillusioned with the Kuomintang and the failing American military and political effort in China, these young diplomats came to embrace their own fanciful dream of what postwar China could and should be like. Ultimate proponents of the view that China had never been America's to lose, they nonetheless gave the impression in 1944 and 1945 that she might be America's to win if only the United States would abandon its feckless support of the exhausted Kuomintang and embrace, as equal partners with Chungking, the increasingly powerful forces of Mao Tse-tung. Their writings and actions bespoke an ultimate unwillingness to see that the Chinese revolution, like the greater Asian revolution of which it was the central part, was a reaction against the whole of past experience. They refused to see that its aim was not merely to replace a corrupt and ineffective indigenous regime but also to repulse the Western powers which had sustained and supported that regime. In their own way these men were as facile in their promises of future success as were those American officials, like Hurley, whom they so bitterly opposed. A China under Mao would go its own way until every vestige of the past was obliterated or subverted, and then, only then, would it renew significant contact with the Western world in a spirit of self-esteem and with a decent sense of self-confidence. The gross injustices and indignities which those men would soon suffer because of their policy recommendations could not alter or modify this brute fact.

George Atcheson, Raymond Ludden, John Paton Davies, and John Stewart Service—the four men most determined to wrench America's China policy onto a different track in late 1944 and early 1945—were all "old China hands." Ludden and Atcheson had been born in the United States, but Atcheson had gone to China in 1920 as a twenty-four-year-old student interpreter and had remained there ever since, save for two very brief tours in the State Department in Washington. Ludden had been in China almost continually since 1932, when he had gone out as a twenty-three-year-old fledgling foreign service officer. Davies and Service had both been born in China of American parents and had spent much of their youth and nearly all of their adult lives amidst the incessant turbulence and chaos that had shaken the unhappy country to its roots ever since the fall of the Manchu Dynasty in 1911.[23] All four understood—or thought they understood—the course of recent Chinese history. All four were acutely sensitive to China's torment. All four eagerly—even desperately—searched for a way out.

Between July and October of 1944 Service, Ludden, and Davies went up to Yenan as part of the sixteen-man observer group that an uneasy Chiang had permitted to travel to the Communist stronghold. Swiftly "impressed by the dynamism of the Communist directorate," Ludden decided in October to see for himself whether the vitality and discipline of headquarters extended to the Communist-controlled hinterlands. Early in the month he and four or five other members of the American observer group left Yenan and traveled for several months by foot and mule, escorted by anywhere from fifty to nine hundred Communist regulars, depending upon how close they came to Japanese lines. On the road and in villages and towns Ludden received the same impression: the Communists had come as patriots, not revolutionaries, and they had rejuvenated the morale and rekindled the hopes of a formerly crushed and apathetic people.[24]

Back at Yenan, Service and later Davies were struck by the difference in physical and moral climate between the crude but vibrant Communist camp and Chungking. Chungking had been sultry, oppressive; Yenan was the opposite—blue sky, dry, sparkling climate, the hills like those of California, the Communist leadership eager to continue the fight against the Japanese invaders.[25] Soon Service began dispatching rather idyllic cables back to Chungking. The telegram of August 29, 1944, was typical and deserves extended quotation, not only for its intrinsic interest and the light that it sheds on Service's thinking at the time, but also because it began a great chain of unforeseen events that would decisively and disastrously influence the course not only of its author's life, but of the life and diplomacy of the nation he served.

> We are now enough acquainted with conditions in China, and sufficiently experienced in cooperation with the Kuomintang, to say that the Kuomintang—as it is today—is weak, incompetent and uncooperative.
>
> The chief concern of the politically blind and thoroughly selfish leaders of the Kuomintang is to preserve their tottering power. Lacking popular support and afraid to carry out reforms necessary to gain it, the Kuomintang knows that its miserable and dispirited conscript armies cannot stand combat against the Japanese. But its power depends, in its present narrow view, on the preservation of those armies and the equipment which it hopes we will give them. Lacking any effective economic policies, the Kuomintang is allowing the country to drift rapidly toward an economic collapse. It fears that this process will be accelerated by any large-scale military operations—by itself or by us—in China.
>
> The Kuomintang therefore fears, and seeks to avoid, the further attrition of its resources by large-scale involvement in the war. It wants to have the war won for it—outside China. It fears, second only to its fear of Russian participation, a large-scale extension of American military operations onto the Chinese mainland.
>
> The situation as far as the Chinese Communists are concerned, is just the opposite. The war has given them a chance to grow and greatly expand their influence. They have acquired real popular

support and mobilized an important part of the population of North China by convincing the people that this is their war and that they must take part in it. The fact that their aggressive participation in the war against Japan has given the Communists their chance to come to by far their greatest power is of great importance. The Communists realize that if they play a major part in winning this war they will greatly strengthen not only their domestic, but also their international position. For these, if for no other more idealistic and patriotic reasons, the Communists really want to fight.

Against this background, the following conclusions can be drawn:

(a) The limitation of our support and supplies to the Kuomintang will not win us an effective and whole-hearted ally.

(b) Instead, it will only encourage the Kuomintang in its present undemocratic tendencies. While it may help us to prolong the Kuomintang's precarious power, it is doubtful, as long as the Kuomintang refuses to reform, whether it can for long delay the inevitable internal crisis. It may even encourage its Fascist-minded leaders to embark on a civil war which could only be disastrous to China, to post-war peace in this part of the world, and to our peaceful interests here.

(c) The impartial support of both Kuomintang and Communists will make effective at least one force, the Communists, which is really interested in fighting.

(d) Such impartial support will actually be a constructive influence in China. The Kuomintang will be forced to compete not only for our support but for that of the Chinese people. We may thus help to stimulate the Kuomintang toward reform.

(e) Finally, the aid we give the Communists will almost certainly make it impossible for the Kuomintang to start a civil war. At the same time we will not likely be contributing to a Communist-provoked civil war; their policies are against civil war, the weapons they want from us (in contrast to those asked for by the Kuomintang) are light and simple rather than heavy offensive weapons, and, if the progress of the Kuomintang which our policy should promote is realized, civil war will be unnecessary.

Summing up: If the Kuomintang is actually what it claims to be—democratic and sincerely anxious to defeat the Japanese as quickly as possible—it should not oppose our insistence on giving at least proportional aid to the Communists. It is not too much to say that the strength of Kuomintang opposition will be a measure of the desirability of support of the Communists.[26]

For a time it appeared that Service was speaking the conventional wisdom on China. His friend Davies appeared in Yenan in late October, the day before Service completed his mission, and soon joined in the call for a much more active American-Communist relationship. Davies was depressed by thoughts of heightened Soviet pressures and ambitions in Northeast Asia once Russia came into the Pacific war. But unlike Hurley, Harriman, Kennan, and others, he swiftly became convinced that the Chinese Communists were not under Russia's heel. After discussions with Mao and his lieutenants, Davies drew up a report to Wedemeyer, which has apparently disappeared, proposing Chinese Communist support of a hypothetical American landing on the north China coast, which would inevitably neutralize most of whatever territorial gains the Russians might expect from an entry into the war against Japan. Davies sent the report off to Chungking on November 2 or 3, 1944.[27] Within days Hurley himself came to Yenan to negotiate some sort of Communist-Kuomintang rapprochement that would at last permit a unified China to make some significant contribution to the war effort.

It was a bad time for the Kuomintang. The great Japanese "East China offensive" had pitilessly revealed once more the military ineptitude of the Nationalist forces at a time when Allied arms were on the offensive everywhere else. Very probably Hurley was momentarily disillusioned with the Chungking regime. In the later words of John Service, which are supported by other sources not at all friendly to his perspective, Hurley

went up to Yenan in November 1944 with some terms he had worked out which were agreeable to the Nationalist Government. But when he got to Yenan the Communists convinced him those terms were quite unreasonable and that there needed to be a really broad-based government in which the Communists would have a voice, some share, and if such a government were set up then they would turn over control of their armies to that government. Hurley bought this completely and threw in a great deal of language of his own—government of the people, by the people, for the people, writ of habeas corpus, four freedoms, and so on—came back to Chungking and was astounded to find that the Generalissimo would not buy it. T. V. Soong [Chinese Foreign Minister and Chiang's brother-in-law] said: "you have been sold a bill of goods." Hurley continued to believe that the Communists were quite reasonable, but by that time he had convinced himself that he had to support Chiang Kai-shek and he was never able to get Chiang Kai-shek to be reasonable.[28]

In truth there seemed no valid reason after Yalta to concentrate America's entire effort in China on a Nationalist-Communist reconciliation and coalition. For at the Crimea Roosevelt had seemingly removed the great threat of Soviet intervention in postwar Chinese affairs once and for all. To be sure, Stalin demanded and got territorial satisfaction on the borders of China. But in return the Soviet leader reiterated his pledge to support the Kuomintang as *the* postwar government of China and promised to conclude a treaty of friendship with Chungking, embodying the Yalta Far Eastern Accords. American support of the Kuomintang thus became a matter of highest policy, intimately tied in as it now was to the Grand Alliance with Russia. Hurley's mandate to support the Kuomintang as the legitimate government of China was greatly strengthened. Hurley did not learn of the Yalta agreements until he returned to Washington in March and then he expressed shock that Roosevelt had given away so much to obtain Stalin's support for Chiang. But the ambassador never wavered in his support for the Kuomintang. Thus when Service and Davies and Ludden returned from Yenan near the end of February, they quickly discovered that Hurley remained openly hostile to any suggestion that the United States weaken its commitment to the Kuomintang. "Hurley's displeasure with what he was hearing was manifested by heckling Ludden about authorization" for his trip, "for which Ludden had orders," Davies bitterly recalled in later years.[29]

It is against this background, then, that we must view Hurley's rage when he discovered, while on leave in Washington, that his recalcitrant subordinates in Chungking were going behind his back, urging the State Department to reverse its China policy and accord Yenan at least equal status with the Kuomintang. The flashpoint of conflict was the famous Atcheson telegram of February 28, 1945.

Atcheson was Counselor of Embassy at Chungking and had assumed the post of Chargé d'Affaires on February 20 when Hurley departed for the United States. Six days later Atcheson cabled Washington that since the conclusion of the recent and fruitless negotiations between Communist and Nationalist leaders arranged by Hurley the previous November "there has been a growing impression among observers here that for various reasons the Generalissimo [Chiang] has greatly stiffened his attitude toward the Communists and toward the continuing faint hopes held by some liberals that a settlement might still eventually be possible."[30] This was followed two days later by a cable which sought, in the words of John Service, one of its drafters, "to give the Department a more full, complete and objective picture of the situation in China."[31]

The cable opened innocuously enough with the observation that "the situation in China appears to be developing in some ways that are not conducive to effective prosecution of the war, nor to China's future peace and unity." But the young foreign service officers soon warmed to their theme. If the high military authorities of the American government agreed that some cooperation with the Communists and other groups who had proved themselves willing to fight the Japanese would be necessary and desirable, "we believe that the immediate and paramount consideration of military necessity should be made the basis for a further step in American policy. The presence of General Wedemeyer in Washington as well as General Hurley should be a favorable opportunity for discussion of this matter." The "further step" which Atcheson and his cohorts sought to press on Washington officialdom was the equal military support and encouragement—and thus implicitly equal political recognition as well—of the Chinese Communists with the Kuomintang. Chiang should be privately informed that from now on Communist forces would receive equal aid, and the word would soon travel around the country. "This, we believe, would have profound and desirable political effects in China," for "there is tremendous internal pressure in China for unity based on a reasonable compromise with the Communists and a chance for the presently repressed liberal groups to express themselves." There was no question, the cable concluded, "that such a policy would be greatly welcomed by the vast majority of the Chinese people (although not by the very small reactionary minority in control of the Kuomintang) and that it would raise American prestige" because "the majority of Chinese believe that the settlement of China's internal problem is not so much a matter of mutual concessions as reform of the Kuomintang itself. They also declare, with justification, that American 'non-intervention' in China cannot help but be in fact intervention in favor of the present conservative leadership."[32]

When queried about this telegram years later, Service revealed the degree to which he and his colleagues were convinced that they could control events in China through manipulation of Chinese policies. Had their advice been taken, Service said, Chiang would have had to admit the Communists to positions of influence. ''There would have to be some form of a broader based government, whether one called it a coalition government or something else. . . . Furthermore, since we would actually be in the field with the Communists, we could police things and be in position to check movements toward civil war by either party. And it would not be necessary for us to order the Japanese to surrender only to the Nationalist government forces because the other group, the Communists, would also by this time be Nationalist government forces.''[33] In their own way Service, Atcheson, Davies, and the other young men were as blinded to the realities of China as was Hurley.

When Hurley reached Washington and learned of the Atcheson telegram, he ''hit the roof,'' and it was apparently at this moment that earlier suspicions in his suggestible mind that the young officers were seeking to subvert his mission hardened into conviction. The fact that the head of the Division of Chinese Affairs in the State Department, John Carter Vincent, was making the same kind of suggestions, made little difference save to later deepen a tragic affair.[34] From Washington's perspective Yalta had seemingly arranged postwar events in Asia as well as Europe. Russia and America were now both committed to the support of Chiang, and it would not do for refractory junior foreign service officers in the field to suggest a wrenching reversal of policy at such a late date. The suggestion in the Atcheson cable that United States support for the Chinese Communists might further serve to preclude Yenan's turning to Moscow for succor seems not to have survived Hurley's wrath. The ambassador had just told reporters during the course of a press conference ''that there could be no unification of China as long as there were armed war lords, armed gangs, or armed political parties who were strong enough to challenge the authority of the Government of the Republic of China.'' And he would later remind a Senate investigating committee that from the beginning of his mission he ''was of the opinion that lend-lease supplies, equipment, and munitions given to any organization in China other than the National Government of the Republic was weakening the Government and would bring about what I was sent to China to prevent, the collapse of the Republic of China.''[35]

The battle lines were thus drawn between an arrogant and emotional ambassador and a determined group of subordinates. When Hurley returned to Chungking, the atmosphere in the embassy quickly became charged with venom. According to one account, Hurley had already become profoundly frustrated by events, and his behavior now became explosive. He lost all control, "raging and cursing, disrupting every Embassy routine and alienating the staff to the point of complete and mutual distrust."[36] There was no question as to the outcome. As Barbara Tuchman has written, the American government was "by nature nervous of the new," and Hurley was upheld. By early summer 1945 nearly all of the young men had left or were about to leave China.[37] Hurley was permitted to continue the policy of supporting Chiang while desultorily seeking some solution for the ever-widening and ever-more-bitter division between the Chungking government and the Yenan Communists, whose suspicion of America deepened with each departure of their former champions. And as war's end neared and America's China policy became ever weaker, Hurley felt his own prestige and influence slip away. The temptation to lash out publicly at former subordinates and tormentors became increasingly difficult to resist. At this point some of the roots of a vast Asian tragedy began to appear. At the same time other roots were being laid to the south in the jungles, hills, and paddies of Indochina, where a century of French rule had been temporarily breached by the tide of Japanese conquest and was now being challenged by an indigenous movement for independence.

The relative beneficence of French rule over the ancient states of Tonkin, Annam, Cochinchina, Cambodia, and Laos has been a topic of rather warm debate in recent years, but of native resistance to French dominance there can be no doubt. In 1930 and 1931 desperate and exploited Annamese Communists staged a large and stirring revolt, which finally became "quite a large military operation" before Paris was able to suppress it. According-to one American expert, nearly all of the nationalist leaders of the uprising were killed with the exception of Ho Chi Minh, Vo Nguyen Giap, "and a few others of the Communist group," who to some undetermined degree had encouraged the uprising from their current place of exile in Hong Kong. Ten years later, during the Japanese drive into the region, another, smaller revolt occurred, which the Japanese allowed the French to put down before moving in for the kill.[38] Thereafter for nearly four years the French population of Indochina under the Decoux administration acted, in the words of one student of the region and period, "as hosts to the Japanese" while a world war raged about them all. Frenchmen officially kept the administration in operation while the Japanese invaders practically ran the country. There was nothing the French could do, but they went along in order to retain some sort of power and influence.[39] The few remaining nationalist leaders and forces dispersed. Some individuals apparently chose to lie low for a time in the villages, others waged sporadic and forlorn guerrilla warfare from mountain and jungle redoubts, still others drifted north into China and after a time made contact with the American military and intelligence units which rushed in after Pearl Harbor to aid the Kuomintang government against Japan.

Portentous decisions were meanwhile being made in the world that lay beyond Saigon and Hue and Hanoi. The fall of France in 1940 and the subsequent emergence of two competing groups claiming legitimacy as successors to the Third Republic—the German-sanctioned government at Vichy and the Free French forces in exile in London under Charles de Gaulle—immensely complicated the task of American diplomacy. For over two years after the collapse of France the American government maintained diplomatic relations with Vichy, justifying its action largely on the basis of tradition and of the value of maintaining a listening post inside occupied Europe.[40] And even after the invasion of North Africa it seemed to the perpetually weak and suspicious Free French in London that Roosevelt and Eisenhower were fatally attracted to deals with such morally and politically questionable characters as Darlan and Giraud.

In fact, FDR never liked de Gaulle personally, and while by mid-1944 he had grudgingly thrown the weight of his administration and government behind the Free French, he was determined not to support the often grandiose pretensions of their leader. Much to de Gaulle's chagrin and fury, he was not informed about the cross-Channel assault against the Normandy beaches until hours before the event. Roosevelt also kept the Gaullist government away from Yalta, informing it of the Crimean decisions only after the meetings of the Big Three had been concluded.[41] Personality conflict with the emerging leader of postwar France thus found a congenial place in Roosevelt's mind with his long-standing prejudice against European colonialism in East Asia.

By 1943 and 1944 the President was making it abundantly clear to colleagues and Allies alike that if he had his way postwar Indochina would become a trust of the United Nations, not part of a rejuvenated French empire. Roosevelt pressed home this point to the British in January of the latter year. "I saw Halifax last week," the President informed his Secretary of State,

and told him quite frankly that it was perfectly true that I had, for over a year, expressed the opinion that Indo-China should not go back to France but that it should be administered by an international trusteeship. France has had the country—thirty million inhabitants for nearly one hundred years, and the people are worse off than they were at the beginning.

As a matter of interest, I am wholeheartedly supported in this view by Generalissimo Chiang Kai-shek and by Marshal Stalin. I see no reason to play in with the British Foreign Office in this matter . . . the case of Indo-China is perfectly clear. France has milked it for one hundred years. The people of Indo-China are entitled to something better than that.[42]

The following month, in a memorandum to the White House, the State Department proposed that American diplomacy proceed on the assumption that to some extent France herself would free Indochina from Japanese rule, ''and that it would be desirable in the civil affairs administration of the country to employ French nationals having an intimate knowledge of the country.'' Back from the presidential desk came the simple and succinct order: ''No French help in Indochina—country on trusteeship.''[43] The following September the Division of Southwest Pacific Affairs— which had been newly created by the State Department to assume joint responsibility for Southeast Asia alongside the British Commonwealth and Western European bureaus—drafted several position papers for the President to take to the Second Quebec Conference with Churchill. One of these papers bluntly repeated ''persistent reports of a British desire to create a Southeast Asia federation of Burma, Malaya, Thailand, and Indochina under British aegis if not direct control.'' And the paper concluded soberly that ''All reports'' from American observers within the British-dominated Southeast Asia Command, headed by Admiral Lord Louis Mountbatten, indicated that SEAC's military operations were ''aimed primarily at the resurgence of British political and economic ascendancy in Southeast Asia and the restoration of British prestige.'' Removal of American identification with the ''restoration of British imperialism'' was imperative. The second paper urged early and total self-rule and economic independence for the peoples of all Southeast Asia in the postwar world. ''The President warmly approved the idea,'' but apparently did not press it on an obstinate Churchill, whose national resources and influence, to say nothing of personal friendship, Roosevelt continued to cherish.[44] Nonetheless the President of the United States was clearly on record by 1944 as favoring a program of positive support for and cooperation with the burgeoning nationalistic movements of Southeast Asia, including Indochina, and he enjoyed widespread, if not unanimous, support in many areas of government in Washington as well as from those officers in the field attached to the Southeast Asia Command.

Of the major regional commands established by the Allies during World War II, that of Southeast Asia—which stretched from India and Ceylon through Burma, round to Malaya, Indochina, and the Dutch East Indies—was probably the most obscure and comparatively quiescent despite the incorporation of large numbers of British troops and a handful of American, Dutch, and later, French forces. As early as the autumn of 1943 most American officers attached to SEAC had concluded that while the fearful tides of total war were sweeping the rest of the world, they had become stuck in a quiet backwater presided over by British cousins who pursued traditional imperial habits—tennis and polo in the afternoons, pink gins on the terrace at five, formal dinners at eight, and weekly dances at the Officers' Club—as if there were no tomorrow and had been no yesterday. Indeed many Yanks were becoming increasingly alarmed at mounting evidence of British—and French and Dutch—determination to restore the prewar colonial status quo throughout the region in flagrant opposition to both the ideals of the Atlantic Charter and the realities of the great revolt in Asia.

In October 1943, for example, an official of the American Office of War Information in New Delhi cabled Washington that current reports from Burma frankly admitted "that there is no point in underestimating the 'enthusiasm' created in Burma by Japan's handling of the political situation" there. The latest craze in that occupied country was "Japan's promise of independence," and as a result "the Japanese have been able to gain for themselves in Burma more 'cannon fodder' than the British were ever able to gain for themselves." Standing solidly against this ominous development was the force of imperial tradition. Conversations with British officials in New Delhi "revealed a completely imperialistic attitude in British thinking toward propaganda problems in Southeast Asia." The Americans were bluntly told that the "only effective bulwark against Southward expansion of Asiatic interests is the maintenance of British power" and that the United States should accept this fact and work for the maintenance of British power "by accepting British plans for organization in this region." If such views could be accepted as representing British consensus, the report concluded, then "we may have no illusions concerning the fundamental British policy behind their propaganda in and towards Southeast Asia regardless of whatever superficial slogans they may use.''[45]

The American response to these manifestations of reemerging European imperialism was prompt and generously idealistic. At the recently concluded First Quebec Conference, Roosevelt and Churchill had agreed to a recommendation by the Combined Chiefs of Staff that emergency committees be established to coordinate Allied war propaganda across the world. Committees were already about to function in London and Washington, and one was in process of formation at New Delhi as well. From November of 1943 to January of 1944 officials in both the State Department and the Office of War Information sought to extricate the United States from membership on the New Delhi committee. Their chief spokesman came to be former presidential speechwriter and renowned playwright, Robert E. Sherwood, then attached to the OWI. Sherwood seems to have gotten to Roosevelt some time at the end of 1943 with a memorandum urging American withdrawal, and, in the opinion of his colleagues, he always enjoyed "easy access to the President and should be able to choose a suitable time to talk to the President about the matter."

By the first week in January 1944 another memorandum was circulated among members of the Washington committee urging that "political warfare matters affecting China and Indo-China should be dealt with by the Washington Committee." A month later the Joint Chiefs of Staff, to whom had been entrusted the task of assigning American personnel to the propaganda committee, drafted their own letter to FDR urging outright abolition of the New Delhi committee and transfer of its functions to the Washington group. The reasoning behind the recommendation was purely anti-imperial:

> It has become evident that differences between the interests and objectives of the United States and Great Britain in Southeast Asia raise serious objections to the continuance of the New Delhi Committee. . . .
>
> American representation on the New Delhi Committee tends to create or confirm suspicion among Far Eastern peoples that the political policies of the United States with respect to this area conform to those of Great Britain. The State Department has consistently taken the position of opposing any integration of our propaganda program for the India-Burma region with the program of the British, and the

attitude of the Office of War Information conforms to that taken by the State Department . . . an increased or even continued United States representation on the New Delhi Committee may lower the regard in which Far Eastern peoples hold United States policies and intentions, and ultimately may hamper our military operations in the Far East. With regard to the latter point, the Commanding General, U.S. Army Forces in China-Burma-India [Stilwell] has expressed concern to the War Department as to United States representation on the Committee.

The letter closed with the statement that the Secretary of State and the director of the OWI concurred with the recommendations and reasoning of the Joint Chiefs, and a penciled notation in the margin indicates that the highly influential personal chief of staff to the President, Admiral William D. Leahy, concurred also. At this moment of total war—six months before the Normandy landings, the greatest Russian offensives, and the certainty of ultimate victory in the Pacific—American adherence to the Atlantic Charter remained firm and undeviating.[46]

The further passage of time did nothing to alleviate the suspicions of American officials in Southeast Asia toward their European allies. Nineteen forty-four saw a decisive turn in the fortunes of war in favor of the Grand Alliance, and this development whetted rather than dampened British, French, and Dutch imperialist appetites. In early November the American consul at Colombo, Ceylon, dispatched a long and gloomy memorandum to the State Department in Washington, and his words were promptly passed on to the Secretary with a covering memorandum to the President. The gist of Max Bishop's memorandum was simply that there existed a growing "danger of serious difficulties between orientals and occidentals unless the Western powers, notably the United States, the United Kingdom, the Netherlands, and France pursue an enlightened policy and succeed in convincing orientals that imperialism and exploitation of the East by the West are things of the past." The body of the memorandum set forth the enormous obstacles in the path of such a policy.

In the first place, the entire Southeast Asian region was a colonial area with the exception of neutral Thailand, which had already attracted the mordant suspicion and antipathy of the British, who were conducting clandestine operations of a quasi-political, quasi-military nature within her borders. Within the command itself mutual dislike between British and American officers and men had steadily grown to the point where any real degree of comradeship had dissipated. Mountbatten had engaged in a running feud with Stilwell for months over conflicting command responsibilities between SEAC and CBI. The latter's removal in October dampened without destroying Anglo-American friction. On lower levels Americans were "disturbed by the inactivity of SEAC, by the comparatively luxurious surroundings at SEAC headquarters, by the exceptionally active social life, and by the 'country club' atmosphere. . . ." Americans felt they lived in a British-controlled environment "of intrigue, plot and counterplot." Such an attitude, the consul readily admitted, "may possibly result from the highly commendable desire of American officers to 'get things done.' They often become impatient with the more apathetic attitude of their British friends toward opening the [Burma] road to China where United States forces need supplies." Beyond these complaints lay others of a more mundane nature: British misuse of American matériel, "British carelessness and profligate waste in handling Lend-Lease supplies, the alleged inadequacy of British facilities, . . ." SEAC "badly needs a major victory" to wipe out the bitterness and sense of lost morale—to destroy the angry quip that the initials of the command really stood for " 'Supreme Example of Allied Confusion.' "

But military triumph alone would not be sufficient. For while the British seemingly refused to play seriously at war, they played the game of imperial restoration with relish and effect, thereby further stimulating American aggravation and mistrust. Consul Bishop noted that SEAC contained a large political staff under the direction of two British Foreign Office officials "with the assimilated ranks of Major General and Brigadier," who acted as political advisers to Mountbatten. There was, the consul added pointedly, no American political adviser. Moreover, "As early as last July, British SOE [Special Operations Executive—roughly equivalent to the OSS and later CIA] sent into Indochina a representative, Baron François deLanglade, carrying a handwritten letter from de Gaulle. DeLanglade has been working closely with the British for about two years." But most disturbing of all was "the latest political maneuver by SEAC [which] has been to bring to its headquarters a large French mission. . . . It is believed that this mission was conceived and the groundwork laid without prior notification to the Government of the United States"despite British protestations to the contrary.

American officers in position to know have become convinced that one of the primary political objectives of SEAC is to restore British prestige and influence in southeast Asia and nearby areas. There is evidence also that the British, French and Dutch have reached a working arrangement if not an agreement on basic policies for this part of the world. There are many indications that the British desire to gain predominant influence over the post-war government or "administration" of Thailand. If unity in policies and in programs for Malaya, Thailand, Indochina, the Netherlands East Indies [Indonesia], and Burma is established under British aegis, the predominance of British influence in this area will be assured so long as the native populations are kept in line.

And the British were in no mood to encourage native aspirations. "Many examples are found in their psychological warfare and a specific example may be cited in the directive of the British Foreign Office that clandestine organizations (SOE) are to have nothing to do with Anamites or other native groups in Indochina." As for the Chinese representatives at SEAC, they "are not trusted and play no significant political or military part."

The United States was thus in great danger of losing its separate identity in both military and political matters within the vast SEAC area. "In the eyes of Asiatics and colonial peoples, we are apt to become politically indistinguishable from European colonial powers." And beyond this immediate dilemma lay another: the possible postwar influence of Soviet Russia upon restless and impatient native political leaders. "Soviet Russia's policies and ideologies have gained a real hold over many progressive leaders in Asia and nearby areas," Bishop warned, and "a feeling of sympathetic receptivity toward Soviet Russia's leadership is widespread." If Russia could be persuaded to remain within the Grand Alliance with all the political, territorial, and ideological restraints implied in that membership, then generous U.S. postwar policies in Southeast Asia "can hardly fail." But if U.S. policies were not ultimately acceptable to the Kremlin, "the sooner and more clearly this fact is made known the better the opportunity afforded to adjust differences."

But Russia was of peripheral concern at this moment. What was of overriding importance was to exert American influence upon Britain, France, and the Netherlands to conform to the principles of the Atlantic Charter. Bishop closed his lengthy cable with the observation that, as the British Empire would clearly emerge from the war "a poor third" in terms of power to both Russia and America, "It would seem highly desirable to seek at once collaboration and agreement with the British, the Dutch, and the French in the declaration and subsequent operation of a progressive and forward-looking program for non-self-governing peoples." As in China, so in Southeast Asia, American officials believed that with a little foresight, fortitude, and fortune, "the United States and its allies could obtain and maintain leadership of the political development of presently dependent peoples and could expect at least 'to hold their own' in winning converts to their principles and in eliciting native cooperation." This was not the arrogance of power, but rather the arrogance of the politically innocent. It would lead to measureless grief.[47]

As the last calendar year of the war opened, policy makers in Washington uneasily watched the further deterioration of Anglo-American relations in SEAC and accelerated British efforts to pressure the Thai government into ceding strategic territory. They steadfastly refused to appoint an American political adviser to Mountbatten's staff, fearing, in Stilwell's earlier words, that such an officer would be corrupted willingly or not by the British, thereby identifying American interests ever more firmly with those of European imperialism. At the same time the American bureaucracy continued to believe, in the words of one memorandum on national interest in Southeast Asia, in the "Extension of American Political and Social Concepts throughout the World." In a policy paper dated January 17, 1945, drafted by Abbot Low Moffat, a long-time specialist on Southeast Asia, it was argued that "unless substantial modification of prewar colonial policies takes place, continual unrest and instability will be inevitable" throughout the area.

> Our present policy of attempting to maintain, except in military matters, our separate identity in the Southeast Asia Command theater in order to avoid identification with the colonial policies of the European powers, with which we are constantly linked by Japanese propaganda, is not sufficient to protect our interests. We should also endeavor to secure from the colonial powers assurances of a more liberal policy towards their dependencies in Southeast Asia, in harmony, if possible, with our own policy towards the Philippines. The British, French and Netherlands governments have each made indefinite promises of greater self-government. More explicit commitments are now needed.

The colonial powers should be forced to make "specific commitments" and ''concerted announcements'' as to when they would grant either outright independence or ''complete autonomous self-government'' to the colonial peoples of the area, and America should do its part by reaffirming her determination to grant the Philippines complete independence on July 4, 1946. The nascent United Nations might well be utilized as the agency through which continued pressure could be applied on the imperial powers to withdraw from colonialism.[48]

Thereafter events began to move with enormous velocity. The war in Asia, as in Europe, was reaching its climax. More and more Japanese-held territories were falling to the Allies or were becoming so weakened by blockade as to stimulate both native unrest and imperial appetite. Roosevelt had been furious when told of the establishment of the French mission within SEAC, and he directed that no American approval be given to Mountbatten's initiative. ''All our people and also the British, Dutch, and French must understand that we expected to be consulted on the future of Indochina'' at the very least. And, the President added, ''We have made no final decisions on the future of Indochina.'' Roosevelt ostensibly maintained his deep interest and concern with colonial matters after his return from the Yalta conference, but in fact a rapidly failing body was sapping his former mental vigor and his instinctive combativeness. At the Crimea Roosevelt had agreed that the liberation of New Guinea and the Netherlands East Indies was to be a British responsibility, as he had earlier acquiesced in a unilateral British return to Malaya. After breakfast with the President sometime in March, an aide confided to Moffat that Roosevelt had given in and had agreed that France might administer any postwar trusteeship over Indochina. On April 3 Secretary of State Stettinius issued a statement with presidential approval that the United States, as a result of the Yalta talks, looked to trusteeship as a postwar arrangement only for territories taken from the enemy and such territories as might voluntarily be placed under trusteeship. Years later Moffat sadly observed that since the French ''clearly had no intention of voluntarily placing Indochina under trusteeship, Mr. Stettinius' statement marked the public end of Mr. Roosevelt's earlier hope for a trusteeship for Indochina.''[49]

It would ease the historian's task immensely if such statements of policy automatically reflected and were translated into coherent action in the field. But such is seldom the case, and it seems almost never to have been the case with respect to the long and melancholy American involvement with East Asia between 1941 and 1975. For the fact is that even as

Roosevelt seemed to be preparing the way for a return of colonialism to Southeast Asia, developments both in Washington and in parts of the field were leading events in a contrary direction.

On the night of March 9, as American bombers laid fiery waste to their capital of Tokyo far to the north, Japanese forces suddenly swept down on the French administration of Indochina and obliterated it, rounding up and interning nearly the entire European civil and military establishment. Fear of an early Allied landing on the coast and of the rebirth of French opposition in the wake of the liberation of the homeland seems to have provoked the Japanese action, though desire to rally support of the restless native population in the face of mounting disasters elsewhere may also have played a part.[50] De Gaulle himself personally requested American aid for the few remaining French units, which were fighting to extricate themselves from Tonkin in order to escape into south China. French officials in Washington pressed the case, but Roosevelt resisted. He would not sign a public statement pledging the United States to "do all it can to be of assistance in the present situation, consistent with plans to which it is already committed and with the operations now taking place in the Pacific."[51] Admiral Leahy did take responsibility on his own to clear a few previously scheduled flights with relief supplies from China to the Tonkin "undergrounders" provided, as the President himself had earlier stipulated, that such aid "involved no interference with our operations against the Japanese."[52] But publicly the American government continued to stand aloof from identification with French interests and aims in Indochina, despite Roosevelt's rather vague promise two weeks later to let the French handle the postwar trusteeship over the region.

The unforeseen result of this policy was to hasten the emergence of an already well-developed and vivacious Vietnamese nationalist movement under the direction of Ho Chi Minh. After an obscure life of revolutionary failure and wanderings through both the Western and Eastern worlds, Ho had surfaced in south China during 1940 to lead a cabal of Vietnamese revolutionaries, who were determined not only to drive the Japanese invader but also the French master from their homeland. Prominent within this cabal were the remnants of the small prewar Indochina Communist Party, or Viet-Minh, to whom Ho had acted for years as exiled leader, planner, and father figure. Jailed in July of 1942 by the chronically suspicious Marshal Fa-kwei of the Kuomintang, Ho nonetheless possessed competent lieutenants, who proceeded to build an effective intelligence network throughout Tonkin. This network ultimately came to the attention of Fa-kwei, who had been an old comrade of Ho's during the twenties when Ho had been part of the Chinese Communist group within the Kuomintang. Fa-kwei released Ho in 1943 and paid him a fair sum to engage in espionage operations in Indochina in the apparent hope that Ho might become a useful puppet and agent of mounting Kuomintang designs on postwar Indochina. Expanding his operations and funneling every cent he received into them, Ho broke with his Chinese patron in late 1944. He then contacted OSS headquarters for south China, located in the city of Kunming, and offered his nascent Viet-Minh organization to the Americans. OSS officials, weary and suspicious of dealing with the French after experiences in North Africa, accepted the offer with initial skepticism and growing pleasure. By March of 1945 Ho and his followers, led by Vo Nguyen Giap, were securely ensconced in Tonkin. The decimation of French forces in Indochina by the Japanese that month left ''only one major underground force . . . in Indochinese territory—the Viet Minh,'' which now enjoyed OSS support. Significantly, however, OSS headquarters in south China was itself becoming divided over further support for Ho. Some Americans feared that the Annamese revolutionary might decide to turn the small amount of arms given him on the French rather than on the Japanese.[53]

The roots of America's Asian tragedy were not confined to China and Indochina during the final chaotic months of the war. They reached right across the Pacific to Washington itself, where increasingly exasperated and hostile government bureaucrats were clumsily fending off the demands of pretentious Korean nationalists led by Syngman Rhee.

Never before had American interest in the Land of the Morning Calm risen above the minimal. As early as the Portsmouth Conference of 1905 Theodore Roosevelt had successfully obtained Russian acknowledgment of Japan's paramount interest in Korea, an interest which the United States itself subsequently accepted in the Taft-Katsura agreement later that year in exchange for Japanese disavowal of aggressive intent upon the Philippines. In 1910 Washington readily acquiesced in the Japanese annexation of Korea. With assurances from Tokyo that existing rights of the few American nationals and of the minuscule American trade would not be affected, the United States had allowed Korea to slip into the Japanese orbit without significant comment. In August of 1914, as World War I broke out in Europe, the American government, along with other treaty powers, had agreed to the outright abolition of foreign settlements in Korea's treaty ports. American disinterest in Chosen—as the Japanese renamed the country—had thus become complete. In 1919, when nationalist agitation broke out on the peninsula—as it did over much of Asia, partly in response to Woodrow Wilson's idealistic call for self-determination of all peoples— the State Department instructed the ambassador in Japan to inform the consulate at Seoul "not to encourage any belief that the United States will assist the Korean nationalists in carrying out their plans." Moreover, the consul "should not do anything which may cause Japanese authorities to suspect [the] American Government sympathizes with Korean Nationalist movement."⁵⁴

Japanese authorities ruthlessly suppressed and harried the predominantly young Korean nationalists who had organized the "Mansei movement," sending most of them fleeing into a twenty-five-year-long exile, which simply strengthened their resolve to the point of fanaticism. Some went to China and ultimately established a "Korean Provisional Government" (KPG), first in Shanghai under Syngman Rhee and later amidst the crowded misery of wartime Chungking. Others, ultimately led by Rhee himself, went on to America where they established a persistent, if impuissant, lobby group designated by their colleagues in Nationalist China the "Korean Commission in Washington."

Between July 1941 and February 1942 Rhee sought to obtain American diplomatic recognition for the KPG, but the best he could obtain was State Department acknowledgment of "the plans and objectives" of the Chungking Koreans and a brief comment by Acting Secretary of State Sumner Welles in a March 1942 press conference that Korean nationalist activities were viewed in Washington with "utmost sympathy." As with political settlements elsewhere across the Eurasian land mass, the instinct of the Roosevelt administration with respect to Korea was to procrastinate and defer hard decisions until World War II had reached a victorious climax. Only the vague Cairo Declaration of December 1, 1943, agreed to by Roosevelt, Churchill and Chiang—later by Stalin at Tehran—pledging "that in due course Korea shall become free and independent," saved the Korean exiles from utter despair, though Roosevelt, unbeknownst to Rhee and his colleagues, returned from the Cairo and Tehran conferences convinced that the "Big Three" should exercise a forty-year trusteeship over the peninsula because "the Koreans are not yet capable of exercising and maintaining independent government."⁵⁵

In fact, the trusteeship idea grew steadily more attractive to State Department planners in the fifteen months between Cairo-Tehran and Yalta. A State Department briefing paper prepared in January 1945 for the

Crimea conference suggested the possibility that an "interim international administration or trusteeship" be established for Korea either within or beyond the UN framework and that the United States, Britain, China, and Russia be included in any such arrangement.[56] Evidence indicates that the tired and distracted Roosevelt very probably never got around to reading this document. He nonetheless discussed the question of a Korean trusteeship with Stalin at Yalta on February 8, and the Generalissimo agreed to it, the major point of conflict being that the President did not wish British participation while Stalin did, arguing that Churchill would be highly and rightly offended if his country were not offered participatory rights. Indeed, Stalin "said the Prime Minister might 'kill us' " should British participation not be actively sought. The Generalissimo also took mild issue with Roosevelt's suggestion of a twenty-five to thirty-year trusteeship. "Marshal Stalin said the shorter the period the better. . . ."[57]

The Korean exiles watched what seemed to be the bartering away of their own and their country's future with mounting anxiety. Their efforts to promote their cause by obtaining arms and training their followers in China to fight the Japanese had been politely rebuffed time and again. Nor would the United States recognize their provisional government, even after China and France had practically done so. Washington steadfastly refused to utilize the provisional government as a conduit to aid resistance groups within Korea or to support any invitation to representatives of that government to attend the UN Charter meeting at San Francisco in the late spring and early summer of 1945.

But, above all, the members of the KPG in both China and the United States watched the growth of the Yalta and immediate post-Yalta Soviet-American *entente cordiale* with the greatest dread. In the week after Yalta, Rhee wrote the State Department of his fears. "Ever since December 7, 1941," he said, "we have been witnessing along with the authorities of the Department of State, the repeated and unmistakable signs of the danger that the Korean Communist Army maintained in Siberia by Russia might rush into Korea at an opportune moment and overrun the entire Peninsula, before the Korean Nationalist Democratic Government in Exile could find a chance to return to Korea." Rhee's fears in this matter were purely his own and those of his colleagues in Chungking and Washington; neither the State Department nor the by now chronically suspicious American embassy in Moscow shared them. As late as April 17, 1945, George Kennan cabled the Secretary of State that the consulate had "heard neither report nor rumor of existence in Vlad[ivostok] of so-called

Korean Liberation Committee and it appears unlikely that an organization of that sort would be created in such obviously unnatural surroundings." Koreans living in the Soviet maritime provinces as late as 1937 had been removed into distant Kazakhstan. Kennan suggested that "any potential rival to Korean Provisional Government located in Chungking would probably make its first appearance in Northwest China region controlled by Chinese Communists at some later date. . . ."[58] Kennan's assessment proved to be relatively accurate. Throughout the 1930s various small Korean Communist parties pursued precarious, uneasy, and divisive careers under the control of the Japanese in Korea and Manchuria, the Chinese Communists in Yenan, and the Russians in the maritime provinces. Discrimination, frustration, and failure was their lot. Only with the coming of the Russians to Korea in 1945 and the sudden emergence of new young leadership would Communist fortunes change.[59]

Rhee and his compatriots were not appeased by Kennan's observations. They suspected that some sort of deal had been arranged between Roosevelt and Stalin at Yalta, and on May 15, 1945, Rhee wrote to President Truman of his fears. Rhee's letter was referred by the White House to the State Department for a reply, which was sent out on June 5 by Frank P. Lockhart, the acting director of the Office of Far Eastern Affairs. Lockhart's tone was blunt to the point of insult and seemed to indicate beyond a doubt that the U.S. government had abandoned any pretense of sympathy with the aspirations of the KPG. Lockhart began his letter by condemning as "unfounded" the "reports that commitments were entered into at the Crimea Conference in regard to Korea which are inconsistent with the Cairo Declaration." Korea would be liberated and "the Cairo Declaration will be carried out," Lockhart asserted. He then turned to the question of KPG representation at the founding Conference of the United Nations then sitting at San Francisco. Only "legally constituted governing authorities" could be accredited, and "the 'Korean Provisional Government' and other Korean organizations do not possess the qualifications requisite for obtaining recognition by the United States as a governing authority." If this were not cruel enough, Lockhart proceeded to cross his *t*'s and dot his *i*'s. The provisional government had never had administrative authority over any part of Korea "nor can it be considered representative of the Korean people of today." Its following, even among exiled Koreans, "is limited," and it was the policy of the American government under such circumstances to avoid taking action which might compromise the right of the people of Korea to choose their own leadership and form of government when victory in the Pacific was at last achieved. In closing, Lockhart stooped to outright condescension: "I am sure," he told Rhee,

you will realize that the foregoing review of the Department's position in this connection carries no implication whatsoever of a lack of sympathy for the people of Korea and their aspirations for freedom. The officers of the Department have spent a great deal of time in studying the problems relating to Korea and have talked at length with you and with other individuals interested in the welfare of Korea and the Koreans and have endeavored to explain this Government's responsibility in such matters and to give a clear indication of the lines along which this responsibility is being fulfilled.[60]

Lockhart's letter was remarkable on two counts. First, of course, Rhee was absolutely right in assuming that a tacit "deal" had been made by Roosevelt and Stalin, if not Churchill, at Yalta. FDR had presumed the establishment of a lengthy Great Power trusteeship over the peninsula, which was certainly at variance with the spirit, if not the letter, of the admittedly vague Cairo pledge to a free and independent Korea. Moreover, unbeknownst to Rhee and his colleagues, that presumption had become reality at the end of May when Truman's envoy, Harry Hopkins, had journeyed to Moscow for talks with Stalin aimed at resolving a number of critical issues confronting the Grand Alliance. During the course of several lengthy conversations Stalin and Hopkins agreed firmly on the need for a joint Anglo-Chinese-Soviet-American postwar trusteeship for the peninsula.[61]

Second, despite Lockhart's lofty comment concerning the amount of time that department officials had spent studying Korean affairs, there is no evidence of any intensive efforts to study the Korean political scene in order to sort out, encourage, and nurture as potential forces for postwar leadership specific groups or interests among the nationalist elements in the United States, China, or within Korea itself. Recalling years later the confusion of postwar planning in wartime Washington, Rodney C. Loehr, a historical officer for the Joint Chiefs of Staff, stated that the chiefs never once discussed Japanese, much less Korean, occupation policy. ". . . the war in Europe was the one that got the attention from the chiefs. And the thought was that the war in the Pacific—that was supposed to be about an eight-year war to begin—this would last long enough after the European war was over so there would be time to think about that. So the main attention was to Germany.''[62] After years of indifference and ignorance, the United States would enter postwar Korea totally blind, knowing only what and who it did not want. Washington had, moreover, deeply antagonized the only truly organized Korean political group then under some sort of Western influence.

In his angry and lengthy reply of July 25 Rhee shrewdly chose to emphasize anti-Communism as the leitmotif of his patriotic concern for his country. At one point the Korean scornfully thanked Lockhart for his assertion that it was American policy to take no action toward recognition of any group before victory. ''This seems to confirm our belief that the State Department has been delaying the recognition of the Korean Provisional Government in order to give the Korean Communists a chance to form a Lublin Government. . . .''[63] Whether Rhee spoke from expediency or conviction, whether he knew or merely sensed that the Grand Alliance would soon die in cold war, his militant anti-Communist posture would soon serve him well. For when at last events forced the American government to turn to him for some sort of indigenous order and support, Rhee would, not unnaturally, seek to extract every advantage from his position in both peace and war.

Washington's initial and cavalier dismissal in the summer of 1945 of the admittedly unpalatable Rhee group without any corresponding effort to promote the influence and legitimacy of other Korean nationalist elements thus proved to be a crucial element in the emerging tragedy of Korea. The decision to divide the peninsula—temporarily it was assumed—into Soviet and American zones of occupation provided an equal impetus toward tragedy.

The question of a four-power Korean trusteeship, which Roosevelt had raised with Stalin at Yalta, was not seriously pursued by the Big Three at Potsdam five months later. The Russians did raise the issue in a general paper on trusteeships, which was circulated during the course of the conference, but the Three quickly bogged down in a discussion of trusteeships for the former Italian colonies in North Africa, and Korea was never discussed.[64] In a memorandum to the President, Secretary of War Henry L. Stimson on July 16 echoed Rhee's fears of Soviet designs on the peninsula. ''The Russians, I am also informed, have already trained one or two divisions of Koreans, and, I assume intend to use them in Korea,'' the old man warned Truman. ''If an international trusteeship is not set up in Korea,'' he continued, ''and perhaps even if it is, these Korean divisions will probably gain control, and influence the setting up of a Soviet dominated local government, rather than [an] independent one. This,'' he concluded, in an ominous echo of what Rhee had earlier hinted to Lockhart, ''is the Polish question transplanted to the Far East.''[65]

Truman and his diplomatic and military colleagues chose to ignore or forget the warning. At the Soviet-American military talks on July 24 General Antonov asked General Marshall and Admiral King if it would be possible for U. S. forces ''to operate against the shores of Korea'' in conjunction ''with the Russian forces which would be making an offensive against the peninsula.'' Here was a perfect opportunity for the United States to exert an early massive influence on Korean destiny by applying military power. But Marshall turned it aside. Amphibious operations against the Korean coast had not been contemplated, he told the Russians, and were moreover beyond even America's enormous resources, all of which would be needed to subdue Japan by anticipated successive invasions of Kyushu and Honshu.[66] All of Korea thus seemed about to fall naturally into the Soviet orbit.

Atomic bombs and Russia's entry into the Pacific war changed circumstances in Northeast Asia with dramatic suddenness. Less than a fortnight after Truman had bade Stalin and Attlee farewell at Potsdam, Japan sued for peace, and World War II came to an abrupt, unforeseen close. The problem of Korea could not be evaded. Either we would allow the peninsula to fall by default to Soviet arms, or it would be necessary to draw zonal boundaries in haste, obtain Soviet acceptance, and then make good our claims by the dispatch of at least a token occupation force. Thus it was that during the feverish days of August 10-15, while Tokyo was making its last desperate and fruitless efforts to avoid unconditional surrender, the State-War-Navy Coordinating Committee, then composed of the undersecretaries of the respective departments, held several long sessions on arrangements for the Japanese surrender in the islands of the Pacific, the home islands, and the Asian mainland including Korea.

According to President Truman, the State Department urged that American troops take the surrender of Japanese forces in all of Korea. Secretary of State Byrnes, whose suspicion of Soviet intentions went back at least as far as Yalta, urged that U.S. forces receive the Japanese surrender ''as far north as practicable.'' The military, faced with a scarcity of forces for Korea and aware that the margin of security for the troops landing in Japan was paper thin, given the existence of a two-million-man Japanese army, countered with the argument that ''time and space factors . . . would make it difficult to reach very far north'' in Korea before ''Soviet troops could enter the area.'' According to the recollection of Dean Rusk, who in 1945 was the Assistant Secretary of State for Far Eastern Affairs, ''The military view was that if our proposals for receiving the surrender greatly over-reached our probable military capabilities, there would be little likelihood of Soviet acceptance—and speed was the essence of the problem.'' Rusk and Colonel Bonesteel of the War Department's general staff were ordered to come up with an immediate proposal. Retiring to a room in the spacious old State Department building across the narrow street from the White House, the two agreed that the consideration of overriding importance was ''to include the capital of Korea,'' Seoul, ''in the area of responsibility of American troops.'' The thirty-eighth parallel ran across the peninsula roughly twenty miles north of the city and was quickly proposed as the most natural point of division ''even though it was further north than could be realistically reached by U.S. forces in the event of Soviet disagreement. . . .'' But to Rusk's surprise, on August 16 Moscow agreed without complaint to the American proposal.[67]

And why not? Like the White House, the Kremlin had what seemed at the time to be more important matters on its mind: the possibility of a postwar loan from the United States, the imposition of Communist rule over the countries of Eastern Europe, the possibility of a trusteeship over one or more of the former Italian colonies in North Africa, revision of the Montreux Convention in order to obtain base rights in the Dardanelles, perhaps even participation in the military occupation of Japan. Korea was a minor issue compared to these objectives. Possibly also the industrially weakened Soviets had become aware that before and especially during World War II Japan had expanded enormously the heavy industrial and hydroelectric resources of Korea, which lay well north of the thirty-eighth parallel.[68] Moreover the cold war, which would emerge with terrifying suddenness in the months immediately following the end of World War II, had not yet taken sufficient shape and dimension to disabuse either Washington or Moscow of the notion that Soviet-American cooperation could and would continue long into the postwar era. So Korea was bisected at the thirty-eighth parallel, and the United States rushed into the south without any real knowledge of the political, social, or economic configuration of the land it was to govern, apparently having rejected the chief native political group at hand which might aid it in its efforts.

The battle lines between revolution and reaction, nationalism and imperialism, were thus clearly drawn all across East Asia as World War II came to a close. Aspiration would oppose tradition; new would oppose old; East would oppose West throughout the area. Only in the extreme southwest corner of the region would imperialism surrender swiftly and with some grace to nationalism. Fearful of becoming permanently embroiled in the murderous religious conflicts of the Indian subcontinent, recognizing the prohibitive cost of trying to hold the restless and alienated people of Burma within a tired colonial structure, impatient to engineer some sort of modest and nonviolent social and economic revolution amidst the ruins at home, the Labour government in Britain by mid-1946 was clearly making ready to quit its two richest imperial holdings east of Suez. At the same time the United States—which viewed the unfolding drama of Indian and Burmese nationalism with general satisatisfaction—prepared to fulfill its long-standing commitment to total independence for the Philippines. American interest in India, Pakistan, Burma, and the Philippines did not cease with the winning of independence by these nations. Indeed it grew in direct proportion to the intensification of the cold war against what was conceived to be an international Communist conspiracy. But the Indians, Burmese, Pakistanis, and Filipinos had won their struggles for independence; henceforth they would be treated, courted, respected, pressured, and cajoled as sovereign peoples.

Elsewhere throughout the early postwar Far East—in Indochina, Indonesia, Korea, and China—the struggle between old and new raged on. America stood somewhere in the middle, herself ostensibly the bearer of a rich revolutionary tradition, uneasy and unsure of her new-found power and unprepared to exercise it confidently in pursuit of well-conceived and well-designed policies. Supposedly committed to ending Asia's long colonial bondage, yet instinctively, culturally, and materially aligned with the old order of Europe, America remained an unknown force in the unfolding political drama of Asia. Which way would she bend? How would she behave? To whom would she listen? In August and September of 1945 the answers began to emerge.

NOTES

1. Sidney Shallet, " 'Stability by Evolution. . . ,' " *New York Times*, 11 November 1945, p. E5; Harold R. Isaacs, *No Peace for Asia* (New York: Macmillan Co., 1947).

2. For a contrary view of Japan's role in stimulating the great revolt in Asia, see Isaacs, *No Peace for Asia*, p. 1. I believe that time, perspective, the availability

of a rich documentation, and mature scholarship has served drastically to modify Isaacs's contemporary impressions, valuable as they have proved.

3. John King Fairbank, *The United States and China*, rev. ed. (Cambridge, Mass.: Harvard University Press, 1971), pp. 122-239 passim; John Paton Davies, Jr., *Dragon by the Tail* (New York: W. W. Norton & Co., 1972), pp. 35-159; Leslie H. Palmer, *Indonesia and the Dutch* (London: Oxford University Press, 1962), pp. 1-40 passim; Zainu' ddin, *A Short History of Indonesia* (New York: Praeger Publishers, 1968), pp. 138-204 passim; J. D. Legge, *Indonesia* (Englewood Cliffs, N.J.: Prentice-Hall, 1964), pp. 112-136 passim; Bernard Fall, *The Two Vietnams: A Political and Military Analysis*, 2nd ed. rev. (New York: Frederick A. Praeger, Publishers, 1967), pp. 9-103 passim; Jean Lacouture, *Ho Chi Minh: A Political Biography*, trans. Peter Wiles (New York: Random House, 1968), pp. 5-84; Lennox A. Mills et al., *The New World of Southeast Asia* (Minneapolis: University of Minnesota Press, 1949); Lawrence K. Rosinger et al., *The State of Asia* (New York: Alfred Knopf, 1951), esp. pp. 3-21; Guy Wint, *Spotlight on Asia*, rev. ed. (London: Penguin Books, 1959); Vera Micheles Dean, *The Nature of the Non-Western World* (New York: New American Library, 1957), pp. 115-153; Isaacs, *No Peace for Asia*, pp. 126-128. The quotation from the enraged American is in Royal Arch Gunnison, *So Sorry, No Peace* (New York: Viking Press, 1944), p. vii. See also Cecil Brown, *From Suez to Singapore* (New York: Random House, 1942), pp. 131-533 passim; Manilal B. Nanvati, introduction to "India Speaking," a collection of essays comprising *The Annals of the American Academy of Political and Social Science* 133 (May 1944):4.

4. "Memorandum Prepared in the Office of British Commonwealth and North European Affairs, March 19, 1945," Bureau of European Affairs Files, Cab. 109-111, Matthews-Hickerson Files, Lot 5, Records of the Department of State, U.S. Department of State, Washington, D.C.

5. Winston S. Churchill, *Triumph and Tragedy* (New York: Bantam Books, 1962), pp. 334-335.

6. Lisle A. Rose, *Dubious Victory: The United States and the End of World War II* (Kent, Ohio: Kent State University Press, 1973), pp. 113-120.

7. Charles de Gaulle, *War Memoirs*, 6 vols. (New York: Simon & Schuster, 1960), vol. 6: *Salvation, 1944-1946, Documents*, pp. 279-280, 293.

8. Eric F. Goldman, *The Crucial Decade—And After: America, 1945-1960* (New York: Vintage Books, 1960), p. 4.

9. *The Atomic Age Opens* (New York: Pocket Books, 1945), pp. 46-60, 168-171.

10. Fairbank, *United States and China*, pp. 142-149, 290-291, 300-303.

11. Samuel Grafton, *An American Diary* (New York: Doubleday, Doran & Co., 1943), pp. 76-77.

12. Herbert Feis, *The Road to Pearl Harbor* (Princeton, N.J.: Princeton

University Press, 1950); William L. Langer and S. Everett Gleason, *The Undeclared War, 1940-1941* (New York: Harper & Brothers, Publishers, 1953), pp. 292-330, 464-493, 625-662, 693-731, 836-941; Robert A. Divine, *Roosevelt and World War II* (Baltimore: Johns Hopkins University Press, 1969), pp. 5-77 passim.

13. "Statement by John S. Service, 21 July 1971," in U.S. Congress, Senate, *United States-China Relations: Hearing before the Committee on Foreign Relations*, 92d Cong., 1st Sess. (Washington, D.C.: U.S. Government Printing Office, 1971), p. 8 (hereinafter cited as *United States-China Relations*); "Statement by Raymond P. Ludden, 7 February 1972," in U.S. Congress, Senate, *China and the United States Today and Yesterday: Hearings before the Committee on Foreign Relations*, 92d Cong., 2d Sess. (Washington, D.C.: U.S. Government Printing Office, 1972), p. 36 (hereinafter cited as *China and the United States Today and Yesterday*); Theodore H. White, editorial notes to Chapter 11 of *The Stilwell Papers* (New York: William Sloane and Associates, 1948), p. 323.

14. "Statement of James C. Thomson, 28 June 1971," in U.S. Congress, Senate, *United States Relations with the People's Republic of China: Hearings before the Committee on Foreign Relations*, 92d Cong., 1st Sess. (Washington, D.C.: U.S. Government Printing Office, 1972), p. 177.

15. "Statement by Service, 21 July 1971," *United States-China Relations*, p. 5.

16. Comments by Senators Case (N.J.) and Cooper (Ky.), 7 February 1972, *China and the United States Today and Yesterday*, pp. 40-41.

17. John Paton Davies, quoted in David Halberstam, *The Best and the Brightest* (New York: Random House, 1972), p. 384.

18. Ibid., p. 551.

19. Stilwell's unhappy stewardship in China is amply recounted in Barbara W. Tuchman, *Stilwell and the American Experience in China* (New York: Macmillan Co., 1971).

20. "Statement by Service, 21 July 1971," *United States-China Relations*, pp. 6, 12-13.

21. The best biography of Hurley is Russell D. Buhite's judicious but sympathetic *Patrick J. Hurley and American Foreign Policy* (Ithaca, N.Y.: Cornell University Press, 1973).

22. Herbert Feis, *The China Tangle: The American Effort in China from Pearl Harbor to the Marshall Mission* (New York: Atheneum Press, 1965), pp. 178, 214-225; U.S. Department of State, *United States Relations with China with Special Reference to the Period 1944-1949*, reprinted as *China White Paper*, 2 vols. (Stanford, Calif.: Stanford University Press, 1967), 1:71-72, 93-98; Edward R. Stettinius, Jr., *Roosevelt and the Russians* (Garden City, N.Y.: Doubleday & Co., 1949), pp. 309-311; U.S. Congress, Senate, *Military Situation in the Far*

East, August 1951, Part 5: Hearings before the Committee on Armed Services and the Committee on Foreign Relations, 82d Cong., 1st Sess., pp. 3336-3337, 3341-3342; Charles F. Romanus and Riley Sunderland, *Time Runs Out in CBI* (Washington, D.C.: Department of the Army, 1959), pp. 249-254, 338-339; U.S. Department of State, *Foreign Relations of the United States, 1945: Diplomatic Papers*, 9 vols. (Washington, D.C.: U.S. Government Printing Office, 1967-1969), 7:329-332, 338-340, 342-344 (hereinafter cited as *FR, 1945: Diplomatic Papers*); George F. Kennan, *Memoirs, 1925-1950* (New York: Bantam Books, 1969), pp. 250-251; William D. Leahy, *I Was There* (New York: Whittlesey House, 1950), p. 369; Hurley to the Secretary of State, 4 February 1945, Secretary of State to Hurley, 24 April 1945, in Record Group 84, Foreign Service Post File (Chungking), 710 Series, Records of the Department of State, National Archives, Washington, D.C.

23. *Biographical Register of the Department of State, October 1, 1945* (Washington, D.C.: U.S. Government Printing Office, 1945).

24. Davies, *Dragon by the Tail*, p. 402.

25. "Statement by Service, 21 July 1971," *United States-China Relations*, p. 8.

26. Quoted in U.S. Department of State, *Foreign Relations of the United States, 1944: Diplomatic Papers*, 7 vols. (Washington, D.C.: U.S. Government Printing Office, 1966-1967), 6:619-620.

27. "Statement by John Paton Davies, 21 July 1971," *United States-China Relations*, p. 15.

28. "Statement by Service, 21 July 1971," ibid., p. 20; Tang Tsou, *America's Failure in China, 1941-1950* (Chicago: University of Chicago Press, 1963), pp. 145, 289-290.

29. Davies, *Dragon by the Tail*, p. 403; Buhite, *Hurley*, p. 203.

30. *FR, 1945: Diplomatic Papers*, 7: 239.

31. "Statement by Service, 21 July 1971," *United States-China Relations*, p. 17.

32. *FR, 1945: Diplomatic Papers*, 7:242-246.

33. "Statement by Service, 21 July 1971," *United States-China Relations*, p. 19.

34. Ibid., p. 18; Memorandum by the Chief of the Division of Chinese Affairs (Vincent), Washington, 1 March 1945, *FR, 1945: Diplomatic Papers*, 7:247-249.

35. "Statement by Patrick J. Hurley, 5 December 1945," *United States-China Relations*, p. 74.

36. Tuchman, *Stilwell and the American Experience in China*, pp. 513-514.

37. Ibid., pp. 514-515.

38. Testimony of Abbot Low Moffat, 11 May 1972, in U.S. Congress, Senate,

Causes, Origins, and Lessons of the Vietnam War: Hearings before the Committee on Foreign Relations, 92d Cong., 2d Sess. (Washington, D.C.: U.S. Government Printing Office, 1973), p. 201 (hereinafter cited as *Causes, Origins, and Lessons of the Vietnam War*); Lacouture, *Ho Chi Minh*, pp. 60-62.

39. Moffat testimony, 11 May 1972, *Causes, Origins, and Lessons of the Vietnam War*, p. 194.

40. William L. Langer, *Our Vichy Gamble* (New York: Alfred A. Knopf, 1947); Leahy, *I Was There*, pp. 6-94 passim.

41. Milton Viorst, *Hostile Allies: FDR and Charles de Gaulle* (New York: Macmillan Co., 1965); Rose, *Dubious Victory*, pp. 113-114; Robert Aron, *An Explanation of de Gaulle*, trans. Marianna Sinclair (New York: Harper & Row, Publishers, 1966), pp. 140-155 passim.

42. Quoted in U.S. Department of Defense, *United States-Vietnam Relations, 1945-1967*, 12 vols. (Washington, D.C.: U.S. Government Printing Office, 1971), 1:A-14 (hereinafter cited as *United States-Vietnam Relations*).

43. Moffat testimony, 11 May 1972, *Causes, Origins, and Lessons of the Vietnam War*, pp. 163-164, 185-186.

44. Ibid., pp. 161-163; Abbot Low Moffat, "Memorandum for the President," 1 September 1944, in Philippine and Southeast Asian Affairs Files, Lot 54 D 109, folder: "SEA 1945-1948, Relations with British," Records of the Department of State, U.S. Department of State, Washington, D.C.

45. "Paraphrase of cable from W. D. Carter (OWI, New Delhi) to Elmer Davis, 22 October 1943," Philippine and Southeast Asian Affairs Files, folder: "Washington Combined Emergency Propaganda Committee."

46. "Paraphrase of cable from F. M. Fisher to Robert Sherwood, 9 October 1943"; "Directive for Psychological Warfare Division, SEAC, from Headquarters, Southeast Asia Command, n.d."; "Memorandum circulated in Washington Combined Emergency Propaganda Committee, 16 January 1944"; "Enclosure Draft of Proposed Letter to the President from the Joint Chiefs of Staff, n.d. [marginalia indicates first week or ten days in February 1944]," all in ibid.; "Memorandum, 2 November 1943"; "Memorandum, Subject: Combined Propaganda Committee located in New Delhi, 3 November 1943"; "Memorandum, with further reference to the New Delhi Propaganda Committee, 4 November 1943," all in ibid., folder: "Joint Anglo-Am Plan of Polit Warfare against Japan."

47. "Memorandum of Consul Max W. Bishop on SEAC and Southeast Asia," 10 November 1944, with covering memorandum and two covering letters, ibid., folder: "Southeast Asia Command, 1946-1948, U.S. Policy."

48. "Memorandum from Moffat to Ballantine of FE, 5 January 1945"; "Inadvisability of Assigning an American Political Adviser to SEAC"; "Memorandum from Moffat to anon., 11 January 1945, *inter alia*"; "Reported British Plans for

Peninsula Thailand''; ''Memo drawn up for discussion purposes only by OSS'';
''American National Interests in Southeast Asia, n.d.''; ''Memorandum from
Moffat to anon., The Dependent Territories in Southeast Asia, 17 January 1945,''
all in ibid.

49. Quoted in Moffat testimony, 11 May 1972, *Causes, Origins, and Lessons
of the Vietnam War*, p. 174; *United States-Vietnam Relations*, 1:A-15, A-16.

50. Chester A. Bain, *Vietnam: The Roots of Conflict* (Englewood Cliffs, N.J.:
Prentice-Hall, 1967), p. 103; R. Harris Smith, *OSS: The Secret History of
America's First Central Intelligence Agency* (Berkeley: University of California
Press, 1972), p. 326.

51. The Ambassador in France (Caffery) to the Secretary of State, Night
Action, Urgent, from Paris, 13 March 1945, Telegram #1196, in French-Iberian
Affairs Files, Operating Records of the French Desk, Lot 53 D 246, folder:
''Indochina (1944-1945),'' Records of the Department of State, U.S. Department
of State, Washington, D.C.; Memorandum for the President, 16 March 1945,
Memorandum from William D. Leahy for the Secretary of State, 17 March 1945, in
ibid.; *United States-Vietnam Relations*, 1:A-16-A-18.

52. *United States-Vietnam Relations* 1:A-19.

53. Smith, *OSS*, pp. 320-328; Fall, *The Two Vietnams*, p. 61; Lacouture, *Ho
Chi Minh*, pp. 69-95; *United States-Vietnam Relations*, 1:B-3-B-4; Isaacs, *No
Peace for Asia*, pp. 147-148.

54. Quoted in U.S. Department of State Publication 7446, *A Historical Summary of United States-Korean Relations . . . 1834-1962* (Washington, D.C.:
Historical Office, Bureau of Public Affairs, 1962), pp. 55-56.

55. Quoted in ibid., pp. 57-58; Shannon McCune, ''Korea,'' in Rosinger et al.,
State of Asia, p. 136. See also U.S. Department of State, *Foreign Relations of the
United States, Diplomatic Papers: The Conferences at Cairo and Tehran, 1943*
(Washington, D.C.: U.S. Government Printing Office, 1961), p. 869; Robert K.
Sawyer, *Military Advisers in Korea: KMAG in Peace and War* (Washington,
D.C.: Office of the Chief of Military History, Department of the Army, 1962), p.
6.

56. Quoted in U.S. Department of State, *Foreign Relations of the United
States, 1945: The Conferences at Malta and Yalta* (Washington, D.C.: U.S.
Government Printing Office, 1955), pp. 358-361, 770.

57. Statements of Soon S. Cho, Eric H. Biddle, and Gregory Henderson in
*Conference of Scholars on the Administration of Occupied Areas, 1943-1955:
April 10-11, 1970, at the Harry S. Truman Library* (Independence, Mo.: Harry S.
Truman Library Institute, 1970), pp. 21-23.

58. Quoted in *FR, 1945: Diplomatic Papers*, 6: 1018-1028.

59. Dae-Sook Suh, *The Korean Communist Movement, 1918-1948* (Princeton,
N.J.: Princeton University Press, 1967), pp. 3-255 passim.

60. *FR, 1945: Diplomatic Papers*, 6:1029-1030.

61. *Leahy, I Was There*, p. 381.

62. Quoted in *Conference of Scholars on the Administration of Occupied Areas*, p. 5.

63. *FR, 1945: Diplomatic Papers*, 6:1035.

64. U.S. Department of State, *Foreign Relations of the United States, 1945: Conference of Berlin,* 2 vols. (Washington, D.C.: U.S. Government Printing Office, 1955), 2:44-606 passim. Rhee did cable Truman, Stalin, and Churchill at Potsdam through the medium of the State Department, requesting the Big Three ''to issue a joint statement repudiating any secret agreement that might affect the political, administrative and territorial integrity of Korea, and recognizing 'The Provisional Government of Korea.' '' Byrnes asked Acting Secretary of State Grew to ''make acknowledgment to Rhee in such informal manner and in such terms as you may consider appropriate.'' The Secretary of State to the Acting Secretary of State, Babelsberg, 21 July 1945, ibid., p. 635.

65. Ibid., p. 631.

66. Ibid., p. 351.

67. *FR, 1945: Diplomatic Papers*, 6:1039-1040; U.S. Congress, House, *Background Information on Korea: Report of the Committee on Foreign Affairs Pursuant to H.Res. 206*, 81st Cong., 2nd Sess. (Washington, D.C.: U.S. Government Printing Office, 1950), p. 2; Harry S. Truman, *Memoirs*, 2 vols. (New York: Signet Books, 1965), vol. 2: *Years of Trial and Hope, 1946-1952*, p. 361.

68. McCune, ''Korea,'' pp. 132-133.

chapter 2

The Deference
to Colonialism:
Indochina

On September 5, 1945, Admiral Lord Louis Mountbatten delivered a speech to troops of his Southeast Asia Command stationed in the delightfully exotic old city of Kandy, located high in the forest-carpeted hills of Ceylon. It was, an OSS report noted, ''probably characteristic of a number of similar speeches that he has made from August 10th to September 5th'' to various groups under his command.

Mountbatten stressed the fact that his men still had much work to do and that it might be some time before they would be going home. He, Mountbatten, had a huge area of responsibility. With peace at last restored, his job, and that of his command, was now one of liberation, rehabilitation, and administration. Operations teams had already arrived in Malaya and would shortly arrive in Bangkok and Saigon. SEAC itself expected to move to Singapore within three months. In the meantime the British were '' 'making new arrangements' '' with the Thai government, ''and conferences will be held in the next few days'' with officials of the Netherlands East Indies and the Burma Defense Army and Anti-Fascist Peoples' Freedom League. To the alarmed Americans it appeared that little or nothing stood in the way of the reimposition of European imperialism throughout the entire region. Mountbatten evidently felt a ''relative independence from supervision in Great Britain'' and was quite conscious of "the scope of his local powers." Moreover, "it is well known that Lord Louis has surrounded himself with a group of upper-class Englishmen and of former colonials. Whatever liberal leanings Lord Louis may himself have and may have demonstrated, his staff has certainly not been bred in that aspect of British tradition which returned a labor government [to power]." At the same time the evident indifference to Southeast Asian affairs currently exhibited by the new Labour government in London forbade any corrective to the neo-imperialistic policies being directed from Whitehall. "The remoteness of Russia, the inertia of the U.S. and the undeveloped condition of native cultures," the report gloomily concluded, "all contribute to strengthening British colonialism and a policy of status quo anti [*sic*] bellum at SACSEA-HQ."[1]

In Washington Roosevelt had prepared the way for a repudiation of the anti-imperialist policies still expounded by the ardent young American field officers in SEAC. Now Truman was about to make the repudiation a reality.

At the moment of Roosevelt's death in the spring of 1945 the State Department had no agreed policy regarding Indochina. The European Office and the Western European Division hoped for a postwar resurgence of France and did not wish to place French recovery in jeopardy by threatening to help strip the French of their prewar Southeast Asian empire. The Division of Southeast Asian Affairs, however, argued that the future peace and stability of the entire region depended "on a recognition of the natural aspirations of the peoples of the area" to be free and independent. French settlers and officials in Indochina had, after all, cravenly collaborated with the Japanese conqueror for most of the previous four years; indeed, the French "had not even attempted to honor their protectorate responsibilities." Furthermore it was anticipated that American military power would liberate Indochina from Japan. In light of these realities why should not the United States demand the right to a major role in shaping the postwar history of the extensive region watered by the Mekong? Such, at any rate, was the thinking at the State Department's Southeast Asian desk.[2]

The conflict of viewpoints between the Department's Europeanists and the Southeast Asian desk came to a head a week after Roosevelt's death when the European division tried to ram its ideas through to the White House. The Southeast Asian desk refused concurrence, a compromise paper was ordered, which would somehow weave together the contending Asian and European perspectives and policies, and the result was drift and delay. The report was not ready for consideration and submission until several weeks before Japan had surrendered. And by that time others in both the State Department and the White House had convinced Truman that the cause of France was far more important than the cause of Indochinese nationalism.[3]

One of the most influential champions of France during the early months of the Truman administration was Assistant Secretary of State for European Affairs James Clement Dunn. At the end of April Dunn had journeyed to San Francisco as part of the American delegation to the UN Conference. On May 15, in a letter to William Phillips, the special assistant to the Secretary of State, Dunn forcefully expounded his views on the need to support postwar France as a great power whatever the cost. He began by aligning himself solidly behind the view expressed by the European office to the White House "that it is established American policy to aid France to regain her strength in order that she may be better fitted to share responsibility in maintaining the peace of Europe and of the world." But successful implementation of that policy would be far harder than anyone had imagined. The Americans had been impressed with French Foreign Minister Bidault, but "I don't think any of us had . . . fully appreciated the demoralized position of France until we saw their Delegation in action here." As a result of World War II "France was a badly beaten and humiliated country and in consequence she is suffering from a perfectly remarkable inferiority complex." The French were painfully sensitive, Dunn continued, and this accounted for their frequent bluster and exaggerated rhetoric. They "are constantly on the lookout for any evidence that we feel France has not fully regained her greatness."

The entire American delegation at San Francisco had tried hard to overcome this French feeling—to build up French morale and confidence. Secretary of State Stettinius and Dunn had "several good talks with Bidault. I believe we have gone a considerable distance toward convincing him that the United States wants to help France in every way we can to take her place as a full fledged member of the Big Five. I think we have made Bidault feel that we are genuine in our assertions. . . . It has been difficult, however, to overcome Bidault's suspicions, which I am convinced originate more from his Chief than himself." French help was mandatory if the Americans were to get from the San Francisco Conference all that they hoped in terms of an international security organization. "It is not going to be easy to obtain it to the extent which we need." Therefore, to further exacerbate French emotions by introducing the question of trusteeships over former European holdings in Asia might well defeat what seemed a broader purpose.[4]

Dunn was speaking here within a comfortable procedural framework that had defined American diplomacy throughout the war years. The United States would work for broad agreements with its allies and for the creation of a general international peace-keeping body. Once such agreements and organizations had come into being, specific world problems and disputes could be worked out within the confines of basic agreement. But the world was not prepared to behave in that fashion—to submit to the general and generous design that Washington had worked out for it. American policy makers were already discovering this sad fact in the case of Poland and of German reparations, to name but two outstanding issues of that time. But they continued to prefer and to pursue a policy of drift and deferral where they could. Indochina was so remote, so distant, of such minor concern in comparison with the vast and terrible drama of French decline that there seemed to most government officials little question of priorities. It is true that Truman reacted strongly in the late spring of 1945 against French efforts to obtain a share of the German occupation and to reestablish prewar influence and power in the Mideast. But as we shall see, when de Gaulle later argued that American humiliation of French aspirations in Europe and Lebanon must not extend to Indochina, Truman quickly—and somewhat abashedly—agreed.

Throughout the summer of 1945 American policy toward Indochina drifted ever closer to outright acceptance of French return with few if any strings attached. In early June the State Department cabled Hurley in China that decisions taken at the San Francisco UN Conference "would preclude the establishment of a trusteeship in Indochina except with the consent of the French Government. The latter seems unlikely. Nevertheless it is the President's intention at some appropriate time to ask that the French Government give some positive indication of its intentions in regard to the establishment of civil liberties and increasing measures of self-government in Indochina before formulating further declarations of policy in this respect."[5]

In the meantime the situation inside Indochina had deteriorated disastrously. Despite repeated French pleas for meaningful aid, Truman left all such decisions up to his military commanders. As a result American military activity was restricted to occasional heavy air strikes against Haiphong and other port cities, which only served, as in Europe, to cripple transportation and supply networks and disrupt the flow of badly needed food from one part of the country to the other. In addition, the rice crop in northern Vietnam failed miserably that year. So it was that instead of grasping the opportunity for rebellion, the young Vietnamese nationalist leaders beyond the reach of Ho Chi Minh indulged in unchecked political pretensions and ''childish vanity in an orgy of demonstrations, processions and public meetings which contributed toward the paralysis of the administrative machine.''[6] ''*Doc-Lap*,'' independence, became a travesty. Upwards of a million people began the long descent into fatal starvation that summer while the Japanese, ''preoccupied with their own forthcoming doom, did little but plunder valuables and seek to escape from prospective Allied war-crimes trials.''[7]

The outer world intruded very little into this chaotic power vacuum. British agents from SEAC flew a number of missions over Indochina from March to July, but in ever-dwindling numbers as their organization began to be thinned out after the termination of the war in Europe. French agents in SEAC apparently did nothing to pave the way for their country's return. The Americans in SEAC were equally quiescent.[8]

Not until midway through the Potsdam conference did the great world again take any notice of Indochina. On July 24 Churchill and Truman approved an earlier decision by the Combined British and American Chiefs of Staff that Indochina south of the sixteenth parallel was to be included in Mountbatten's Southeast Asia Command, while the area to the north of that line would be included in the China theater.[9] Therefore when Japan at last capitulated, her forces south of the sixteenth parallel would surrender to SEAC, those to the north of the line to the Chinese. At the same time Washington was seriously considering whether or not to retain official representation within SEAC. A report prepared for the State-War-Navy Coordinating Committee in mid-August, just seventy-two hours after V-J Day, reviewed the question and concluded ''That there should continue to be American participation in SEAC after the cessation of Japanese resistance lasting at least until United States Foreign Service officers are established at regular posts in Thailand and other places.'' Since the United States would continue to be represented in SEAC yet did not wish to seriously contest the return of French rule to Indochina and had no career foreign service people of great stature and experience available to enter the area, it was natural that the OSS would assume the role of political observer in both parts of Indochina. OSS officers would be attached to the British and French forces entering Saigon from SEAC and to Chinese forces entering Hanoi from the north.[10]

Five days after submission of this report and a week after a delirious America had celebrated the end of mankind's most gruesome adventure in mutual mass slaughter, Charles de Gaulle traveled to Washington to again press French claims to greatness upon a burdened and inexperienced American President, immersed in dreadfully complex problems of reconversion from war to peace. Out of this meeting would issue a casual American commitment which rivaled in tragic consequences the earlier decision to employ the unlimited power of atomic weaponry in pursuit of total triumph.

Truman and de Gaulle met twice on August 22. Most of their conversation was taken up with European matters. De Gaulle pressed for an even greater dismemberment of Germany than had been agreed to the previous month at Potsdam. He asked for four-power occupation and internationalization of the Ruhr and outright transfer of the Rhineland from German hands to French sovereignty or, failing that, the transmutation of the area into an autonomous state. The American response was casual, as befitted a nation basking in the glow of recent victory obtained by atomic power. According to the French minutes Truman said that the Russians had raised the Ruhr question at Potsdam, but the American delegation had refused to consider four-power occupation, which was "an excessive claim." Then, according to the American minutes, Truman added: "the prime requisite for world security is understanding of the Allies working together in an effective international organization. Furthermore, the atomic bomb will give pause to countries which might be tempted to commit aggression."

According to the American record the Truman-de Gaulle talks closed with a general presidential pledge to help the French return to a status of greatness and power in international life. Two further days of talks between Secretary of State Byrnes and Ambassador Bidault concentrated entirely on Europe and the Middle East. The French minutes of the Truman-de Gaulle talks, however, contain a crucial addendum. At the very close of their discussion de Gaulle "mentioned the Levant and the deplorable British intervention" there against France the previous spring. The general added that it was most regrettable that the United States had seen fit to support the intervention and therefore London's efforts to suppress French colonial aims in the Middle East. Truman rather uncomfortably, it would seem, "admitted that the British had presented their case in such a way that the attitude of the United States had been influenced.'' Then the President hastened to ''stress that in the case of Indo-China, the American Government would do nothing to prevent the return of France.''[11] The commitment had been made, the hands symbolically clasped.

American officials were left with no sense of pain or betrayal; they had been prepared to surrender whatever influence they might have chosen to exercise in postwar Indochina even before de Gaulle appeared at the White House. A briefing paper prepared for the President and Secretary of State sometime earlier in August stated the postwar American position toward Indochina with great clarity. ''It should be made clear to General de Gaulle that this government has no thought of opposing the reestablishment of French control in Indo-China.'' However, because of American sacrifices in lives and resources in the Far East during the recent war, ''our major responsibility for post-war maintenance of peace and stability in that area'' and a belief that failure to recognize the dynamic trend toward self-government among the peoples of Asia could jeopardize U.S. objectives, the Truman administration felt ''entitled'' to ask de Gaulle to give some positive indication of French intentions. Specifically Truman was to request the French to voluntarily initiate a significant movement toward Indochinese self-government so that ''within a reasonable period'' the region might be autonomous ''except in matters of common concern to the contemplated French Union'' and that even in those matters ''the Indo-Chinese may have a reasonable voice.'' Truman was to ask for other concessions as well, all of them designed to loosen, in one way or another, the French imperial grip upon Southeast Asia. ''It should be made clear to General de Gaulle,'' this portion of the briefing paper concluded, ''that this Government will not assist the French to reestablish their control over Indo-China by force, and that our willingness to see their control reestablished is predicated on the assumption that their claim to have the support of the population of Indo-China is borne out by future events.''[12] Brave words. But there is no indication that either Truman or Byrnes ever sought to translate them into national policy during the three days of talks with the French. Instead, in an offhand fashion late in the evening of August 22, 1945, Harry Truman gave his temperamental ally, Charles de Gaulle, practical carte blanche in Indochina.[13]

But, of course, no one seems to have thought to inform the Americans in the field. In mid-July various units of the OSS began to penetrate Indochina, appearing in both Hanoi and Saigon. The young and inexperienced Americans were soon immersed in the confusion and chaos of that time and place, and chance and circumstance combined to produce one of those ironies with which history abounds. For while the OSS people in Saigon became identified with the French colonial cause, those in Hanoi supported Ho Chi Minh with ever mounting enthusiasm.

On May 16, 1945, Major Allison K. Thomas, then in south China, was ordered to head an intelligence and sabotage unit which would be parachuted into Tonkin to operate, according to his orders, "with Chinese units as assigned." For some reason the "Deer mission," as it was labeled, did not parachute into Tonkin until July 17, 1945, there to be met on the landing ground by native guerrillas, who promptly took the Americans to their leader—one "Hoe," according to Thomas's first report. Thomas and Ho seem to have taken to one another immediately. Ho baldly informed Thomas that the remnants of the French forces which had fled Indochina in the wake of the March 9 Japanese coup had "shot and gassed many political prisoners" on their way out of the country and that while he personally liked some of the French he had met, his men did not. The Deer mission was apparently designed as an advance group to pave the way for a much larger infusion of French forces and of Annamese loyalists, but Ho told Thomas he would have none of it. Thomas and his men could go anywhere they liked, and Ho would give them as many men and as much aid and support as was needed, but there were to be no French and no Annamese lackeys allowed. Thomas seems to have been a very ambitious and resourceful fellow, and he immediately realized that Ho was offering him a great opportunity to shape events. Thomas radioed back to China that the impatient French and Annamese waiting to jump back into Tonkin should be held back as Ho wished and further OSS units, supplies, and ammunition should be sent instead, including materials for propaganda production. Thomas concluded by telling his superiors in Kunming: "Forget the Communist Bogy. VML [Viet-Minh League] is *not* Communist. Stands for freedom and reforms from French harshness. VML would be willing to talk to some High Ranking French officer (General Sebotier [*sic*], eg [*sic*]) and see what French would have to offer. If French go part way with them they might work with French—particularly if Sebatier [*sic*] would come here. It might be done."[14]

Three days later Thomas was again on the radio to China. The "first fact" he told his superiors was that "all the French and Annamese" waiting to jump into Tonkin "will have to be eliminated or we will have to go back." The Viet-Minh was dominant in Tonkin and one could not work without them. Moreover Ho and his followers "have a long list of grievances against the French.'' According to Thomas these included the facts that the French had seized Ho's wife and children and had burned his lands, that retreating French forces on leaving Tonkin had ''gassed and shot political prisoners,'' and that the French had been guilty of levying excessive taxes, forcing the sale of opium and alcohol upon the native population, and denying civil and political liberties to the natives. Thomas reiterated Ho's earlier invitation to the exiled French to send ''some high ranking'' officials into Tonkin to negotiate a political settlement, but there was to be no capitulation to French rule by the Viet-Minh. Once again Thomas closed his message with the assertion that neither Ho nor the Viet-Minh were ''Communist or Communist controlled or Communist led.''[15]

Three weeks later Japan surrendered and the pace of events quickened. The dropping of the atomic bombs galvanized the various OSS missions in SEAC. Plans were immediately made to send what were then called ''city teams'' into all the capitals of Japanese-occupied Southeast Asia, because it was clear that there would be no other intelligence groups available to send reports on the orderly surrender of Japanese forces back to the appropriate departments in Washington. As one former OSS officer recalled to a later generation, ''there were as yet no State Department officers there; there were no consulates; nobody was there representing U.S. interests in that part of the world.''

As OSS teams prepared to move into Saigon from the south, members of the Deer mission prepared to follow Ho Chi Minh into Hanoi. Some ten days after Thomas's message to China, the Deer group had received a slight augmentation of personnel, including an OSS medic named Paul Hoagland, who found Ho desperately ill. Sulfa and quinine sufficed to restore the Viet-Minh leader's health in an astonishingly short period of time and possibly prevented a rupture between the Americans and the Viet-Minh when Ho discovered that one of the new arrivals was really a French officer. Tragedy was avoided and harmony was retained; the Frenchman was simply marched back to the Chinese border under guard, and the incident was overlooked. With news of the atomic raids on Japan Ho moved swiftly. The Indochinese Communist party hurriedly convened a national conference in Tonkin and called for a general insurrection against the Japanese; on August 16 a National Liberation committee was formed, and a contingent of Viet-Minh guerrillas appeared in the streets of Hanoi; the following day the French flag on the balcony of the Hanoi Municipal Theater was run down and the Viet-Minh banner run up in its place. Simultaneously Ho transmitted a message to OSS headquarters in China using equipment furnished by the ever-willing Deer mission. The United States was to inform the United Nations that the Viet-Minh had been fighting the Japanese alongside other UN forces. Now that the war was drawing to an end, "We beg United Nations to realize their solemn promise that all nationalities will be given democracy and independence."[16]

As Ho's forces moved into Hanoi in late August and the first days of September, members of the Deer mission were not far behind, seemingly giving de facto American recognition to Ho's men as the governing body of Indochina. Whether Ho was emboldened by the American presence or whether he was determined in any case to master a fluid situation before his opponents recovered is quite unclear. But it is a matter of record that on the same day—September 2, 1945—on which Douglas MacArthur formally received Japan's surrender on the broad quarterdeck of the battleship *Missouri* far to the north, Ho Chi Minh proclaimed the Democratic Republic of Vietnam from a Hanoi balcony. Emperor Bao Dai, the Japanese puppet, swiftly gave allegiance to the new government and offered to serve as advisor. Ho's "republic" was to stand unchallenged for seven days while the dazed "victors" over Japan collected both their wits and their forces for a suitable riposte.[17]

On August 17, while Ho was broadcasting his appeal to the United States and United Nations on Major Thomas's radio, de Gaulle met in Paris with his Committee of National Defense to discuss plans to reoccupy Indochina. The land forces, it was discovered, were ready to leave in three echelons during September, October, and November. The Madagascar brigade could leave immediately. In all, France would pledge the lives of over 60,000 of its young men in a desperate bid to regain imperial stature. The following month, while Ho's Democratic Republic of Vietnam apparently continued to hold undisputed sway over Tonkin, Annam, and Cochinchina, de Gaulle moved to support force with diplomacy. He summoned Chinese Foreign Minister T. V. Soong to his office in the Elysée Palace and in lofty, elliptical language asked the Chinese to quit Tonkin as rapidly as possible.

The situation in French Indo-China and particularly in Tonkin seemed confused at the moment. In this district there were more or less improvised organizations which had sprung up in the name of Annamite Governments. These organizations were composed,

mainly, of people who had been with the Japanese before the capitulation, as well as Communists who there, as elsewhere, came into
prominent positions before the war ended. These organizations were
incapable of dealing with the extremely difficult economic
situation—a situation made worse by the indifference of the
authorities on the spot, the disorganization of communications and in
general the consequences of the occupation and military operations.

According to the Potsdam agreement on Indochina, the legal "authorities
on the spot" in Tonkin were, of course, Chinese, and de Gaulle implied to
his Chinese listener that Chiang's armies were not only not evacuating fast
enough nor gracefully enough as the first few Frenchmen returned, but
were indeed hindering the restoration of French rule by their very presence.
Soong replied in equally lofty and somewhat evasive language that China
would maintain her pledge to leave Indochina to the French as soon as a
sufficiently large garrison could be established out there. He told de Gaulle
that he had just received a telegram from Chiang reaffirming China's
commitment. De Gaulle had done all that he could for the moment. Troops
were being sent out; the Chinese had been warned. Now decisions would
be made in the field, not in Paris.[18]
   Two days before de Gaulle's interview with Soong the Deer mission had
returned to Kunming from Hanoi. Thomas and his men had observed the
Viet-Minh's successful battle against Japanese forces at Thai Nguyen
between August 20 and 26, had "comfortably" rested in the town's
provincial governor's quarters, "well fed and cared for by the Viet-Minh
. . . getting fat, getting a suntan" between August 27 and September 9,
and then had moved on into Hanoi where they spent their final week in
Tonkin, "seeing the city, buying souvenirs, saying good-bye to our
VIETMINH friends, and making arrangements to return to Kunming."
There Major Thomas wrote a lengthy, surprisingly objective report in
which he carefully balanced vociferous Viet-Minh denials of Communist
affiliation with his own observations and those of others that if Ho and his
men were not outright followers of Communism, they at least held Communist sympathies. "If not out-right communists, they were definitely
leftists," Thomas concluded. He also noted, however, that all parties and
persons seemed united for independence, apparently accepted the claim
that the Viet-Minh "represents at least 85% of the population of Annam,
Cochin-China, Tonkin and Cambodia," and stressed the fact that

Viet-Minh leaders were ready and eager to talk to French officials about meaningful civil and political reforms within Indochina.[19]

So the Deer mission passed into history, but not OSS interest in events at Hanoi. Even as Thomas and his men observed the battle at Thai Nguyen, another OSS group, headed by Major Archimedes L. A. Patti, who headed the North Indochina desk in Kunming, flew into Hanoi's Gia Lam airfield on August 22. The seven Americans were accompanied by five French officers, headed by Jean Sainteny of French intelligence. Wedemeyer, the American commander-in-chief of the China theater, had not wanted to send Patti and his group south, fearing that the team would become involved in politics. The French officers with the American party became convinced of this soon after their arrival in Hanoi. While they observed that the city was festooned with Viet-Minh flags and while any and all French were kept locked up in "golden cages" by the Japanese, who feared a bloodbath should Frenchmen and Tonkinese meet, the American group was comfortably ensconced in the Hotel Metropole, where its members, particularly one "Roberts," held long and—to the suspicious French—sympathetic conversations with Ho and his lieutenants. Sainteny and his men whiled away their enforced, if pleasant, bondage "dispatching radio messages to Kunming deploring their misfortune." Actually, as R. Harris Smith has revealed, the Americans were divided in outlook. Some, notably Lucien Conein, whose name would appear again in the annals of American-Vietnamese history, were sympathetic to both sides. Others had taken up with Vietnamese girls, whose physical attractions not unnaturally shaped their lovers' political outlooks. Nonetheless, when Ho proclaimed September 2, 1945, as Vietnam Independence Day and stated that the Democratic Republic of Vietnam would exist "within the French Union," Colonel Patti and "Roberts" stood behind him.[20]

With the coming of Chinese troops on September 9, however, American influence in Hanoi began to erode rapidly. The Americans were few, the Chinese many, and the threat of a massive French return loomed large. Gradually the OSS contingent began to dribble away. "Roberts," who had become convinced that Ho was a great man and a great patriot,[21] stayed the longest, to the growing dismay of Wedemeyer's headquarters in China. "Roberts" sought to form some extralegal organizations to encourage the Viet-Minh, symbolically if nothing else. Finally on October 25 the restless Wedemeyer ordered "Roberts" back to China.[22] Still a third small OSS contingent would come to Hanoi, but any possible American opportunity to influence events had disappeared, as the new observers quickly concluded. Meanwhile, to the south, in Saigon, events had taken a very different and far from genial turn.

Between September 2 and 4, 1945, nine young OSS agents deplaned in Saigon after a long journey from their headquarters in Ceylon. This was "Detachment 404," an American unit attached to Mountbatten's Southeast Asia Command, ordered into French Indochina to investigate war crimes, process American POWs in the region and investigate the condition of U.S. properties.[23] By mid-September Detachment 404 had accomplished a number of objectives. Cargo planes had been brought in from India to evacuate 214 American POWs. A local French residence had been acquired as detachment headquarters, a household staff of servants had been obtained, some local French officers had been entertained at dinner, four more officers had come in from India, and, most important of all, members of the detachment had begun informal conversations with several Viet-Minh leaders.[24]

The commanding officer of the detachment was a young twenty-eight-year-old former journalist and writer named A. Peter Dewey, who had operated in behind-the-lines OSS projects in France in 1944 and whose father was at the time a banker and conservative Republican congressman from Illinois.[25] Once the American POWs had been taken care of, Dewey and his men had been ordered to remain in Saigon to "represent American interests," which meant primarily political surveillance for the State Department.[26] Dewey was, in fact, a poor man for the job. He simply possessed too many conflicting loyalties. He had studied French history as a Yale undergraduate and held France in the greatest esteem. Yet he shared with so many of his American colleagues in SEAC an equally profound repugnance for European colonialism. With divided loyalties such as these he was suddenly thrust into the midst of revolutionary upheaval. That tragedy would be the consequence should elicit no surprise.

The situation in the southern portion of Indochina at this time was far different from that which prevailed in the north, where Ho and the Viet-Minh held sway with at least tacit Chinese support. In Cochinchina the Viet-Minh was considerably weaker, the forces of native nationalism frightfully fragmented. But news of Hiroshima and of an impending Japanese surrender forced all such groups into an uneasy coalition called the "Committee for the South," which had taken over in Saigon and proclaimed itself the legitimate government some days before the Americans landed.[27] Dewey tried to remain aloof from the turmoil about him, but this proved impossible. He was impressed by Committee efforts to maintain public order and dismayed by the blind opposition of French and other Vietnamese nationalists to Committee efforts. ''Nightly clandestine midnight'' meetings between OSS and Viet-Minh officials were held in these early weeks, and an unmistakable sympathy for the Viet-Minh grew within the detachment, which paralleled the sentiments held by OSS personnel in Hanoi and which crept into intelligence reports on Indochina prepared by the special intelligence branch in China.[28]

But things began to change on September 13, when British General Douglas Gracey flew into Saigon from SEAC headquarters to take command of the area south of the sixteenth parallel in accordance with MacArthur's General Order No. 1 regarding the surrender of Japanese forces in Asia and the Pacific. Gracey found ''Vietnamese, Frenchmen, Japanese, Indians, Englishmen, Chinese, and Americans mingling uneasily in the city streets.'' Restricted by Mountbatten's orders to disarm the Japanese, Gracey immediately became determined to ''restore order,'' which practically translated into preparations to restore French rule. The Americans, who had been happily mingling with French officers by day even as they covertly spoke to Viet-Minh officials by the light of the moon, were caught in the middle. Bluechel, the second in command of Detachment 404, had had an interview with Viet-Minh ''Foreign Minister'' Pham Ngec Thach on the fifteenth, in which Thach had claimed that his party sought only to obtain ''self government for the Annamese people by peaceable means.'' The party was sufficiently well-organized, Thach continued, to assume immediate government of ''Viet Nam,'' i.e., the coastal provinces of Cochinchina, Annam, and Tonkin. Laos and Cambodia were considered separate countries, but an entente could be arranged with them. The overriding objective, however, ''was to rid the Annamites of French rule, immediately if possible, gradually if necessary,'' and Thach frequently alluded with great enthusiasm to the American plan for gradual independence for the Philippines as a suitable model for the future development of French Indochina. Thach added that such a scheme was by no means incompatible with French desires ''for French commercial interests would remain. In fact he stated that the Viet Minh wanted and needed French interests to develop the country.'' American interests, he said, would also be welcomed.

According to Thach the aims of the Viet-Minh would be presented to the French and also to British and American representatives, who, it was hoped, would assist as disinterested neutrals in subsequent negotiations.[29]

But the hope, if such it was, was chimerical in the extreme. After years of occupation, defeat, and humiliation both at home and in Indochina, Frenchmen were not about to surrender their colonial prerogatives, privileges, and power at the behest of what seemed to them a motley crew of native revolutionaries. And General Gracey, who detested the very thought of Asian nationalism, was in Saigon with his Ghurkas ready to give his French colleagues all the help they required. While recognizing various Viet-Minh leaders as heads of respective political parties, Gracey took complete charge of affairs in Saigon, completely undercutting the Committee of the South. Within four days the drift of his policy had become so clear that desperate Vietnamese nationalists rebelled, and the great thirty-year war for Indochina began.

It commenced on September 17, when the Committee for the South declared what was in effect a general strike.[30] The rationale behind this move, as explained to OSS agents by Viet-Minh leaders, was essentially defensive. Gracey had refused to receive Viet-Minh petitioners, and the party had been forced to evacuate the public buildings which it and its allies in the coalition Committee for the South had been using for their government. "A passive course of action" was deemed best, and so the general strike was called. Five days later, under further "dreadful provocation," the Viet-Minh ordered the evacuation of as many of their Annamese followers as possible from the Saigon-Cholon area to "headquarters in the country," where the struggle for Vietnamese independence could continue. A chilling pattern of warfare was already taking shape.[31]

The "dreadful provocation" was the sudden release from previous detention of over a thousand armed French colonial troops by the " 'impartial' " Gracey in retaliation for the native general strike. The troops seized all government buildings and sought without success to arrest the members of the Committee of the South who fled to the rice paddies and villages of the countryside. The armed uprising in turn stimulated a wild rampage by the French civilian population against the natives in the streets of Saigon. Any Vietnamese who appeared was insulted, attacked, or arrested and subjected to brutal treatment by the enraged French citizenry. British and French soldiers looked on stolidly.

Dewey was completely alienated by Gracey's action. The OSS detachment was quietly headquartered on the outskirts of the city and took no active part in the events of September 22, but Dewey did publicly criticize Gracey's behavior. The British general, who had excitedly concluded that the Americans were supporting the Committee of the South, declared

Dewey persona non grata on September 25 and ordered him to leave Indochina the following day. Gracey undoubtedly allowed whatever reason he possessed to be overwhelmed by the passions of the moment, for in a subsequent report filed by Bluechel on events in Saigon between September 15 and 30, the barbarous behavior of the French was drastically played down.[32] Dewey nonetheless prepared to depart Saigon on September 26. He was never to leave. For on that morning, on a road between the city and Ton Son Nhut airfield, the young OSS commander was murdered. His death destroyed any faint possibility that the Vietnamese-Anglo-French dispute over the future of Indochina could be resolved short of blood and fire.

Available accounts of what happened on the day of Dewey's murder differ on at least one crucial point. There is agreement that Dewey and his second-in-command, Bluechel, departed for Ton Son Nhut airfield early in the morning of September 26 so that Dewey could catch a 9:30 plane sent to take him back to OSS headquarters at Kandy, Ceylon. The plane failed to arrive on time, and so Dewey and Bluechel wandered back and forth between the airfield and the city. First Dewey went back to the hotel to finish packing. Then he discovered that he had left his dog tags behind and went back again. Finally, about 12:25 p.m., with the plane still nowhere in sight, Dewey decided he had time to return to the OSS headquarters for lunch. Driving back toward the city, Dewey told Bluechel of his anger over the recent wounding of one of his men in the nearby countryside by some Vietnamese nationalists who had been chased out of Saigon by the French rampage. In 1945 Bluechel swore that though Dewey was obviously "upset," he did not precipitate the attack on him; he was suddenly machine-gunned to death on the road by Vietnamese forces and died so swiftly that he had no time to react. A quarter of a century later Bluechel told OSS historian R. Harris Smith that Dewey was not killed before sighting the armed Vietnamese and screaming some obscenities at them in French, thus inviting murder.[33] Dewey's mental state and behavior in the brief moments before his death thus remain an enigma—and one with enormous consequences for both the immediate and long-term future of Indochina. There seems no way to resolve the discrepancy between what Bluechel told his superiors in Saigon at the time and what he told Smith twenty-five years later.

As to what happened thereafter, available accounts are in substantial agreement. The jeep in which Dewey and Bluechel were riding careened into the ditch with Bluechel jumping or being thrown clear. Bluechel returned the Vietnamese fire for a time, and then, after assuring himself that Dewey was indeed dead, he raced back to the OSS compound with the Vietnamese in hot pursuit. Alerting his men, Bluechel prepared a defense against the Vietnamese, who took positions on a golf course fronting the OSS building, and there for two hours a desultory fire fight ensued, in which a number of Vietnamese were hit. For the handful of residents inside the small compound it was a terrifying time. As the tropic sun beat down upon a semi-silence, punctuated by frequent blasts of small-arms fire, the Americans were given long moments to reflect that they dwelt at the edge of a strange city in a foreign land, surrounded by hostile natives, their only hope being eventual rescue by resentful allies, their only touch with reality being the ghostly whispers coming through the radio transmitter linking them with Kandy, hundreds of miles away.

At mid-afternoon the Vietnamese asked for a truce to care for their wounded, and Bluechel permitted two of his men to slip away for help down a drainage ditch. It was at this point that the Vietnamese apparently realized for the first time that they had not been shooting at Englishmen or Frenchmen, but at Americans. At least they claimed this to some of the OSS men they met. The fight broke off, and arrangements were made to go back for Dewey's body. But at this moment of growing calm British Ghurkas suddenly appeared, and the Americans were informed in no uncertain terms that the British were determined to destroy the Vietnamese root and branch. Gracey—who had borne Dewey no love and who, along with the French, had expressed open and frequent resentment at OSS contacts with the Viet-Minh—had at last found his "incident" and would exploit it to the hilt.[34] The day after Dewey's death Gracey arrested the Japanese commander in Saigon and "threatened to have him tried as a war criminal if his troops did not aid in battling the Vietnamese."[35] Bluechel's moderate assessments of the incident, including his stress on the fact that the jeep had not flown an American flag, carried no weight. Bluechel told his superiors in Ceylon "that Americans are not considered to belong in the classification 'Europeans.' Americans are considered to be a separate people, and the Viet-Minh leaders expressed the hope that Americans would view favorably their bid for independence. . . ." It was all to no avail. Gracey had the power to influence events in Saigon; Bluechel did not. A brief truce was arranged between the Viet-Minh and the Europeans on October 2, but it broke down several days later when the first troops arrived from France. A "war of extermination, marked by appalling atrocities on both sides,'' to use the words of one later OSS observer, had begun.[36]

Washington's reaction to Dewey's murder was to prepare the way for a drastic diminution of the OSS role and activities in Saigon. An investigative report of Dewey's death by the Strategic Services Unit of the War Department concluded somewhat drolly that ''General Gracey is not well suited to his assignment. He seems to have adopted a notably bull-like attitude toward the Annamese, calculating that this would cow them. In the light of later experience, he should have realized that in their overly emotional state, they would react violently toward his bluffs.'' British assertions that the OSS headquarters had been provided with sufficient security and that neither Gracey nor his staff should be blamed for what had happened was received with great skepticism by the War Department reporter, who concluded with ''a further gratuitous comment'' that it was highly unlikely that in the future American ''military personnel'' would be in a position to ''secure much valuable intelligence from French Indo-China.'' By the end of 1945 the few OSS men in Saigon found themselves hopelessly mired in an environment of mounting confusion and violence.[37]

At the end of October 1945 the attention of General Wedemeyer and the OSS in China shifted again to Hanoi. ''Roberts's'' departure had left an informational blank that needed to be filled. The man chosen for the assignment was Captain Frank M. White, who had participated in the battle of the OSS compound in Saigon following Dewey's death. His arrival in the Tonkinese capital was delayed by the need to resolve jurisdictional problems between SEAC and Wedemeyer's headquarters in China, and the young man then traveled from Saigon to Hanoi via Manila and Shanghai, arriving in mid-November.

The Hanoi which met his eyes ''was a strange and stricken town, restive, covered with a film of red dust, raised, more often than not, by crowds of tense demonstrators moving in the streets.'' Most of the demonstrators were Viet-Minh, but White noted the ''profusion'' of other, non-Communist groups, less numerous and well-organized, but marching in counter-demonstration to the Ho regime. The continued existence of Ho's ''republic'' was tacitly guaranteed by the Chinese forces under Marshal Lu Han, which had spread all over the area north of the sixteenth parallel, ostensibly to fulfill MacArthur's order to disarm all Japanese forces in the region and prepare them for ultimate shipment back to Japan. In fact, the Chinese ''had devoted themselves to looting the country systematically of everything of value they could find." In the scramble for pelf Ho was simply ignored.[38]

The situation began to change, however, with the arrival of the first French troops in Tonkin on December 19. Shortly after the first units came ashore at Haiphong Ho summoned White to an interview at Le Palais du Gouvernement. The whole thing was rather pathetic. White found Ho completely alone save for a doorman in a large, bare building, apparently devoid of telephones, lieutenants, colleagues, bustle, and all the other accouterments of a functioning government. The two men talked for several hours, first in French, then in English, which Ho was eager to use. He spoke bitterly of the Chinese, who were beginning to stream out of the city now that the French had come. He spoke of the great desire of his people for independence and hoped that White would impress this fact upon distant Washington. He expressed pleasure that White's presence seemed to indicate some American interest in the plight of the native population of Indochina. Finally the little man with the wispy beard expressed very cautious hope that he could negotiate with the French for Vietnamese independence within the French Union.

White could offer little in return. He "had come to report on events then happening in Vietnam and to transmit whatever messages" Ho "might want passed to U.S. authorities in Washington." He was empowered to do no more. Ho's comment that while he had studied Marxist-Leninism in Russia, he did not expect that the Soviet Union either could or would make any kind of real contribution to the building of a "new Vietnam" was pleasant to hear, but did it really mean anything?[39] Did Ho himself really represent any kind of discernible Vietnamese future? Surely the man's surroundings and prospects were not alluring. Asia was throwing up countless "revolutionaries" and "nationalists" in the chaotic days and weeks and months after V-J Day. Who could predict with any degree of accuracy which one of them—if any—might successfully seize and shape the destiny of their peoples?

White took his leave and returned to the hotel. Within moments he had received an invitation to dinner back at Le Palais. When he arrived he found Ho and two colleagues, one of whom turned out to be Vo Nguyen Giap. Soon the other guests arrived. The French party was led by the impressive and imperious General Le Clerc and included Jean Sainteny. Le Clerc and his lieutenants, though superficially cordial, quickly made young White aware "of their irritation and distrust of OSS." The Chinese trooped in next followed by an Englishman, Lieutenant Colonel Wilson, head of MI-5 in Hanoi and Mountbatten's representative in the city. After "glacial" introductions the company sat down to a dinner which proved to be a "horror." The French would not really converse with anyone and were particularly nasty to the Chinese, who promptly got "wildly drunk." Ho sat forlornly at the head of the table with White, as obvious guest of honor, at his side. At one point the young American leaned toward his host, the head of the Democratic Republic of Vietnam, and remarked that there seemed some resentment over the seating arrangements. "I can see that," Ho replied quietly, "but who else would I have to talk to?"[40]

Soon there would be no one for Ho to talk to save his implacable French opponents. For back in Washington the U.S. government was steadily retreating from the vibrant anticolonialism of the high war years as the terrible prospects grew of a cold war with the former Soviet ally. Nonetheless the retreat was a fighting one on the part of some government officials, who refused to tamely submit to the reversal of a policy in which they deeply believed.

Thanks to the popular reception of the heavily edited versions of the "Pentagon papers," it is now a matter of general knowledge that between September of 1945 and the following spring Ho Chi Minh sent some eight letters to the Truman administration, begging for help in securing Vietnamese independence within or beyond a contemplated "French Union," and that Ho on several occasions alluded specifically to America's generous policy toward the Philippines as a suitable model for Vietnamese political development. Washington's response, it has been stated time and again, was complete silence.

Yet, as is usually the case, matters were not that simple. The highest officials in the State Department and administration, it is true, were willing to ignore Ho for the sake of strengthening the French alliance and stiffening French resolve to assume a firm anti-Communist stance in Europe. But more junior officers at State have subsequently expressed great unhappiness at what they were called upon to do a quarter of a century and more ago. For example, on November 15, 1945, Abbot Low Moffat, then director of the Office of Southeast Asian Affairs, dispatched a memorandum to his immediate chief, John Carter Vincent, director of the Bureau of Far Eastern Affairs, in response to the reception by the Department of a number of Ho's pleas. "SEA [Southeast Asian Affairs] considers that no action should be taken on the attached telegram of Ho Chi Minh to the President requesting membership of the so-called Viet-Nam Republic on the Far Eastern Advisory Commission" then in process of creation to generally oversee American occupation policies with respect to Japan.[41] Yet in testimony before the Senate Foreign Relations Committee in 1972 on the general question of any kind of recognition of Ho's regime in 1945-1946, Moffat haltingly stated:

> The position, and we were very sympathetic with Ho Chi Minh who was, in our opinion, perfectly clear—a letter addressed to the President of the United States cannot be answered without, in effect, I mean, other than from the head of another state, without actually involving recognition. We talked with him [Ho], we had all had communications with him, but there was no answer ever sent to a formal inquiry addressed to the President of the United States, and I think if we had, that would have been taken by the French in that case as a really serious affront and possibly a breach of international etiquette. . . . It had nothing to do with his [Ho's] being a Communist. I wrote one of these memos saying we shouldn't answer this.[42]

Other evidence exists suggesting that a number of State Department officials were unhappy with the official American treatment of Ho Chi Minh without knowing quite what to do about it. Moffat, for example, complained in late September of "SEAC actions in Allied name without American concurrence" and cited specifically the "strong anti-Annamese policy in Indochina" which was made to appear "as an Allied decision." At the end of that month a memorandum drawn up in the Office of Far Eastern Affairs circulated the other regional offices in the Department. The memorandum proposed formation of an international commission for Southeast Asia to be composed of representatives of the United States, France, Great Britain, and China. H. Freeman Matthews, director of the Office of European Affairs, protested. Russia was sure to demand inclusion, and the United States, in the wake of the Yalta Far Eastern Accords, could not really refuse, thus creating one more flashpoint of conflict in the mounting contest of wills between East and West.[43] The officers manning the various Far Eastern desks at the State Department, however, continued their cautious fight against wholesale capitulation to Anglo-French imperialism in the face of expressed administration policy. When, for example, Sir George Sansom, British minister in Washington and internationally recognized expert on Japan and the Far East, called on Vincent and Moffat on September 24 to express concern that the outbreak of violence between natives and Europeans in Indochina might spread to "all other colonial areas,'' Vincent and Moffat replied that ''some effort should be made to secure negotiations between the French and moderate Annamese forces.''[44]

But such efforts to modify the emerging pro-French, procolonial policy within the American government were to no avail. President Truman had pledged his word to de Gaulle in late August that this country would not interfere with French efforts to return to Indochina as the legitimate governing agency. On October 1 Acting Secretary of State Dean Acheson renewed the American commitment to French Ambassador Henri Bonnet. Bonnet did not get all he wanted. He first told Acheson that, contrary to what Soong had earlier said to de Gaulle in Paris, the Chinese were not leaving Indochina as yet. In fact, they were reinforcing their garrison in Tonkin, which in the French view was ''unnecessary.'' Could the State Department perhaps cable Wedemeyer in China and through him ''attempt to bring to the attention of the Generalissimo [Chiang Kai-shek] that his orders'' to merely disarm the Japanese garrison and then withdraw ''were not being obeyed?'' Quite impossible, Acheson replied. It ''would be wholly improper and undesirable for us to interfere with the functioning of the Generalissimo's staff. . . .'' Bonnet then turned to the irritating presence of the OSS in Indochina. There were a ''considerable number'' of such officers, and French citizens in Indochina were complaining that the Americans ''were not carrying out our policy of non-opposition to the reestablishment of French control but were talking to the natives in terms of independence.'' Acheson's response was firm, sure, and certainly pleasant to French ears. ''I said that our policy had been very clearly stated along the lines which he [Bonnet] had indicated, which was that we were not opposing the reestablishment of French authority in Indochina. I could not believe that American officers were acting contrary to this announced policy.'' Five days later Acheson cogently spelled out the dimensions of America's Indochina policy in a cable to China, which paraphrased an earlier message sent to New Delhi: ''US has no thought of opposing the reestablishment of French control in Indochina and no official statement by US Govt has questioned even by implication French sovereignty over Indochina. However it is not the policy of this Govt to assist the French to reestablish their control over Indochina by force and the willingness of the US to see French control reestablished assumes that French claim to have the support of the population of Indochina is borne out by future events.''[45]

As late as October 20 Vincent made one last effort to modify somewhat

American policy toward Indochina and Southeast Asia in general. "In Southeast Asia a situation has developed to the liking of none of us, least of all to the British, the French, the Dutch, and, I gather, to the Annamese and Indonesians," Vincent stated in a New York speech.

> With regard to the situation in French Indochina, this Government does not question French sovereignty in that area. Our attitude toward the situation in the Dutch East Indies is similar to that in regard to French Indochina. In both these areas, however, we earnestly hope that an early agreement can be reached between representatives of the governments concerned and the Annamese and Indonesians. It is not our intention to assist or participate in forceful measures for the imposition of control by the territorial sovereigns, but we would be prepared to lend our assistance, if requested to do so, in efforts to reach peaceful agreements in these disturbed areas.[46]

But Truman had long since made up his mind that for the moment at least the great revolt of Asia would be subordinate in American policy making to the emerging imperatives of the cold war in Europe. Two weeks after Vincent's speech the President publicly "praised the British Empire for having a constant foreign policy, always backed by the British people no matter what party was in power." Truman "said he hoped this country could have a foreign policy which will be the policy of the people, not of any party."[47] The President had in mind current British policies in Indonesia, where the Royal Navy and Air Force had just razed a large part of the city of Surabaya in retaliation for the murder of a British general by Indonesian rebels. But the President also made his point with that portion of the administration and bureaucracy which hoped for a sympathetic policy toward the Indochinese. There was to be no public revelation of dissent or division on foreign policy. Vincent, Moffat, and others stilled their criticisms; once more America would stand aside while Europe— now gravely weakened and uncertain—attempted to reimpose its rule over Asia.

Between November 1945 and the following spring de Gaulle moved slowly but surely in Indochina. He refused to issue a statement "announcing France's intention to adopt a far-reaching progressive policy" in Indochina "designed to give the native population much greater authority," as urged upon him by the French mission in India, because, he said, the time was not yet ripe, conditions were too confused.[48] Meanwhile the fighting that had broken out between the Annamese and Europeans in and around Saigon spread through much of Vietnam. By the end of January it had become on the European side an entirely French operation; the accommodating British had withdrawn completely. On March 4, 1946, Mountbatten deactivated Indochina as a territory within SEAC, and the French and Viet-Minh faced each other alone.[49] Only in Tonkin were French aspirations still contested for a time by an outside force—China.

Washington assumed an attitude of interest without comment. Officials who had been in Hanoi and Tonkin during the autumn of 1945 were debriefed in some detail when they arrived home. At the end of January 1946, for example, Brigadier General Philip E. Gallager was queried about conditions in northern Indochina by several State Department officials, whose major concern seemed to be the continued presence of Chinese forces in Tonkin. Gallager assured his listeners that the Chinese probably would leave soon—indeed they were already gone for the most part—and the French could now begin to move into Tonkin without fear of Chinese provocation. As for Ho and the Viet-Minh, Gallager expressed admiration for them. They were young and enthusiastic, but too few in number. Should the French refuse to deal with Ho or should negotiations break down, then the Viet-Minh would undoubtedly take to the hills and commence guerrilla warfare. "Asked how 'communist' the Viet-Minh were, General Gallager replied that they were smart and successfully gave the impression of not being communist. Rather, they emphasized their interest in independence and their Annamese patriotism. Their excellent organization and propaganda techniques, Gallager pointed out, would seem to have the earmarks of some Russian influence. . . . In his opinion, however, the Viet Minh should not be labelled full-fledged doctrinaire communist." As for the French population of Indochina, Gallager expounded at some length upon their bitterness at American "neutrality." Originally these people had hoped that the United States would play the same role in Tonkin that the British had played in Cochinchina, i.e., as a catalyst preparing the way for the return of French rule. Instead, Americans in Tonkin—which was to say the OSS—had tried to maintain contact with both sides, French and native. The result was that "in our neutral role we were thus a disappointment to both sides."[50]

Two days before Gallager's debriefing, Secretary of State Byrnes had ordered the assistant chief of the Southeast Asian Affairs Division, Kenneth Landon, then in Saigon, to proceed to Hanoi in order to report on conditions firsthand and especially to assess the course of French-

Vietnamese negotiations, which Landon had already learned had been proceeding sporadically since November. Landon's subsequent reports from Hanoi—available in the Defense Department version of the Pentagon papers—were written from a distinctly French perspective. Landon certainly spoke with Ho and received two of the ultimately famous eight letters which the Viet-Minh leader addressed to President Truman in the six months following V-J Day. But Landon received most of his news and impressions from French officials—D'Argenlieu, Sainteny, and Le Clerc —and he reported with undeviating consistency his impression that the French wanted to be conciliatory and moderate in their dealings with Ho, even to the point of offering outright Vietnamese independence within the framework of a new French colonial union. All in all the impression which emerged from Landon's cables from Hanoi in February 1946 was of a French government seeking to accommodate itself to new realities and of a stubborn and therefore unreasonable native revolutionary determined to fight to the death if he did not obtain everything he demanded.[51]

Only once had the Truman administration abandoned its ostentatiously neutral position. On November 5, 1945, France had formally requested permission to purchase surplus military equipment from U.S. stores in the Philippines for use in Indochina. Moffat blocked the proposal with respect to aircraft by pointing to what he described as "US policy of not assisting the French to reestablish their control over Indochina by force. . . ." In January, however, the French were able to obtain jeeps for Indochina by going through the British, who requested eight hundred such vehicles of *lend lease* origin for their French ally in Indochina. So long as the provisions of wartime lend lease aid could cover such a transaction, leading State Department officials were apparently satisfied that legality had been served.[52] By March even this pretense was abandoned. While Moffat bravely issued a "Policy and Information Statement on French Indochina," which stated in part that the United States would not compromise "the natural political aspirations of the colonial peoples in Southeast Asia," a draft *aide-memoire* was circulating through the State Department, in which the Secretary of State was to tell the French government of American willingness to sell some twenty-five surplus landing craft then in Philippine waters for use in Indochina.[53]

As fighting between French and Viet-Minh forces spread throughout Indochina in the spring of 1946, however, the United States sought to revert to its position of firm neutrality. The Chinese had at last agreed to quit northern Indochina at the end of March, and France was faced with a burgeoning civil war.[54] The Chinese did not leave the Hanoi area for some months, and as late as the end of June French officials were calling at the State Department to complain of their presence and behavior.[55] Ho himself was no happier than the French with the Chinese presence, very probably because he was as anxious as the Europeans to settle the future of Indochina once and for all.[56] However, the United States shrank from further involvement. Even as the draft *aide-memoire* on French purchase of surplus landing craft wended its way through the Department, Secretary of State Byrnes received a further recommendation from the Bureau of Western European Affairs that he call in the French ambassador ''and inform him orally that while we sympathize with their desire to bring about stable conditions in Indo-China, we are unable at this time to comply with his Government's request to purchase American equipment for use in that area, with the exception of approximately $220,000 worth of medical supplies.'' Furthermore, the French should be pressured continually to seek some sort of peaceful resolution of the conflict.[57]

On March 6 French officials reached a tentative accord with Ho's DRV, in which ''The French Government recognizes the Vietnamese Republic as a Free State having its own Government, its own Parliament, its own Army and its own Finances, forming part of the Indochinese Federation of the French Union.'' On the other hand, Ho had been forced to accept an ominous provision, which read, ''The Vietnamese Government declares itself ready to welcome amicably the French Army when, conforming to international agreements, it relieves the Chinese troops . . . .''[58] On March 18 French forces exercised this prerogative and occupied Hanoi. Fighting between French forces and rebels continued in the countryside, and Viet-Minh extremists carried out several assassinations of more moderate Vietnamese political figures, while negotiations to define precisely the new status of the DRV opened in Dalat on April 3. By April 10 all vestiges of Allied occupation in Indochina—including the American presence—had been officially swept away, while French forces were positioned in all the major cities of Vietnam,[59] ready to pounce on the native rebels once negotiations broke down as, given the mutual implacability and dislike of the principals, they were certain to do. The Indochinese segment of the great revolt appeared to have been halted for a time, due in no small measure to the policy of a distant and indifferent United States, which had bent to the strongest pressures and acquiesced in the return of a weak and vengeful ally to the Asian quagmire.

And yet, why not? It seemed the best—indeed the only—viable policy at the time. Few knew who the Viet-Minh were; everyone knew of the desperate straits in which France was fixed at the close of World War II. Yet a stable and increasingly powerful France was absolutely essential for the future peace and well-being of Western Europe. French obstructionism on the Allied Control Commission for Germany had complicated the already immense problems of occupation in that country.[60] The cold war between Russia and the West was growing more apparent daily, climaxed in March by the Iranian crisis, in which the world seemed to be moving as close to war as at the time of Munich. A vast and terrible holocaust had ended only months before. Now a new one—whose violent dimensions could scarcely be conceived in the new age of atomic power—seemed inevitable. It was a time to scramble for allies and to clasp in warm embrace those who were already friends. So the great revolt was to be ignored as it worked its way out in Indochina. Neither the French nor the Viet-Minh truly wished peace short of the total capitulation of their opponents. Negotiations held first at Dalat and later—at Fontainebleau in France— were devoid of meaning or spirit. They were broken off on August 2 by the Viet-Minh, and a week later Moffat wrote Vincent that ''Recent developments indicate that the French are moving to regain a large measure of their control in Indochina in violation of the spirit of the March 6 convention.''[61] In November the French navy shelled Haiphong, killing thousands. Within months the Viet-Minh crept away to the villages, hills, and jungles of the interior, carrying with them the respect and admiration, if not the support, of much of Washington's officialdom.[62] When Ho and his men reappeared in strength in later years they would be viewed in the chill atmosphere of global cold war, not with sympathy but in fear, not as an essentially nationalist anticolonial group but as an arm of ''the international Communist conspiracy.''

NOTES

1. Report by the Headquarters, Office of Strategic Services, India Burma Theatre, in Philippine and Southeast Asian Affairs Files, Lot 54 D 109, folder: ''Southeast Asia Command,'' Records of the Department of State, U.S. Department of State, Washington, D.C.

2. Testimony of Abbot Low Moffat, 11 May 1972, in U.S. Congress, Senate, *Causes, Origins, and Lessons of the Vietnam War: Hearings before the Committee*

on Foreign Relations, 92d Cong., 2d Sess. (Washington, D.C.: U.S. Government Printing Office, 1973), pp. 174-175 (hereinafter cited as *Causes, Origins, and Lessons of the Vietnam War*); "Memorandum by James C. H. Bonbright (WE) to the President," 30 April 1945, in French-Iberian Affairs Files, Operating Records of the French Desk, Lot 53 D 246, folder: "Indochina, 1945," Records of the Department of State, U.S. Department of State, Washington, D.C.

3. Moffat testimony, 11 May 1972, in *Causes, Origins, and Lessons of the Vietnam War*, pp. 175-177.

4. James Dunn to William Phillips, 15 May 1945, in French-Iberian Affairs Files, folder: "Indochina (1944-1945)."

5. Quoted in U.S. Department of Defense, *United States-Vietnam Relations, 1945-1967*, 12 vols. (Washington, D.C.: U.S. Government Printing Office, 1971), 1:A-21 (hereinafter cited as *United States-Vietnam Relations*).

6. Donald Lancaster, quoted in Bernard Fall, *The Two Vietnams: A Political and Military Analysis*, 2d ed. rev. (New York: Frederick A. Praeger, Publishers, 1967), p. 61.

7. Ibid.

8. Report entitled "Clandestine Activities in French Indochina Directed from SEAC," in Philippine and Southeast Asian Affairs Files, folder: "Southeast Asia Command."

9. *United States-Vietnam Relations*, 1:A-22, 8:39-44.

10. Report for the State-War-Navy Coordinating Committee, entitled "American Participation in SEAC after Cessation of Japanese Resistance," Philippine and Southeast Asian Affairs Files, folder: "Southeast Asia Command."

11. The American minutes of the Franco-American talks of 22-24 August 1945 may be found in U.S. Department of State, *Foreign Relations of the United States, 1945: Diplomatic Papers*, 9 vols. (Washington, D.C.: U.S. Government Printing Office, 1967-1969), 4:707-724. The French record is in Charles de Gaulle, *War Memoirs*, 6 vols. (New York: Simon & Schuster, 1960), vol. 6: *Salvation, 1944-1946, Documents*, pp. 282-289.

12. "Memorandum for the President and the Secretary of State, Subject: Recommendations with Respect to Topics for Possible Discussion with General de Gaulle. . . , August 1945," in French-Iberian Affairs Files, folder: "Indochina, U.S. Policy Towards, 1945-1946."

13. The twelve-volume Department of Defense version of the Pentagon papers contains a memorandum from OSS Director William J. Donavan to Byrnes, dated 22 August 1945, the day of the Truman-de Gaulle talks on Indochina, enclosing a report from OSS officials in Kunming, flatly asserting that "The French Government has decided to adopt a passive diplomatic attitude toward the reoccupation of Indo-China because of their inability to make an entry with a powerful show of arms." From what General de Gaulle has since told us in his *Memoirs*, this report was probably false. Yet it is significant that neither Byrnes nor Truman chose to

explore the possibility raised by the memorandum of modifying ultimate French designs upon the region. *United States-Vietnam Relations,* 8:46-48.

14. "The 'Deer' Mission to Viet Minh Headquarters, July-September, 1945," in *Causes, Origins, and Lessons of the Vietnam War,* pp. 243-247.

15. Ibid., pp. 248-249.

16. Quoted in R. Harris Smith, *OSS: The Secret History of America's First Central Intelligence Agency* (Berkeley: University of California Press, 1972), pp. 332-335.

17. Moffat testimony, 11 May 1972, "Report on the 'Deer' Mission," both in *Causes, Origins, and Lessons of the Vietnam War,* pp. 168, 271-272; *United States-Vietnam Relations,* 1:A-22.

18. De Gaulle, *Salvation, Documents,* pp. 282, 299-300.

19. "Report on the 'Deer' Mission," in *Causes, Origins, and Lessons of the Vietnam War,* pp. 261-272.

20. Smith, *OSS,* pp. 348-356; "Statement of Frank M. White, Former Major, Office of Strategic Services," in *Causes, Origins, and Lessons of the Vietnam War,* p. 147.

21. See unsigned memorandum entitled "Interview with Ho Chi Minh," dated 19 September 1945, which would seem to have been written by "Roberts," in *Causes, Origins, and Lessons of the Vietnam War,* pp. 306-307.

22. Smith, *OSS,* pp. 356-359.

23. Memorandum by Major A. Peter Dewey to Lt. Col. Moscrip, Subject: "Operation EMBANKMENT," 25 August 1945, in *Causes, Origins, and Lessons of the Vietnam War,* p. 281.

24. "Report by Major Herbert J. Bluechel, Adjutant 404 Detachment to Commanding Officer OSS Detachment 404, Saigon FIC [Dewey], 17 September 1945," in ibid., p. 282.

25. Smith, *OSS,* p. 192; *Biographical Directory of the American Congress, 1774-1971* (Washington, D.C.: U.S. Government Printing Office, 1971), p. 854.

26. Smith, *OSS,* p. 338.

27. Ibid., p. 336.

28. Ibid., pp. 336-341; "Report on the Provisional Government, FIC," Office of Strategic Services China Theater, SI Branch, 20 September 1945, in *Causes, Origins, and Lessons of the Vietnam War,* pp. 308-311. Harold Isaacs, who appeared in Saigon during the course of that tumultuous autumn after the French had succeeded in restoring their rule, reported the unsurprising fact that recently freed French nationals had convinced themselves that the Viet-Minh were a puppet guerrilla force left behind by defeated but fanatically defiant Japanese. Harold R. Isaacs, *No Peace for Asia* (New York: Macmillan Co., 1947), pp. 135, 141, 154-156.

29. "Political Aims and Philosophy of the Viet Minh Government of French

Indo-China,'' report by Major Bleuchel, from Saigon, 30 September 1945, in *Causes, Origins, and Lessons of the Vietnam War*, pp. 283-284.

30. Smith, *OSS*, p. 341.

31. Bluechel, ''Political Aims and Philosophy of the Viet Minh Government,'' in *Causes, Origins, and Lessons of the Vietnam War*, pp. 283-284.

32. Smith, *OSS*, pp. 341-342; Bluechel, ''Political Aims and Philosophy of the Viet Minh Government,'' in *Causes, Origins, and Lessons of the Vietnam War*, pp. 282-283.

33. ''AFFADAVIT . . . by Captain Herbert J. Bluechel. . . , Saigon, Indochina, 13 October 1945,'' in *Causes, Origins, and Lessons of the Vietnam War*, pp. 286-287; Smith, *OSS*, pp. 344, 415.

34. Bluechel Affadavit; ''AFFADAVIT . . . of Captain Frank M. White. . . , Saigon French Indochina, 13 October 1945''; and White testimony, 11 May 1972, all in *Causes, Origins, and Lessons of the Vietnam War*, pp. 183-184, 286-295. See also Smith, *OSS*, pp. 344-345.

35. Smith, *OSS*, p. 345.

36. Ibid., pp. 345-346; Bluechel, ''Political Aims and Philosophy of the Viet Minh Government,'' in *Causes, Origins, and Lessons of the Vietnam War*, pp. 283-284; Isaacs, *No Peace for Asia*, pp. 134-140, 160-162.

37. ''Memorandum; Subject: Investigation of Death of Major Peter Dewey,'' Strategic Services Unit, War Department, in *Causes, Origins, and Lessons of the Vietnam War*, pp. 296-298; Smith, *OSS*, pp. 346-347.

38. ''Statement of Frank M. White. . . ,'' 11 May 1972, in *Causes, Origins, and Lessons of the Vietnam War*, p. 147.

39. Ibid., pp. 148-150.

40. Ibid., pp. 151-152. Ho's remark is quoted in Smith, *OSS*, pp. 358-360.

41. *United States-Vietnam Relations*, 1:C-71.

42. Moffat testimony, 11 May 1972, in *Causes, Origins, and Lessons of the Vietnam War*, p. 187.

43. Memorandum by Moffat to John Carter Vincent, 22 September 1945, in Philippine and Southeast Asian Affairs Files, folder: ''Southeast Asia Command''; Memorandum by J. C. H. Bonbright of the Office of Western European Affairs to Matthews, 2 October 1945, in French-Iberian Affairs Files, folder: ''Indochina (generally 1940-1945).''

44. *FR, 1945: Diplomatic Papers*, 6:313.

45. ''Memorandum of Conversation, by the Acting Secretary of State (Acheson), 1 October 1945,'' in French-Iberian Affairs Files, folder: ''Indochina, U.S. Policy Towards, 1945-1946''; *FR, 1945: Diplomatic Papers*, 6: 313.

46. ''Address by John Carter Vincent Made at the Foreign Policy Association Forum, 'Between War and Peace,' in New York City, 20 October 1945,'' U.S. Department of State *Bulletin* 13 (21 October 1945):646.

47. Quoted in an editorial in the *St. Louis Post-Dispatch*, 12 November 1945, clipping in Official File #385, Harry S. Truman Papers, Harry S. Truman Library, Independence, Mo. The President's remarks were made at a state dinner for British Prime Minister Attlee, who had come to Washington for talks with the President and Canadian Prime Minister Mackenzie King on the atomic bomb.

48. Ambassador in France (Caffery) to Secretary of State, 28 November 1945, *FR, 1945: Diplomatic Papers*, 6:314-315; *United States-Vietnam Relations*, 1:A-23.

49. *United States-Vietnam Relations*, 1:A-24.

50. Memorandum of Conversation between General Gallager, Charles S. Reed, FSO, and Woodroof Wallner of WE, 30 January 1946, French-Iberian Affairs Files, folder: "Indochina, 1946-1948"; U.S. Department of State, *Foreign Relations of the United States, 1946*, 11 vols. (Washington, D.C.: U.S. Government Printing Office, 1969-1972), 8:15-20 (hereinafter cited as *FR, 1946*); *United States-Vietnam Relations*, 8:53-57.

51. *United States-Vietnam Relations*, 8:59, 61.

52. Memorandum by Moffat to Morgan of AV, 28 November 1945, French-Iberian Affairs Files, folder: "Indochina (1940-1945)"; Hubert F. Havli, Chief, Lend Lease and Surplus War Property Affairs Office, to General Donald G. Shingler, 23 January 1946, ibid., folder: "Indochina (1946-1948)." Truman personally approved the transfer in late January after discussing the matter in very routine fashion with Acheson. The memorandum of the conversation in the Pentagon papers imparts the distinct impression that both Truman and Acheson treated the incident as a very minor matter, which in the context of those tumultuous times it certainly was. *United States-Vietnam Relations*, 8:52.

53. Moffat's draft policy statement and the draft *aide-memoire* are in the Philippine and Southeast Asian Affairs Files, folder: "Indochina, Political Policy, United States."

54. *FR, 1946*, 8:21-30 passim.

55. Memorandum of Conversation with Jean-Claude Winckler, 28 June 1946, Philippine and Southeast Asian Affairs Files, folder: "Indochina: Chinese Relations, 1945-1949."

56. See Memorandum: "Chinese Forces in Indochina," 15 May 1946, ibid., folder: "Political Misc."

57. Memorandum of Conversation between Ambassador Bonnet, Mr. Acheson, Mr. Culberton, 16 February 1946; Memorandum by J. C. H. Bonbright and H. Freeman Matthews to the Secretary of State, 2 March 1946, both in French-Iberian Affairs Files, folder: "Indochina (1946-1948)."

58. Quoted in *United States-Vietnam Relations*, 1:A-25; see also cable by Consul Reed at Saigon to Secretary of State, 7 March 1946, *FR, 1946*, 8:32.

59. *United States-Vietnam Relations*, 1:A-24-A-26; *FR, 1946*, 8:34.

60. John Gimbel, *The American Occupation of Germany: Politics and the*

Military, 1945-1949 (Stanford, Calif.: Stanford University Press, 1968), pp. 23-26; *FR, 1945: Diplomatic Papers*, 3:841-852; *FR, 1946*, 5:496-516.

61. *FR, 1946*, 8:48-54 passim.

62. As late as January 1947 Moffat and his subordinates in PSA strove to get their department and government to initiate or at least support some kind of effort to bring the French and the rebels back to serious and meaningful negotiations. When this proposal was debated within the State Department, it was quickly accepted for three reasons: (1) the view that a clear-cut victory for either side would threaten the long-term stability of Southeast Asia, (2) because it was felt something ought to be done to neutralize growing Soviet propaganda in support of the Vietnamese, and (3) a mounting fear that French recalcitrance and possible rebel successes in Indochina might give renewed vigor to the national movement in Indonesia. Concrete proposals were few and timid, however, centering around the idea that either Chinese, British, and American officials on the spot ought to jointly offer their ''good offices'' to the warring parties, or that the United States should support a UN resolution to the same effect. Needless to say, nothing of significance emerged from these efforts and discussions. Memorandum of Conversation with Tswen-ling Tsui, Counselor, Chinese Embassy, 3 January 1947, in Philippine and Southeast Asian Affairs Files, folder: "Indochina: Chinese Relations, 1945-1949"; Memorandum from Kenneth P. Landon of SEA to John Carter Vincent, 14 January 1947, ibid., folder: "Indochina, Original Memoranda to Mr. Vincent."

chapter 3

The Deference to Colonialism: Indonesia

As France groped its way back into Indochina the Dutch endeavored to restore their power and prestige in the lush, mineral-rich islands of Indonesia. Here the story was far more complex, and American interest proved less intense. Nonetheless the Truman administration could not escape entirely the terrible pressures generated by the great revolt in this remote but important corner of Asia.

Nationalism had first emerged in Indonesia early in the century and had become an organized movement shortly after World War I. From the beginning of their rule the Dutch had been content to govern the East Indies indirectly through hereditary local leaders. At the same time Dutch authorities had ostentatiously recognized and preserved the diverse cultural and ethnic traditions of the islands, the better to divide and rule the native peoples. Although the Indonesians did possess a semblance of self-government through the *Volksraad*, an ostensibly popular assembly, this institution actually hindered the formation of a nationalist impulse since a large proportion of the membership was appointed and the remainder were chosen by a very narrow franchise. But in a number of ways the Dutch, like their European counterparts elsewhere in East Asia, had sewn the seeds of their own defeat. Although European education had been restricted to a handful of Indonesians—only 6 percent of the native population was literate in any sense as late as 1945—the small elite still found it increasingly difficult to obtain places in either the civil service or business economy of the islands and as a result grew increasingly restive.

Moreover, Dutch disinclination to either Christianize or Westernize the Indonesian population permitted the Moslems to gradually complete their penetration of the islands, which had begun centuries before. Thus a patina of religious universalism bound the diverse peoples and cultures of Java, Sumatra, and the other islands of the East Indies by the first decade of this century, when Javanese merchants, using their religion as a symbol of social unity, organized the first significant nationalist movement in reaction to economic dominance by Chinese and European business interests. This initial impulse waned in the early 1920s to be replaced first by futile Communist-led agitation and then by a firmer and more attractive nationalist movement, which was neither completely communistic nor Islamic in orientation. This movement, under the Westernized leadership of men such as Achmed Sukarno, Hatta, and others, was based upon more or less clandestine study mlubs and "wild schools" in East Indian cities and villages.

Dutch authorities responded with consistent repression. Force and mass arrests defeated the earliest outbreaks of nationalism in 1926-1927, and the young rebels themselves remained torn between the competing images of communism and Islam even as they revealed a consensual predisposition to the collectivist approach to economic and social problems. But despite defeat, dissension, and jail, Indonesia's native leadership clung tenaciously to its dreams, and by the time of the Japanese invasion nationalist leaders of all stripes, conservative and radical, democratic and socialist and even Marxist, had all won a significant, if not always legal, place in the life of the islands. The Japanese conquest, while producing economic chaos and new miseries for the people, brought the nationalists one step closer to power. While political independence remained chimerical, Japanese authorities assiduously courted the favor and enlisted the collaboration of leading nationalists including Sukarno. Only a very few recognized leaders—most notably the socialist Sjahrir—resisted Japanese importunities and blandishments.[1]

Doubt and confusion surround the birth of the self-proclaimed Indonesian Republic at the close of World War II. According to the most respectable accounts, those radical nationalists who had collaborated to a greater or lesser degree with Japan, including Sukarno, immediately found themselves under pressure to establish an independent Indonesian Republic from more moderate nationalist elements "anxious to avoid acquiring independence as a gift" from the defeated and discredited Japanese. As early as August 17, only seventy-two hours after Japan's formal agreement to surrender, Sukarno rushed a native government into being, and when British troops from the Southeast Asia Command landed in Java on September 29 as the spearhead of the Allied reconquest, "they found a functioning administration in existence."[2]

The British quickly concluded that they had stumbled into an impossible situation. A Foreign Office official reminded Ambassador Winant in London on November 7 "that Java was only included in SEAC on August 15 and that Britain did not have readily available sufficient troops and munition or adequate flow of intelligence from Java which would have prepared them for task they would face."[3] By the end of October no more than three battalions of Indian troops had been landed in Java, where they concentrated in the major cities of Batavia and Surabaya. Unfortunately a thousand Dutch troops and Ambonese mercenaries were permitted to debark from a British transport off Batavia during the first week of October. Equipped with American lend lease weapons and uniforms, these troops promptly went berserk, shooting, beating, and looting the native population of the city and surrounding native compounds.[4] Under these trying curcumstances Mountbatten assumed a deliberately detached posture. As early as September 28 he flatly told the Dutch representative at his headquarters that British forces could not be permitted to become involved in the internal politics of the Indies and that British forces were in Java solely for the purposes of securing key cities, controlling Japanese headquarters, disarming Japanese troops, and recovering Allied prisoners of war. According to U.S. political adviser Charles Yost, Mountbatten then urged the Dutch representative to go to Batavia immediately and confer with leaders of the Indonesian Republic while the Dutch government at home should issue an immediate pronouncement for "some degree of independence."[5]

The Dutch government responded on October 1 with a press statement from The Hague. Admitting that the ravages of the recently concluded war in Europe had "continually slowed up" the dispatch of Dutch forces to the Far East, the government adamantly refused to recognize the Indonesian Republic as the de facto government in the Indies or to negotiate the future political fate of the islands with Sukarno or his followers. "Soekarno has allowed himself to be the tool and puppet of the Japanese for which he has received a high Japanese imperial decoration. This man, with his fascist tendencies, has systematically preached hatred against the Allies." This fervent reaction apparently rattled the British Chiefs of Staff, who promptly cabled Kandy, asking Mountbatten to define the extent, if any, "to which he considered he could ensure law and order outside Batavia and Surabaya with the forces he planned to place in Java."[6]

Mountbatten remained unmoved, however. He refused to allow himself, his command, or his handful of troops in Java to become embroiled in an incipient civil war between stubborn Dutchmen and determined Indonesians. A British embassy official calling at the State Department in mid-October revealed that Mountbatten and his colleages at SEAC "appear to be in complete accord that a meeting of all Indonesian leaders must be held to discuss conditions in Java" and to inform Indonesians of Queen Wilhelmina's proclamation of 1942 calling for a postwar Dutch commonwealth, including Indonesia, that would guarantee a large measure of local self-government to its various members. Mountbatten was aware that the Indonesians were in control of Java and that if the Dutch refused to negotiate the islands' future, violence was certain to result. Sukarno's power and influence would have to be recognized. "Admiral Mountbatten stated that in his opinion, if Soekarno continued to be excluded by the Dutch from all Indonesian meetings, civil war would result. . . ." It was essential, British officials in Java reported, to bring pressure on both the Dutch and Indonesians to see reason; "considerable deflation" of the excessive expectations of both sides was required.[7]

The United States was swiftly drawn into the Indonesian drama not only because of its now-predominant role across Oceania, but also because some 5,000 Dutch marines were currently in training at Quantico, Virginia, and American lend lease equipment was being used by British forces in Java. An obscure American colonel apparently had been the first Westerner to contact Sukarno in mid-September, after the first Dutch official to visit the islands had been forced to return to his ship off Batavia. The colonel had then gone ashore and learned from Sukarno personally that Allied forces would be permitted ashore only if no political interference with the Indonesian Republic was contemplated; if prompt attention was given to disarming the Japanese and evacuating prisoners; and if no Dutch representatives or armed forces were landed. According to the colonel the British quickly accepted these provisions and thus were permitted ashore.[8]

Early in September, meanwhile, Rear Admiral Van der Kun of the Dutch navy had called on Admiral Leahy "to make an urgent request" that the Dutch marines at Quantico be permitted to complete their training, despite the end of the war, "and then be transported to the Netherlands East Indies." Leahy promised to pass on this request to the Joint Chiefs of Staff, who approved it. When Van der Kun called on Leahy again at the end of

October, he found that the U.S. Navy had "made all arrangements for the shipment" of the Dutch troops to Southeast Asia "except the destination, which must be prescribed by Admiral Mountbatten as the East Indies are in his area."[9]

Mountbatten was by now hard-pressed. As early as mid-October, while he was still building up his small, lend lease-equipped forces on Java, Indonesian extremists had called for war on the Dutch. According to press reports Mountbatten's deputy at Batavia, General Sir A. F. P. Christison, had ordered the still-armed Japanese garrison to rout the rebels, who were harassing Japanese as well as European troops.[10] A week later reports reached the United States that Ghurkas under Christison's command had skirmished with Indonesian forces near the town of Semerang, Java. On October 29 the sputtering conflict flared into full-scale crisis. British Ghurkas at the Surabaya naval base found themselves surrounded by armed Indonesians and ordered the rebels to disarm. The Indonesians rejected the order and opened fire. Brigadier General A. W. Mallaby, in immediate command of British forces at the base, set out for Indonesian lines to try to arrange a cease fire and was shot down. The enraged British promptly threatened to "bring the whole weight of land, sea and air forces" in the area and "all the weapons of modern war" against the Indonesians unless the surrender of those guilty of "murdering" General Mallaby was immediately arranged. The British promptly enforced this threat by ordering RAF and Royal Navy units to the Java area.[11]

The United States found itself increasingly drawn into the controversy. On October 21 Sukarno had bitterly denounced the Americans for providing the British and Dutch forces with "Guns and Uniforms,"[12] a charge quite impossible to refute since the Europeans in their battles with the rebels were employing lend lease equipment obtained from the United States during the past five years of world war. During the week and a half after Mallaby's death, while Java lay wrapped in an oppressive atmosphere of dreadful anticipation, and the British government sought to pressure the Dutch into bargaining with all rebel elements, including Sukarno, Washington took several steps of its own to force the Netherlands government toward meaningful negotiations. Possibly in direct response to Sukarno's charges, an order was sent out prohibiting the shipment to Java of ammunition stocks purchased by the Dutch, while authorities in the Philippines were forbidden to equip several thousand released Dutch prisoners of war waiting to be transported back to Java.

Meanwhile British forces and the few Dutchmen who had landed in

Java were formally requested to remove U.S. emblems from all their lend lease equipment, and the American government formally condemned the use of lend lease material "in any way that has a political connotation."[13] Dutch officials in Java, under instructions from The Hague, were loath to meet with Sukarno and steadfastly clung to the view that most Indonesians were "moderate" in outlook. But both they and their government in Europe were poignantly aware of the dangerous situation, hemmed in as they were by the Anglo-American desire to see an end to bloodshed and rebel determination to perpetuate it should meaningful negotiations fail to materialize. During the first week in November Washington learned from its ambassadors in both Britain and the Netherlands that the Dutch were apparently prepared to make serious proposals to the rebels. These included promises of substantial if not total internal self-government for Indonesia, participation by Indonesians in the affairs of the Dutch kingdom as a whole and specifically in the Dutch Foreign Service, the abolition of existing racial discrimination in Indonesia, symbolized by the existence of a separate court system, and expansion of economic and educational opportunities.[14] But would these proposals suffice to stifle the rebel impulse, and would they be made in time? On November 10 came the melancholy answer to the second question.

The British command, employing both warships and land-based artillery, shelled the center of Surabaya in retaliation for rebel unwillingness or inability to deliver up Mallaby's assassin and lay down their arms. Press reports stated that the shelling was intense, and an "Indonesian spokesman" claimed that many natives were killed or wounded. The following day the British continued to press their advantage; planes and warships blasted the city's naval base, while Ghurkas moved through the town.[15] Thereafter fighting between Asians and Europeans lasted five terrible weeks with no mercy asked or given on either side. British patrols were swiftly and silently dispatched by machete and knife while ignorant villages perished under rocket and napalm assaults from often lowering skies. Before order was restored 900 Ghurkas and British and 6,000 Indonesians had been killed or injured.[16]

Liberal opinion in America was shocked. "The reports from Soerabaja bear a sickening resemblance to the news from Warsaw, Rotterdam, Belgrade, Athens, Coventry and London when they were subjected to the bombs of the Nazis," the *St. Louis Post-Dispatch* editorialized on November 12, adding that the British were "doing the dirty work for the rich islands' overlords." The Netherlands had ruthlessly exploited the

Indies for years, and now the British, "fearing that a successful revolt in Java would be a bad example to their own colonies, rush to put down the nationalists." Was the United States following that "people's foreign policy" in Indonesia which Truman had expansively proclaimed in his recent speech before Prime Minister Attlee? It appeared not. The concerned citizen who sent the editorial to Truman added that there was an "increasing feeling of insecurity which citizens in all walks of life are coming to have over events in the Far East. There is grave apprehension that our country may be dangerously involved so that we will be doing acts and standing for, and apparently approving, policies diametrically opposed to the principles that we fought for. I must confess," he concluded loquaciously, "that I have not heard anyone voice views on this subject who has not expressed the keenest regret that we seem to be fighting with or aiding those who are fighting against those who are eager to obtain and enjoy civil rights and freedoms which are elementary with us and which have been denied to them. The strong hope is constantly expressed that we may find at least some way to withdraw from what seems to be, for the average person, the side of the oppressor."[17] There is no evidence that the President either saw or responded to the letter.

Instead, the American government doggedly pursued its policy of minimal pressure on the contestants, concentrating on the far more accessible British and Dutch. On November 20, without alluding to the recent violence at Surabaya, Secretary Byrnes cabled Ambassador Winant in London that "Since the Indies are primarily Brit zone of military responsibility and continuing confusion of events there renders any accurate judgment extremely difficult, we have not desired to take any early or premature action in regard to the situation." However, further deterioration of the situation in Indonesia "cannot fail to have an unfavorable effect on general situation in East Asia." Therefore at his discretion Winant was to ask British officials whether a little more American pressure at The Hague might help push the Dutch toward negotiations.[18]

The British reply, sent through Winant on December 1, was cautiously hopeful. Although Whitehall tactfully chose not to say it, the shelling of Surabaya had temporarily shocked both the Dutch and Indonesian moderates. Even as fighting raged in Java the cabinet of the rebel Indonesian Republic was completely reshuffled. Sukarno retained his presidential title, but was stripped of much of his power, while the moderates, led by thirty-six-year-old Soetan Sjahrir assumed practical control of the nationalist movement. Western chancelleries were pleased and hopeful.

"The new Cabinet," Abbot Low Moffat wrote to John Carter Vincent, "is composed mainly of men who were educated in Holland; not a single Japanese collaborator is included; several of the group are decidedly moderate in their views." Yet none could be considered potential lackeys of the Dutch. Sjahrir himself, though trained as a lawyer in Amsterdam, was an "ardent nationalist," who had emerged as head of the native labor movement in the early thirties and had been arrested and exiled to New Guinea for his efforts. "The moderate and non-collaborationist character of the new group will probably satisfy Dutch objections to negotiating with Soekarno," Moffat concluded prophetically.[19]

The chief Dutch official in Java, Van Moek, promptly met with Indonesian leaders on November 17 to present his government's proposals. Apparently they were not sufficiently attractive to lure the Indonesians into formal negotiations. According to the Foreign Office, "Present difficulties are said to be unwillingness of Indonesian leaders to attend further meetings with Dutch and their inability to control the extremists which has resulted in serious deterioration of situation throughout Java." In those circumstances it was obviously useless to pressure the Dutch government any further. The British asked whether the State Department would be willing to issue a general statement, not addressed specifically to either side, "but expressing concern at the cessation of conversations which seem to have made a promising start."[20]

As Department officials pondered this query, Ambassador Stanley Hornbeck in the Netherlands sought to move them to a more sympathetic consideration of the merits of the old colonial regime. Hornbeck warned that if Dutch political control in Indonesia weakened or disappeared and if there were no adequate substitution of British or American prestige, another, more sinister influence might emerge. In the nature of things, political trends being what they were, "that new influence would likely to be oriental rather than occidental; the chances would be in favor of its being Chinese or Japanese; and, as between these two, the greater likelihood would be that it would be Japanese."[21] This warning, delivered only a little more than one hundred days after the end of World War II, was sober indeed. Hornbeck added that even the Soviet Union might seek to exploit any power vacuum in Indonesia that would emerge as the result of a Dutch defeat. Indeed, the Soviet press had already hailed "national liberation movements" in both Indochina and Indonesia and had charged British officials with using force to restore European colonial rule and oppression in both areas. "The sympathy of progressive forces of the entire world is unqualifiedly on the side of the popular masses aspiring to freedom and possessing the right to freedom,'' a Soviet journalist proclaimed at the beginning of November.[22] This was apparently the first time in the postwar era that the Soviet government would applaud and support ''wars of national liberation.'' It was not, of course, to be the last. Hornbeck, however, was haunted not by the spectre of communism, but of revived Japanese militarism. ''More and more,'' he wrote in his peculiarly convoluted prose,

> the evidence which becomes available indicates that the present situation in the Netherlands East Indies is a product of Japanese inspiration and a projection of the Japanese war effort. . . . There is potentially in the making a political alignment of the peoples of the world in two great and conflicting groups: on one hand the ''white'' peoples of the Occident together with those ''colored'' peoples in various parts of the world who remain under their influence and partake of their ways of thinking, and on the other those ''colored'' peoples who reject or escape from the influence of the ''white'' and Occidental peoples and who, entertaining and committed to concepts contrary thereto, are suceptible to the influence of a leadership such as Japan has for four decades offered, has recently attempted to impose, and may be expected again to try to exert.[23]

At the end of 1945 the American government thus had before it two powerful rationales for a policy of alignment with the old colonial order in Indonesia and, by implication, throughout Southeast Asia. First was the possible future menace of international communism expanding from its power base in the Soviet Union into areas of unrest such as Java, where the old order was powerless to contain movements for local independence. Second was the terrifying possibility of a future resurgence of an imperialist Japan, which would seize once again upon nationalist sentiments and rhetoric to obliterate Western interests and influence throughout East Asia. To state the matter bluntly, both anticommunism and racism had been suggested, implicitly or explicitly, as rationalizations to support a continuing American commitment to the imperialist order in the Far East. Against these arguments stood the fervent wartime commitment to human decency and liberty as summed up in the Four Freedoms, the Atlantic Charter, and the United Nations with their promises of self-determination and self-protection for all the peoples of the earth. The emerging prospect of a terrifying cold or even hot war between the United States and the Soviet Union—between "democracy" and "communism"—immeasurably intensified the pressures on the American government and people to be evenhanded and sympathetic to the nationalist aspirations of the people of Southeast Asia. It would be difficult for American policy makers to condemn brutal, suppressive Russian behavior in Eastern Europe and yet support apparently similar behavior on the part of British and Dutch officials and soldiers in Indonesia. It ill-behooved the Truman administration to precipitately support the colonial powers in Asia simply because their support of American policy was desperately needed in Europe. And by this time Colonel Kennedy, the first Westerner to meet Sukarno and a man who had spent most of September and October in Indonesia, returned to Washington to report that while "the village farmer might prefer to be left alone to cultivate his paddy land in peace, the feeling of nationalism had become sufficiently widespread throughout the Javanese population that the people as a whole could be roused to resist Dutch rule and that none would support the Dutch."[24]

The State Department's initial solution to the dilemma was to do nothing except to reach internal agreement during early December that further sales of surplus arms and military equipment to the Dutch for the express purpose of use in Indonesia should be forbidden.[25] Washington's silence prompted another British request on December 10 for a general statement of conciliation.[26] At last, on December 19, the Department issued the press statement which the British had long sought. It began with a review of the current situation: that the Southeast Asia Command had been assigned the responsibility of accepting the Japanese surrender in the Netherlands East Indies and of freeing prisoners and internees and that "The carrying out of this mandate has been complicated by the differences between Indonesians and the Netherlands authorities." The U.S. government had viewed with "increasing concern" recent developments in the Netherlands East Indies, the statement continued. "It had hoped that conversations between the Indonesians and the Netherlands authorities would have resulted in a peaceful settlement recognizing alike the natural aspirations of the Indonesian peoples and the legitimate rights and interests of the Netherlands. There has apparently been a cessation of these conversations." The "sole desire" of the American government was to "see such peaceful settlement achieved as will best promote world stability and prosperity and the happiness of people. . . . Extremist or irresponsible action—or failure to present or consider specific proposals can lead only to a disastrous situation. The United States earnestly hopes that all parties in the Netherlands Indies will see the necessity of an early resumption of conversations'' which would lead to a peaceful solution of the existing conflict.[27]

It was, all in all, an exquisitely balanced statement and one that implicitly stressed American unwillingness to become involved. The Dutch government responded three days later with a note applauding Washington's call for renewed talks while condemning ''the extreme danger to which many'' in Java ''are exposed as a result of unpardonable excesses committed by extremist elements.''[28] The Indonesians replied on Christmas Day, stressing the fact that their republic had come into being in response to the will of the people: ''Taking advantage of the confusion into which the Japanese here were thrown'' at the time of Tokyo's surrender, ''we seized power and proclaimed our freedom.'' The UN mandate to the Southeast Asia Command and its ''Anglo-Dutch Army of Occupation'' did ''not give the British the right to reimpose the Dutch on the Indonesians,'' the note continued. ''Unfortunately that is what has been and is being done.'' Tension was mounting and necessary measures of rehabilitation were retarded. ''We look to you,'' the Indonesians concluded, ''as the . . . country that has always been in the forefront of the fight for liberty, justice and self-determination, to use the benefit of your influence to stop the present bloodshed in Indonesia.''[29] In fact, as the Dutch note had concluded, conversations between Dutch negotiator Van Moek and Indonesian Prime Minister Sjahrir had already resumed without any American pressure.

In the first place, the Dutch quickly discovered that they did not possess the resources to return to Indonesia in force. At the end of December there were only 20,000 Dutch troops in the islands, yet The Hague had concluded that at least 75,000 would be needed to subdue the rebels, a force that it was estimated could not be mustered before October 1946. Second, the rebels had proved that their hold over people and territory was indeed tenacious. The British shelling and consequent occupation of Surabaya had obviously not led to native collapse. Instead, throughout December there was fierce fighting. Third, even before the Surabaya incident moderate elements, led by Sjahrir, had gained control of the Indonesian Republic. Sukarno was simply too intractable and excitable to lead his people into anything less than a long, drawn-out bloodbath, and the Dutch regarded Sjahrir as a man with whom they could negotiate responsibly. And, finally, there was the cool attitude of the British, who had their own problems with their own colonial and mandated areas in Asia and the Middle East after a long and dreadfully debilitating war. Some Dutchmen—as well as American Consul-General Foote at Batavia—also believed that overt British sympathy for Indonesian aspirations was due to a desire on the part of greedy English businessmen to supplant their Dutch and American rivals in the East Indies economy by flattering and supporting rebel demands for independence. Mountbatten's headquarters at Singapore, meanwhile, publicly condemned what it described as atrocities by Dutch forces against the native population of Indonesia. Available evidence would suggest that Lord Louis was indulging in rather gross hypocrisy; the strafing and burning of native villages throughout November and December was apparently carried out largely by Ghurkas and the RAF. Nonetheless the British were obviously unwilling to remain in Java for long months in order to rescue Dutch imperialism. At the end of December and into January British and Dutch officials meeting in Britain emerged with a joint communiqué to the effect that the right of Indonesia to independence should be recognized, and a high British official, Sir Archibald Clark-Kerr, was sent to Djakarta to assist in renewed Dutch-Indonesian talks. Thereafter negotiations would take precedence over violence, though they did not end it.[30]

Washington did add a kind of exclamation point to the attempts of Europeans and Asians to end the blood-letting in Indonesia. On January 23 the State Department again asserted that "it is not in accord with policy this Govt to employ American flag-vessels or aircraft to transport troops of any nationality to or from Netherlands East Indies or French Indochina nor to permit use of such craft to carry arms, ammunition or military equipment to these areas."[31] Sometime later the Soviet Union, the Ukraine, and Egypt proposed to the United Nations the creation of an investigatory commission for Indonesia to end what was called "a threat to the maintenance of international peace and security" by "regular British troops." The American Ambassador to the United Nations, Edward R. Stettinius, contributed to the death of this proposal by pointing out that the Dutch-Indonesian negotiations had resumed and might be imperiled by such a commission.[32]

As Dutch troops began to replace British in Java and Sumatra after April 1946, negotiations between the native republicans and Dutch continued, oscillating between deep pessimism and cautious hope,[33] until on November 15, 1946 the Linggadjati Agreement, named for its place of signature, a hill resort in Java, was tentatively accepted by both sides. The Netherlands would recognize the Indonesian Republic as the de facto authority in both Java and Sumatra, and both governments pledged themselves to cooperate in establishing a United States of Indonesia, embracing the rest of the archipelago including Borneo. Final agreement was reached by Dutch and Indonesian negotiators in March 1947. Not surprisingly, both sides followed their own interpretations of the agreement. The Dutch established puppet states in the reaches of the Indies beyond Java and Sumatra, while the republic extended its foreign relations to a point which the Dutch felt compromised the eventual establishment of the all-Indonesian state stipulated by Linggadjati. As one authority has written, the simple passage of time "favoured those people on both sides who did not want compromise." By late 1947 fighting had broken out again, and the final struggle for Indonesian independence was under way.[34]

What contribution had the United States made to the struggle for Indonesia? None at all beyond calling upon the three principals—Britain, the Netherlands, and the Indonesians—to negotiate their differences. American Far Eastern policy in the weeks and months immediately following the end of World War II was summarized by the knowledgeable *New York Times* correspondent Sidney Shallet as "Stability by Evolution." Assessing the "collective utterances" of State, War, and Navy Department officials from August to early November 1945, Shallet discovered a threefold aim, which stressed, above all, "long-range security for this nation," defined not in terms of a future communist menace so much as in terms of a recollected Japanese threat. America "never again" wanted "a situation to develop in which an aggressor nation, such as Japan was, can reach out to threaten us." Beyond that Washington "would like to see democracy in the Far East," though it recognized that democracy was something a people had to willingly accept "and not have forced on them by the decrees of a stronger party." Finally, the Truman administration would like to see established "stability in the seething, faction-ridden, economically bankrupt countries of the Far East." Stability had become the "keynote" of policy to prevent future aggression and to obliterate the threat of future attack in the Pacific.[35]

Because stability meant more to American policy makers and to millions of ordinary citizens than anything else, the American government never seriously contested the right of the old European colonial order to attempt a revival in the lands of the East. The new voices of Asia would be ignored. A State Department memorandum prepared at the close of 1945 for UN Ambassador Stettinius made this point clear enough. "Primary responsibility" for arriving at an agreement with the Indonesian republic "lies with the Netherlands authorities."[36] Stettinius promptly cast his vote with the majority when the world organization decided some weeks later to assign the Dutch full responsibility for resolving the Indonesian crisis without first consulting the rebel republic.

Nor did American policy toward the Dutch in Indonesia change markedly prior to the end of 1948. During 1947, in response to a renewed outbreak of hostilities between Indonesian military extremists and the equally pugnacious Dutch, the United Nations created a "Good Offices Committee," of which the United States was a part, to attempt a final mediation of the Indonesian crisis. On the last day of that year, in response to repeated calls for policy guidance from Frank Parker Graham, the chief American delegate on the committee, Acting Secretary of State Robert A. Lovett set forth the "major considerations of US policy which should determine the ambit of choice of alternatives . . ." facing the peace seekers.

Lovett's first point was that the Netherlands "is strong proponent US policy in Europe. Dept believes that stability present Dutch Govt would be seriously undermined if Netherlands fails retain very considerable stake in NEI, and that the political consequences of failure of present Dutch Govt would in all likelihood be prejudicial to US position in Western Europe." However, the United States had also long favored self-government or independence for those people qualified to accept the consequent responsibilities. Moreover, the United States desired the "speediest acceleration" of trade between Indonesia and the rest of the world because of the "tremendous burden imposed on US ability to supply consumer goods under Marshall Plan." Recent studies by the State Department had disclosed the "indispensability" of Indonesia "as supplier of food and other commodities to meet needs under" the European Recovery Program. What was obviously needed in this situation, Lovett continued, was some sort of formula by which the Dutch would recognize the ultimate independence and legitimacy of the Indonesian Republic without surrendering all of their interests and influence over the Indies. The Dutch, therefore, must be allowed "an interim period of continued . . . sovereignty" to prepare themselves for the wrench of final disengagement and also in order to "have opportunity during interim period to convince Indos of their mutual dependence on each other." The United States would thus seek a settlement in which concern for the interests and morale of the old, rather than for the aspirations of the new, would prevail. Moreover, a persistent, if subtle, hostility—or at least skepticism—continued to shape the American response to Indonesian nationalism. The Dutch had surely not been able to maintain law and order during the two years since their return in 1945, yet near the close of his cable to Graham, Lovett demanded that the infant republic be held to such an impossible accountability. The Acting Secretary warned that it "seems equally important that the administrative control of disputed territories be not returned to Republican authorities without adequate guarantees that orderly conditions will in fact prevail." After more than two years of nearly incessant civil conflict, this was an almost impossible demand. Only under pressure of the incipient triumph of communism in China and the corresponding fear that the movement might spread throughout Southeast Asia did the Truman administration in the latter half of 1948 suddenly abandon its Indonesian policy, turning abruptly to the struggling and hapless Dutch with the threat of an immediate suspension of Marshall Plan aid if The Hague did not abandon the islands immediately.[37]

It may be well to pause at this point and ask to what extent American policy was based on purely economic motives—on a desire to expand the influence and domination of U.S. capitalism to a remote and rich corner of the earth. There is no firm or clear-cut answer from available sources. Certainly the highest officials in the American government are on record in June of 1946 as expressing concern that continued violence in Indonesia would threaten U.S. petroleum interests at Palernbany, and the Secretary of State asked the ambassador to the Court of St. James to ensure that the British government and British forces still in Java "will take such steps as may be feasible to assure protection of these assets."[38]

Soon thereafter, however, the American consul-general at Batavia (Djakarta) wrote rather bitterly to his superiors in Washington of his conviction that the British "have some ulterior motive re NEI." In their outspoken contempt for the Dutch and ostensible sympathy for the rebels, British officials and the growing flood of British "real estate owners coming to Java from England" were seeking to maneuver control of the great island of Sumatra into Anglo-Australian-American hands. "Such would leave British and Australs [sic] in control with USA holding empty bag," the consul-general argued. This could only be accomplished if the Dutch hold over all of Indonesia was badly shaken.[39] Still a third perspective on the economic future of Indonesia was offered in April of 1946 by Abbot Low Moffat in a memorandum to the State Department's Central Secretariat. Moffat suggested that consideration might be given to wringing economic concessions from the Dutch in Indonesia in forthcoming lend lease and surplus property settlement negotiations. Such concessions could include provision of dollar exchanges to American concerns in the islands "for such legitimate purposes as amortization, full remission of profits and for purchase of equipment and necessary supplies." The Dutch should also be urged to abandon "unreasonable" taxation policies vis-à-vis American firms in Indonesia, and they should be induced to relax those economic policies and procedures "which make it imperative for American companies in the Netherlands East Indies to register as Dutch firms and not as American firms." Finally, should the "suggested Indonesian Free State" come into being, it should be asked to "assume its share of *all* loans and credits heretofore made on account of the Netherlands East Indies" and not merely those made prior to 1942 as Sjahrir had suggested. Moffat spoke approvingly of the "Open Door" as a traditional objective of American policy in Asia that could and should be applied to postwar Indonesia.[40]

It would be a mistake, however, to assume that such sporadic and fragmentary expressions of opinion and concern represented a well-conceived and coherent line of policy. Moffat, for example, was not only an avowed enemy of European colonialism; he was also a positive supporter of native self-determination, and even if we assume that he had ulterior economic motives—the supplanting of European imperialism in Asia by American capitalism—it is significant that his political and economic suggestions were constantly at odds with America's substantially pro-Dutch policy. Capitalist thinkers and theorizers traditionally have stressed the need for economic stability and law and order to ensure that their system would flourish. Yet Moffat's policy suggestions for Southeast Asia in 1945-46 were consistently based on the assumption that the United States should undertake the immense gamble of supporting the legitimate aims of excitable native revolutionaries. Nor is there any indication from the working files of the State Department that any coherent, well-defined "economic strategy" for Asia was ever proposed, considered, or debated within the American government during the early years of the great revolt in Asia following World War II. The desire of the State Department at the end of 1947 to see a termination of hostilities in Indonesia partly to expand Indonesian trade with war-devastated Europe is as close to an "economic strategy" for Asia as can be found in the tumultuous years between Hiroshima and the outbreak of the Korean War. American policy in Indonesia, as finally in Indochina, was based on a conservatism of instinct and temperament, not of economics.

Yet even as self-styled "liberal" Americans expressed public concern over the conservative course of national policy with respect to Indonesia—and Indochina and even China as well—socially and economically conservative Americans peered into the future with equal unease. The "fate of the colonial system in the most populous area of the world is regarded by U.S. officials as at stake in the outcome of the uprising in Java," a conservative journal observed in late December of 1945. Summarizing recent events in the island, the editors calmly dismissed as "a strange development" the use of Japanese troops and equipment by the hard-pressed British. They stressed once again the apparent rebel tie to the recent Japanese occupation, including "the fact that Achmed Soekarno, the extremist Indonesian leader, had collaborated closely with the Japanese all through the war. . . ." The Indonesian rebellion, then, could be defined as "a 'delayed Japanese time bomb' " set off at the moment of final defeat by a fanatic enemy to embarrass and distract his conquerer. But even conservatives could not ignore or explain away the demonstrably impressive support for the rebellion among the native population by the end of 1945. "Now it is recognized that the movement for independence is widespread and is by no means limited to those who collaborated with Japan." Accurately characterizing American policy as one of "not taking sides," noting that "early in the fighting the British were asked to remove any American labels from the Lend-Lease trucks and weapons they were using," the article closed with the gloomy comment that "signs are multiplying that the old-time system of colonial imperialism may be doomed." Any suggestion that the United States might have either a duty or a right to assist in the transition from imperial dominance and exploitation to national pride and self-sufficiency was as studiously avoided by the editors as it was by their government.[41].

By the end of 1945 the great revolt in Indonesia and elsewhere in Asia had gone far enough to reveal the essential conservatism of American policy, yet paradoxically that policy was not sufficiently coherent and vigorous to mollify conservatives at home. The roots of great tension, conflict, and anxiety—the roots of tragedy, in short—continued to grow month by month as the United States confronted the turbulence that was postwar Asia.

But Indonesia—and Indochina—were comparatively remote from the warm and confortable offices of power in Washington, where affairs of apparently greater significance were distracting American policy makers during the final months of 1945 and on into 1946 and 1947. If East Asia beyond Japan presented a set of serious problems to the United States in the months following the end of World War II, the centers of immediate challenge appeared to lie not in the southeast corner of the region but in Korea and above all in China.

NOTES

1. Paul M. Kattenburg, "Indonesia," in Lawrence K. Rosinger et al., *The State of Asia* (New York: Alfred A. Knopf, 1951), pp. 405-412; Amry Vandenbosch, "Indonesia," in Lennox A. Mills et al., *The New World of Southeast Asia* (Minneapolis: University of Minnesota Press, 1949), pp. 79-125; Gunnar Myrdal, *Asian Drama: An Inquiry into the Poverty of Nations*, 3 vols. (New York: Pantheon, 1968), 1:162-166, 3:1635; J. D. Legge, *Indonesia* (Englewood Cliffs, N.J.: Prentice-Hall, 1964), pp. 103-133.

2. Legge, *Indonesia*, pp. 128-132; Russell H. Fifield, *Americans in Southeast Asia* (New York: Thomas Y. Crowell, 1973), p. 34; Memorandum by the Chief of the Division of Northern European Affairs (Cumming), Washington, 8 October 1945, in U.S. Department of State, *Foreign Relations of the United States, 1945: Diplomatic Papers*, 9 vols. (Washington, D.C.: U.S. Government Printing Office, 1967-1969), 6:1158-1163 (hereinafter cited as *FR, 1945: Diplomatic Papers*).

3. Ambassador in UK to Secretary of State, 7 November 1945, ibid., p. 1168.

4. Harold R. Isaacs, *No Peace for Asia* (New York: Macmillan Co., 1947), pp. 127-131.

5. Quoted in Memorandum by the Chief of the Division of Northern European Affairs, *FR, 1945: Diplomatic Papers*, 6:1159.

6. *FR, 1945: Diplomatic Papers*, 6:1160-1161.

7. Memorandum of Conversation by the Chief of the Division of Southeast Asian Affairs (Moffat), 18 October 1945, ibid., pp. 1165-1167.

8. Memorandum of Conversation by the Chief of the Division of Southeast Asian Affairs (Moffat), 6 December 1945, ibid., p. 1178.

9. Leahy Diary, 6 September 1945, 26 October 1945, William D. Leahy Papers, Library of Congress, Washington, D.C.; *FR, 1945: Diplomatic Papers*, 6:1161.

10. *New York Times*, 14 October 1945, p. 1; see also Isaacs' less careful account in *No Peace for Asia*, p. 131.

11. Quoted in *New York Times*, 29 October 1945, p. 1; 31 October 1945, p. 1; 1 November 1945, p. 1.

12. Ibid., 21 October 1945, p. 1.

13. Ambassador in UK to Secretary of State, 7 November 1945; Ambassador in Netherlands to Secretary of State, 8 November 1945; Memorandum of Conversa-

tion by the Chief of the Division of Southeast Asian Affairs (Moffat), 8 November 1945, all in *FR, 1945: Diplomatic Papers*, 6:1168-1173; "Excerpt from Memorandum from the Press and Radio News Conference, October 24, 1945," in Philippine and Southeast Asian Affairs Files, Lot 54 D 109, folder: "Indonesia General (1945 and 1946)," Records of the Department of State, U.S. Department of State, Washington, D.C.

14. Memorandum of Conversation by the Chief of the Division of Southeast Asian Affairs (Moffat), 6 December 1945, *FR, 1945: Diplomatic Papers*, 6:1178.

15. *New York Times*, 10 November 1945, p. 1; 11 November 1945, p. 1.

16. Isaacs, *No Peace for Asia*, p. 131.

17. Luther Ely Smith to Charles G. Ross, Secretary to the President, with enclosures, 17 November 1945, Official File #386, Harry S. Truman Papers, Harry S. Truman Library, Independence, Mo.

18. *FR, 1946: Diplomatic Papers*, 6:1173.

19. Memorandum from Moffat to Vincent, "The New Cabinet of the 'Indonesian Republic,' " 21 November 1945, Philippine and Southeast Asian Affairs Files, folder: "NEI, September 1944-1947, Indonesian parties and leaders."

20. *FR, 1945: Diplomatic Papers*, 6:1175.

21. Hornbeck to the Secretary of State, 1 December 1945, ibid., p. 1176.

22. Alexander Guver dispatch in *New Times*, 3 November 1945, quoted in *New York Times*, 5 November 1945, p. 1.

23. *FR, 1945: Diplomatic Papers*, 6:1176.

24. Memorandum of Conversation by the Chief of the Division of Southeast Asian Affairs (Moffat), 6 December 1945, ibid., p. 1179.

25. SEA Draft Memorandum, "NEI and FIC," 18 December 1945; "Draft Memorandum for the President," 22 December 1945, both in Philippine and Southeast Asian Affairs Files, folder: "NEI-Arms—Surplus Property Disposal."

26. Memorandum of Conversation by the Secretary of State, 10 December 1945, *FR, 1945: Diplomatic Papers*, 6:1181.

27. Acting Secretary of State to the Consul General at Batavia, 19 December 1945, ibid., pp. 1182-1183.

28. Ambassador in the Netherlands to the Secretary of State, 22 December 1945, ibid., pp. 1184-1185.

29. Mr. Soetan Sjahrjr to President Truman, Batavia, Christmas Day, 1945, ibid., pp. 1186-1188.

30. Leslie H. Palmer, *Indonesia and the Dutch* (London: Oxford University Press, 1962), pp. 49-51; Zainu' ddin, *A Short History of Indonesia* (New York: Praeger Publishers, 1968), pp. 225-229; U.S. Department of State, *Foreign Relations of the United States, 1946*, 11 vols. (Washington, D.C.: U.S. Government Printing Office, 1969-1972), 8:789, 792-797, 801-803, 806, 809-810, 832-833 (hereinafter cited as *FR, 1946*).

31. *FR, 1946*, p. 800.

32. Ibid., pp. 804-806.

33. See the Memoranda entitled "Weekly Review" of 3, 31 July and 9 October 1946 in Philippine and Southeast Asian Affairs Files, folder: "Political Misc."; *FR, 1946*, 8:820-852.

34. Palmer, *Indonesia and the Dutch*, pp. 53-56; Fifield, *Americans in Southeast Asia*, p. 82.

35. *New York Times*, 11 November 1945, p. E5.

36. *FR, 1946*, 8:787.

37. U.S. Department of State, *Foreign Relations of the United States, 1947*, 8 vols. (Washington, D.C.: U.S. Government Printing Office, 1971-1973), 6:962-983, 1099-1101; Fifield, *Americans in Southeast Asia*, pp. 82-86; Myrdal, *Asian Drama*, 1:167.

38. Secretary of State to the Ambassador in the United Kingdom (Harriman), 12 June 1946, *FR, 1946*, 8:826-827.

39. The Consul General at Batavia (Foote) to the Secretary of State, 10 July 1946, ibid., pp. 832-833.

40. Memorandum from Moffat to Central Secretariat entitled "The Netherlands Committee . . . ," 10 April 1946, Philippine and Southeast Asian Affairs Files, folder: NEI-Arms—Surplus Property Disposal."

41. *United States News* 29 (December 28, 1945):16.

chapter *4*

The Stillbirth of Korea

Americans had entered Indochina and Indonesia as comparatively detached observers; they went to Korea as conquerors, charged with all the responsibilities of an occupying power. Not only was the United States responsible for the immediate political destiny of southern Korea, she had opened her doors years before, as had her ally Nationalist China, to a determined and outspoken band of Korean nationalist exiles whose assertions of legitimacy had grown, not diminished, with the passage of time. And now there existed as well the vexing problem of a peninsula divided into Soviet and American zones of occupation. How long would such a division last? How could it be ended? What means, if any, could be found to mutually satisfy Communist and non-Communist aspirations regarding Korea's future?

The occupation of southern Korea was to be carried out by the 24th Corps, commanded by Lieutenant General John Hodge, described by one critic as "stocky and pugnacious, with a gimlet eye and a lantern jaw." Hodge and his men went to Korea from the battlefields of the Pacific. For three long years they had trained, lived, and fought as soldiers, not statesmen. And they carried with them all of the prejudices and antagonisms generated by months of bitter warfare and propaganda against an Asian people. They had expected to form part of the spearhead for the invasion of Japan. All of their thinking had been focused upon the beaches of Kyushu, where violence and death beckoned. Now suddenly the war was over, and they were to occupy a strange land and rule an alien people. They were asked to make a wrenching readjustment in life style and perspective from soldier to policeman, from warrior to governor; it was an assignment sufficient to disorient the calmest and most stable personality.

Hodge was disturbed deeply by the vagueness of his assignment. From Manila, where he was awaiting formal orders to enter Korea, he nervously cabled the State Department near the end of August 1945 that no directive regarding the scope of his duties and responsibilities in Korea had been received. He added that apparently the plan was to apply the directive for the occupation of Japan to the peninsula as well, "that is to utilize the Governor General and his Japanese staff for the administration of the country ueder the direction of the American Military Governor." Was this what Washington wished? No one in the Far East could be sure during those first hectic hours and days after the Japanese surrender. MacArthur had cabled the War Department asking for an immediate directive on Korea, "including the question of relations between the Russian and American occupied sections of the country," but no such directive had arrived.[1]

Nor did it prior to the initial American landings at Inchon on September 8 and the American occupation of Seoul the following day. As late as September 10 the Joint Chiefs of Staff were studying a State-War-Navy "Basic Initial Directive," and Hodge and his men went into Korea backed merely by MacArthur's proclamation of September 7, which noted in passing the "long enslavement of the people of Korea and the determination that in due course Korea shall become free and independent. . . ." The proclamation added that the purpose of the American occupation was to enforce the instrument of surrender just imposed on Japan and to protect the people of the peninsula in their personal and religious rights. But all essential services and all public functionaries and employees would continue as before, thereby ensuring the perpetuation of de facto Japanese control even if under ultimate American authority. The proclamation was obviously a hastily devised instrument designed to give immediate legitimacy to American occupation and no more. It was a poor beginning for a government that had assured Syngman Rhee several months before that the Korean question had been intensively studied.[2]

Meanwhile the "Korean Provisional Government" in Chungking had been actively seeking American aid since the day the war ended. On the afternoon of August 14 the minister for foreign affairs had called at the American embassy to offer his congratulations and to propose cooperation with all the occupying powers, "particularly American." Tjo So-wang added that members of his government wished to assist in disarming "and disposing" of the more than one million Koreans presently in the Japanese army throughout the Far East and to "have a voice where Korean political problems are concerned. . . ." Tjo So-wang was promised that his "remarks" would be reported to Washington, but nothing came of it. On August 31 an unnamed representative of the KPG returned to the embassy and presented a memorandum to American officials calculated to generate concern among anti-Communist members of the Truman administration. Koreans from Russia and Korean Communists from Yenan were entering Korea in large numbers, and they had made it clear that they aimed to set up a government on the peninsula "according to Communist ideals." In view of the frightening possibilities of this pledge, "Korean Democrats, who believe in Anglo-American constitutionalism and who have been fighting for Korean freedom for past 40 years, are losing hope and their chances in Korea are decreasing." The KPG hoped to assist and cooperate with the American occupation forces, the memorandum continued, and wished to mobilize public opinion in favor of the United States "in order to keep law and order." At the very least, the KPG begged U.S. authorities to allow them to enter the country as assistants or interpreters for the occupation forces or in any other manner suitable to the United States. Failure to give the KPG what it wished would "work in favor of Communists"; in addition, the KPG pled for the immediate dispatch of American missionaries to northern Korea, which had been the center of prewar American missionary work. In conclusion, the memorandum pledged that "If United States could assist Korean leaders and send them to Korea, they would do nothing contrary to wishes of United States occupation forces or State Department."[3]

Washington remained unmoved. KPG members were at last allowed to return to their homeland in late September, but they had to obtain State Department visas to do so and had to promise to return as private citizens and not as members of any organized or recognized political group. As for their pleas to enter into political life under American aegis as either assistants or interpreters, Acting Secretary of State Acheson cabled Ambassador Hurley in Chungking on September 21 that American forces in Korea already had interpreters and more were being sent.[4]

Meanwhile Hodge and his troops were beginning their task of governance after a quiet arrival through politely applauding throngs of shining faces along the twenty-mile road from Inchon to Seoul.[5] The American occupation authorities were burdened by ignorance, an impatience to be out and on their way home after years of war, and a contempt for the native population, which had been an all too prevalent reaction among American troops in Asia since Pearl Harbor.[6] To the great majority of the occupation army "Korea was little more than a place on the map—a temporary stopover before they returned home." Japan's dramatic and unforeseen collapse had allowed little time for proper preparation, and the need for haste in securing the American right of occupation through physical presence demanded that MacArthur select units on the basis of availability and transport, not expertise. "Thus the first arrivals had little knowledge of the land and the people they were destined to control," and Hodge "was the only man in history who was appointed a ruler over 20 million people on the basis of shipping time."[7] But the State Department and every other responsible agency in distant Washington was equally blind. Near the end of August Assistant Secretary of State Dunn had admitted that "there is no agreed United States view as to the character of administration of civil affairs in Korea" beyond the fervent hope that the administration of the Soviet and American zones might be combined at an early date.[8]

Hodge and his men soon found themselves facing three sources of trouble. The Korean people as a whole had expected that the end of the war would instantly bring liberation, freedom, and sovereignty; they bitterly resented the continuation of Japanese administration under American authority. Korean political activists maintained a constant state of turmoil as they jockeyed for position and favor with both their own people and the American command. And as the first weeks and months of the occupation passed, Soviet behavior in the north became as ominous as it was elsewhere across the Eurasian land mass.

The decision to retain incumbent Japanese officials in southern Korea "until the Koreans attained more political maturity" was apparently the direct result of American distaste, both at MacArthur's headquarters in Japan and at Seoul, for the excitable behavior of the numerous Korean political parties which had mushroomed since the Japanese surrender. American officials persistently claimed that these native groups lacked the support and confidence of the public as a whole. Hodge had perhaps committed a major blunder as soon as he stepped ashore at Inchon. For in the chaotic days between the Japanese surrender in mid-August and the arrival of American troops, Korean political figures south of the thirty-eighth parallel, led by one Lyuh Woon-Heung, "a famous resistance leader," had hastily formed a provisional committee for Korean independence. The Japanese governor-general of Korea, Noboyuki Abe, had promptly recognized this group. Abe apparently hoped to perpetuate his own rule—or at least escape prison—by urging this group to form a Korean government before the Americans came in. Right-wing leaders refused, and the frantic governor-general turned to the left-wing leader, Lyuh, who agreed, and a firm left-wing government, called the Committee for the Preparation of Korean Independence, was formed on September 6, two days before the American arrival.[9]

But Hodge immediately disavowed this government, claiming it did not adequately represent the Korean people.[10] On September 12 he allowed two representatives of each existing political group in southern Korea to come before him for counsel; more than twelve hundred persons appeared. Amidst growing political turmoil in and around Seoul, H. Merrell Benninghoff, the State Department's political adviser in Korea, cabled Washington on September 15 that "Almost all Koreans have been on a prolonged holiday since August 15. To them independence apparently means freedom from work; no thought is given to the future . . . There has been no show of industry in this area since our arrival and no interest in returning to normal pursuits" so long as the Japanese continued to own or control most business and industrial establishments. Korea was "completely ripe for agitators." Indeed, it could "best be described as a powder keg ready to explode at the application of a spark."[11]

The Americans had discovered that the Koreans really had no concept of the subtle wording of the Cairo Declaration. Most Korean political leaders assumed the term "in due course" meant national freedom and independence within a matter of days or weeks at most, not years.[12] To most Koreans the concept of a four-power trusteeship over their land was anathema. Hodge wrote Washington at the end of 1945 that should a joint trusteeship be imposed on the peninsula "now or at future time, it is believed possible that the Korean people will actually and physically revolt."[13] The general knew whereof he spoke. Harold Isaacs, traveling through the southern part of the peninsula that autumn, was deeply impressed by the bitter disillusionment of the people. They had not expected their fate. Koreans below as well as above the parallel lived "under a military governor general supported by an army of occupation. To a great many [southern] Koreans this looked like anything but 'liberation.' . . . In fact it looked a great deal like the Japanese regime that had just been ousted. Only it was a little more benevolent, slightly more democratic, somewhat less efficient, and it covered only half the country. This was not freedom, nor did it look like any prelude to freedom."[14] The situation was further complicated by the paucity of American troops on the peninsula and the behavior of the Japanese in those areas—notably around Pusan—where the American occupation took hold only slowly and haltingly. Where Japanese and Americans met face to face there was little trouble, although

Isaacs noted that in and around Seoul Japanese soldiers had quickly attempted to insinuate themselves into the American occupation structure. Indeed, during the confused early days some former Japanese police not only continued to stand guard over Japanese property, but even boldly donned armbands marked "USMG" (United States Military Government) and stalked city streets before incredulous and furious Koreans. Hodge soon countermanded the order which had given the former oppressors of Korea such insolent license, but many Koreans never forgave the Americans their initial carelessness. Meanwhile, reports from the extreme southern part of the peninsula during the early postwar weeks indicated that Japanese soldiers and civilians were "looting and intimidating the Koreans and otherwise behaving in characteristic fashion," thereby exacerbating the already "unbelievably bitter" hatred of the Korean people for their former masters. Yet with too few qualified Koreans—or Americans—the need to maintain Japanese in key administrative positions was felt to be acute.[15]

It was indeed fortunate, Benninghoff continued in his telegram of September 15, that in these chaotic circumstances there had been found in Seoul "several hundred conservatives among the older and better educated Koreans. Although many of them have served with the Japanese, that stigma ought eventually to disappear." These conservatives, mostly Korean Christians in their thirties and early forties, favored the return of the KPG, "and although they may not constitute a majority they are probably the largest single group" of capable political leaders available. Benninghoff concluded his report with the suggestion that Japanese administrators be removed in name but retained in fact and that an indigenous police force be trained as soon as possible to take over the burden of maintaining law and order.[16]

Thus did Benninghoff and his handful of beleaguered and ignorant colleagues propose to shape the future of southern Korea along self-consciously conservative lines. A premium would be placed upon stability and orderly procedure at the expense of political competition and experimentation.

On September 14 the Joint Chiefs of Staff and the State-War-Navy Coordinating Committee ordered Hodge to remove from office the Japanese governor-general of Korea, plus all of his bureau chiefs, provincial governors, and police chiefs. Hodge was further directed to "proceed as rapidly as possible with the removal of other Japanese and collaborationist Korean administrators."[17] A month later, however, the SWNCC partially rescinded its order in a lengthy "Basic Initial Directive . . . for the Administration of Civil Affairs in Those Areas of Korea Occupied by U.S. Forces." Hodge was told that Japanese and Korean collaborationists could be used in administrative posts in "exceptional circumstances as determined by you" and only for the briefest time and only after informing the Korean people of the exceptional and transitory nature of their employment. The directive further stipulated that "minimum control and censorship of civilian communications, including the mails, wireless, radio, telephone, telegraph and cables, films and press," should be established immediately, although "Subject to such controls you will facilitate and encourage the distribution of news and information, both domestic and foreign through all channels and media." Moreover, "You will immediately place under control all existing political parties, organizations and societies. Those whose activities are consistent with the requirements of the military occupation and its objectives should be encouraged. Those whose activities are inconsistent with such requirements and objectives should be abolished. Subject to the necessity of maintaining the security of the occupying forces, the formation and activities of democratic political parties with rights of assembly and public discussion will be encouraged." Above all, "You will not extend official recognition to, nor utilize for political purposes, any self-styled Korean provisional government or similar political organizations. . . ."[18]

The occupation policy outlined in the Basic Directive reflected both ignorance and anxiety; ignorance of the various but powerful currents of nationalism sweeping Korea and all of East Asia, and anxiety that should such currents be left unrestrained and uncontrolled, the way would be prepared for an early revival of Japanese imperialism. In these first postwar weeks fear of Russia and consciousness of an emerging worldwide cold war with international communism was decidedly subordinate to fears generated by the recent world war. But the effect on the great revolt as it appeared in Korea was substantially the same. Indigenous political activity would be sharply curtailed and controlled to serve the purposes and appease the anxieties of an ignorant conqueror. One reputable source has claimed that Hodge never received the Korean occupation directive until the end of January of 1946. Nonetheless he had by the end of 1945 begun implementing on his own initiative some of the basic provisions of the tardy directive. A National Defense Agency, a police force, and a constabulary were being created across southern Korea; the basic institutions of a separate state were thus coming into being.[19] And so were at least some of the trappings of a free-enterprise economy, American-style.

Efforts to introduce economic reform into southern Korea in 1945 and 1946 were crude, fumbling, and insensitive. Admittedly, the economic situation in September 1945 was "most difficult to handle." The Americans controlled the best farmlands in the country but were also responsible for feeding two-thirds of Korea's total population. During the autumn of 1945 and into 1946 over a million southern Koreans in Japan returned to their homeland, as did over 100,000 from China. In addition, about a million people from northern Korea moved south in search of better living conditions and greater freedom. There to meet them and to care for the needs of all was an American military government headed by a fifty-two-year-old pipe-smoking general from Golconda, Illinois, who had studied architectural engineering in his youth before passing into the military, where he spent the rest of his days.[20]

Despite such limited credentials as a capitalistic reformer, Hodge determined to plunge ahead. Hoping that "a rapid shove in the direction of free enterprise might start the country's stalled economic machine," yet lacking any positive plan or directive, Hodge in late September lifted all price controls on rice. The results were disruptive. A bumper rice crop was to be harvested in 1945, and for the first time in forty years, half of it was not mortgaged to Japan. Koreans had anticipated that with controlled prices and rationed distribution there would be plenty of food for all. The abrupt abolition of controls changed everything. Speculators bought up all the rice they could find; the comparatively few well-to-do native families hoarded shamelessly; and, most important of all, the farmers kept most of their crop off the market in anticipation of instant wealth. The result was predictable: the sudden emergence of a quasi-legitimate black market, which everyone frequented, and demands upon overworked and short-tempered American officials by furious Koreans that the authorities take drastic measures to obliterate hoarding and black marketeering. Hodge and his subordinates were soon charged—rightly or wrongly—with foot dragging in bringing the disorder to an end, since the principal hoarders were often "respectable" Korean business, professional, and political figures upon whom the American military government relied to provide stability and leadership. Under mounting pressure Hodge finally ordered a survey of rice futures and found the outlook so discouraging that in March 1946 orders were issued to resume rationing and price controls and to establish rice collections under American supervision. Unfortunately, many Korean peasants interpreted this latter initiative as reminiscent of Japanese rule, and despite the ''adamant'' determination of Americans to impose their program, Korean farmers continued to keep their rice off the market. For some months southern Korea wallowed in economic apathy, and the plight of the peasant as well as the town dweller remained as depressed as ever.[21]

Nor was Korean morale significantly lifted by any imaginative American policy of land reform. At war's end the country was dreadfully burdened by the historic evils of landlordism and tenancy, with their accompanying blight of exorbitant rents and usurious interest rates. The ephemeral Provisional Committee for Korean Independence, which had led a brief but influential life in the weeks between Japan's surrender and the arrival of the Americans, had formed a Farmers' Association, which appeared to be a system of private cooperatives. Hodge had abolished this organization and substituted in its stead an Agricultural Association whose aim was to bestow greater market control benefits upon the farmer while at the same time making the Korean farmer cooperate with the military government. Obviously under such a system the structure of agricultural economics and the pace of agricultural reform would be shaped by the occupation authorities, not by the people themselves. And agricultural policy was determinedly conservative. One of Hodge's first actions provided for military government approval of all transactions concerning Japanese private property. The Americans admitted that this policy '' 'complicated and slowed up' property transfers.'' But complexity was compounded by the fact that the order was made retroactive to a week prior to the Japanese surrender, thus invalidating previous transactions made in good faith. Thereafter seized Japanese agricultural property in Korea remained in American hands for over a year, while increasingly suspicious and embittered Koreans claimed it was being held for ultimate disposition to those wealthy landlords and collaborationists most sympathetic to the occupation administration and its policies. About 80 percent of Korea's farmers were tenants and had expected some measure of land reform. ''While only the more radical groups advocated the immediate distribution of large estates, almost all of the Koreans favored steps to eliminate tenancy and increase the number of individual landholders.'' Yet as late as February 1947 ''the United States remained landlord to more tenant farmers than any other property owner in Korea,'' and one official admitted that ''the only property sold by Military Government has been that which could not be protected adequately.'' By this time a ''fierce agitation for land reform'' had gripped the Korean people, and the State Department was moved to declare that henceforth land reform would become a major objective of the military government. But such declarations were too late to prevent a striking alienation between much of the Korean public and its American governors.[22]

Yet a third source of conflict between Koreans and Americans during the early months of the occupation concerned the "New Korea Company." During the first weeks of the occupation Hodge announced that there would be no confiscation of Japanese property. A month later he changed his mind, and the military government took over the "700 million-dollar octopus" known as the Oriental Development Company. This conglomerate was the largest Japanese holding company in Korea. It owned 64 percent of the country's dry lands, 80 percent of its rice lands, and 350,000 acres of forests. It had controlled the shipyards, the textile industry, the iron mines, the shoe factory, and the alcohol refinery. Now it was seized and its assets held against future Japanese reparations and Japanese or Korean payment of American occupation costs in the southern zone. The corporation was renamed the "New Korea Company," and it was quickly restaffed by the old collaborationists who had run the Oriental Development Company for the former Japanese master.

To countless Koreans it seemed as if the callous Americans were reintroducing the worst aspects of the Japanese occupation, and Hodge's people admitted openly that Ordinance 52 of February 1946, establishing the New Korea Company, drew unfavorable press comment. Some contemporary writers expressed the opinion that exploitation by American interests existed. The fact that Hodge had also followed a policy of permitting former Japanese workers in Korean industry to keep their jobs until repatriation had also infuriated many Koreans, and the combination of this policy and "rightist favoritism" led to serious labor strife and reactionary "police riots" during the summer and autumn of 1946. The Koreans—and those who have since echoed their charges—were too clever by half. The New Korea Company did embrace all of the assets of the old Japanese corporation and was thus deeply involved in monopolistic land, as well as industrial, ownership. It was a convenient target for those impatient of the incorporation by the American military government of most of the sinews of southern Korean economic life. Yet Hodge and his colleagues were not set upon establishing an outpost of American capitalism in Asia. They were determined, as were the American government and people thousands of miles away, that in Asia as in Europe, the American taxpayer would not underwrite the reparations burdens and occupation costs of former enemies as had been done after World War I. If the New Korea Company, with its tremendous assets in Korean agricultural and industrial holdings, could be fashioned into a useful reparations instrument, then the American taxpayer would be well served. Of course, this meant that real efforts toward land reform and the creation of a truly new Korean economy based on mass participation in decision making would have to be deferred. The occupation authorities, working with the Japanese-trained and dominated Korean economic bureaucracy, would make the decisions about Korean economic life largely in terms of American needs, not native aspirations. It was a tragically short-sighted perspective, assumed by those who knew little of the land they had come to administer and wished to know less.

By most accounts the morale of American occupation personnel in Korea was dangerously low by September 1946 at the latest. Most Americans merely wished to go home. And while they remained in Korea, they wished order and stability, peace and quiet, above all else.[23] All that was lacking in Korea by January 1946 was an indigenous national leader, and here too, despite the warning of the basic directive against overt support of "any self-styled Korean provisional government," Hodge and the military government in Seoul had moved swiftly to ensure the kind of stable and conservative political atmosphere that the directive advocated.

On September 27, 1945, Acting Secretary of State Acheson had cabled Chargé Robertson at Chungking, reconfirming the fact that permits to return home were being issued to Syngman Rhee and other members of the KPG in both China and the United States. "Outright support of any one political group presently outside Korea is not contemplated," Acheson reiterated, "but because of the chaotic conditions within Korea, elements having constructive ability and willing to work within the framework of military government are encouraged to enter and might be transported by airplanes controlled by the Army when space is available."[24]

Two days later Benninghoff cabled a lengthy political appreciation of recent events in Korea to the State Department. The scene had now crystallized to the point where "Seoul, and perhaps southern Korea as a whole, is at present politically divided into two distinct groups; each is composed of several smaller components, but each follows its own distinct school of political philosophy." On the one hand was the "so-called democratic or conservative group," which included many of the professional and educational leaders of the land, who had been trained either in the United States or in American missionary schools in Korea. In their aims and policies, Benninghoff said, these leaders "demonstrate a desire to follow the western democracies." They also, he added, "almost unanimously desire the early return of Dr. Syngman Rhee and the 'Provisional Government' at Chungking."

Opposing the conservative "democrats" was the "radical or communist group," splintered into several parties ranging in thought "from left of center to radical." However, "the avowed communist group is the most vocal and seems to be supplying the leadership." Doubtless this group included members of the brief left-wing "Korean Government" of September 6-9, which Hodge had disavowed. Emphasizing once more the enormous prestige which Rhee enjoyed throughout the country and the early efforts of the well-organized "radical" group to popularize itself through parades and demonstrations, Benninghoff asserted that the attitude of the American forces was one "of aloofness as long as peace and order is maintained." And he closed with the observation that should Rhee return to Korea, the United States might well stand accused "of favoring the conservatives against the radicals."[25]

Such caveats aside, Benninghoff's depiction of the Korean political scene less than a month after the beginning of the American occupation was so sharply drawn that any intelligent but harassed and preoccupied decision maker in Washington or Tokyo could come to only one conclusion as to which Korean political group to support. Nor did Benninghoff slacken his efforts on behalf of the "conservative" element in Korean politics. On October 10 he dispatched another assessment of Korean politics, this time to George Atcheson, then attached to MacArthur's headquarters. Strong evidence existed that the "Radical or Communist" group in southern Korea was receiving "support and direction from the Soviet Union (perhaps from Koreans formerly resident in Siberia)," Benninghoff asserted. He added that the "Radical" press, which was "most aggressive," had unfavorably contrasted American occupation policies with those of the Soviets north of the thirty-eighth parallel, particularly with respect to the removal of Japanese from administrative posts.[26]

By mid-October Atcheson, who had left Chungking under a cloud of suspicion, had become so alarmed by reports from Seoul that he urged Washington to abandon its policy of political aloofness in Korea and to throw its support behind Rhee. Here was irony, indeed. For within a month the young political adviser would be publicly accused by Hurley as one of the architects of a pro-Communist policy in China. But now Atcheson urged his government's support of Rhee along clear anti-Communist lines.

> I realize that to give open, official approval or support to any one leader, group, or combination is contrary to past American thinking. But . . . unless positive action is taken to give the Koreans a start in governmental participation and organization, our difficulties will increase rather than diminish, and the Communistic group set up and encouraged by the Soviets in northern Korea will manage to extend its influence into southern Korea with results which can readily be envisaged.[27]

Ten days later, on October 25, Secretary of State Byrnes replied, noting first that General Hodge had recently had Rhee as a dinner guest and that Rhee had been "outspoken in his hostility of Soviet policy." Byrnes expressed displeasure at these developments, for he had not yet completely abandoned hope of working with Soviet Russia to preserve the fragile postwar peace, and the behavior of Hodge and Rhee hindered efforts to prevent the imposition of an iron curtain across the thirty-eighth parallel.[28] On November 7 John Carter Vincent sent the War Department a further, sharply worded message on the subject of General Hodge's close identification with Rhee, citing the same objection that Byrnes had earlier expressed.

Six days later Assistant Secretary of War John J. McCloy replied to Vincent's superior, Dean Acheson. McCloy supported Hodge's actions unequivocally. Korea, he aaid, was still on the verge of chaos, and "There is no question but that communist action is actively and intelligently being carried out throughout our zone." Hodge therefore harbored a "legitimate concern . . . that the Communists will seize by direct means the government in our area." He had the right, indeed, he had the duty, McCloy implied, to work with and support whatever indigenous political force he could find that would defeat the Communist purpose. And McCloy supported Rhee as a perfectly suitable anti-Communist instrument. The "local Koreans" who had remained throughout the years of Japanese rule "are most narrow, selfish and confused in their political thought. Each individual conceives himself to be the only local boy untainted by Jap collaborationism." However, thb "exile Koreans," and by that term McCloy clearly meant Rhee and the KPG, enjoyed "great respect and confidence" in southern Korea. Hodge had recently admitted to McCloy that he "had seen quite a bit of Dr. Rhee and had found him helpful. He was using him then in negotiations with the communist leaders" of southern Korea. And why not?

> For us not to make some use, at the discretion of Hodge, of the only stabilizing individuals available to us seems peculiar when it is well known that the Soviets had two divisions of Koreans thoroughly indoctrinated in the Communist creed whom they are reported on good authority to be using in the Soviet zone and perhaps also to good advantage in our own. Should we fear some criticism of our honest efforts to bring Korea to a state where representative government has some chance of success, when at the same time the Soviets have by force of arms replaced all officials, major and minor, in cities, towns, and hamlets in their zone with ardent Korean Communists, armed with tommy guns and protected by the Red Army. . . .[29]

MacArthur had cabled Army Chief of Staff George C. Marshall on November 5 that "The presence of Dr. Syngman Rhee in Korea appears to be having favorable influence toward consolidation of various political parties and toward coalition of ideas. The primary wish of all Koreans is to be independent and to have self-rule which is also helping in coalition."[30]

So the State Department was in effect told that Washington would be excluded from any real influence upon American policy making in Korea. The officers in Seoul, both military and civilian, would assume that responsibility and would pursue a firm and conservative course, centering about order and authority. Despite the fact that Hodge had been forced on October 10 to declare illegal the existence of any native "government" in Korea, as a result of persistent clashes between the "conservative-democratic" and "radical-communist" elements within his zone, Syngman Rhee was already pursuing a shrewdly calculated policy, combining anti-Communism for the Americans with repeated calls for national independence and no trusteeship to rally his fellow Koreans. Rhee's strategy reflected the climate of opinion—both Korean and American—so perfectly that he swiftly expanded and solidified his power and influence with both occidentals and orientals below the thirty-eighth parallel.[31]

Perhaps Rhee's inexorable rise to power at the expense of open political competition could have been avoided, perhaps American rule could have been relaxed had the diplomats in Washington been able to prevent the spread of the cold war to Korea in the autumn and winter of 1945-1946. But such was not to be, and as a result the one-man rule of Syngman Rhee became inevitable.

Within the first two months of the American occupation Hodge's headquarters in Seoul was expressing deep disillusionment with zonal occupation arrangements in general and Soviet behavior in particular. Southern Korea included the ancient capital of the country and its chief agricultural region. But northern Korea contained key mineral deposits, especially coal, as well as the country's small industrial base and its limited source of hydroelectric power along the southern shore of the Yalu River. Yet Soviet authorities had persistently if politely rebuffed every tentative American effort to initiate negotiations leading to an economic and social unification of the country. Moreover, rumors began to flow southward across the parallel of systematic Soviet looting and stripping of the industrial plant and of repressive political behavior, which seemed all too familiar in light of similar reports of Russian behavior across Eastern Europe. [32]

Knowledgeable scholars have so far been unable to agree on the extent of successful Russian manipulation of the political process north of the parallel. Gregory Henderson and Soon S. Cho have stated that Soviet authorities had moved into their zone with well-organized People's Committees of exiled Korean Communists and ''immediately were utilizing the Korean group for implementation of their military government.'' Robert Scalapino and Chong-Sik Lee maintain that the eventual ruler of North Korea, Kim Il-sung, ''was the Russian choice at a time when the Russians had the power to enforce their choice.'' Dae-Sook Suh, however, suggests a confused situation of much greater fluidity throughout Korea in late 1945 and early 1946, in which the obscure Kim Il-sung climbed to eventual power over ''older Communists'' in northern Korea, largely by his own efforts and from a personal past that stemmed more from semiautonomous Chinese guerrilla bands than from a Soviet political training school. [33]

What is obvious is that the dream of a united and autonomous Korea held by Roosevelt—and who is to say not by Stalin as well—was one more terrible casualty, like the Grand Alliance itself, of the vast forces let loose by World War II. No one has stated the case better than Gregory Henderson, who, in stressing the lack of coherent American occupation policy for Korea prior to February 1946, added that Hodge had

no proper policy direction at all for crucial months of time. In that absence he became like the, you know, an intelligent, Illinois farm-boy confronted with the image of people on the other side of the 38th parallel, bringing with him the kind of basic hostility image that a field commander engaged a few weeks previously in a bitter war, would have of people whom he had not met, had not planned with, had no experience with, and thought were Communists. Well, indeed they were. This image, I think, operated very powerfully . . . on the lieutenant colonels that went up to try to contact the Russians in the early days, probably on the Russians themselves who likewise had no operating experience with the Americans in that area, that had been sitting entirely isolated with no kinds of communication in their Army posts in Vladivostok and elsewhere in the Far East. A hostility image easily developed under those circumstances without being encouraged in any way by Washington directives and policy.[34]

The first signs of American disillusionment with the Russians had appeared at Hodge's headquarters by early October. On October 1 Benninghoff reported that the Red Army was forceably replacing spontaneously created "self-rule councils" in northern Korea with "People's Political Committees," in which the dominant positions were given to "minuscule" Communist groups. Meanwhile all efforts by Hodge to try to establish satisfactory relations with the Soviet commander at Pyongyang were met with silence.[35]

Ten days later Hodge reported to MacArthur and the Joint Chiefs of Staff that the Soviet consul in Seoul had returned from Pyongyang, "bearing two letters from the Army Commander to effect that there will be no negotiations on a military level" concerning the economic and social integration of Korea. The Soviet commander had added "that there is no prospect of any negotiations until decisions are made and relationships established between our respective governments." In a separate message the following day Hodge told MacArthur that he was worried about the Soviet presence in Seoul. The consul, his staff, and his family had been legally resident in the Korean capital throughout the war and had been interned for only a few days following the Soviet declaration of hostilities against Japan. Hodge and his people had extended the Soviets every courtesy. "In return, this Headquarters, although treated with 'correctness,' has been rebuffed in all its efforts to reach any kind of an understanding on any subject." Hodge's suspicions had by this time been deeply aroused. "It is considered possible," he told MacArthur, "that the [Soviet] Consul General is assisting the Korean Communist movement in Seoul, and is [working] behind the scenes in apparent attempts to discredit the United States and its occupation policies in the eyes of the Koreans.''[36]

By early November, two months after American troops had disembarked at Inchon, Washington as well as Seoul had become deeply alarmed by developments in Korea. Navy Secretary James Forrestal, an incipient cold warrior, had already gloomily summarized in his diary one of the long dispatches from the peninsula telling of the '' 'chaotically impossible' situation that had resulted from 'the splitting of Korea into two parts for occupation by forces of nations operating under widely divergent policies and with no common command.' Russian infiltration and looting, on top of all of the legacies of war destruction, financial disorder, Korean political immaturity and the presence of the still undemobilized Japanese army, added up to an appalling situation.''[37] Admiral Leahy wrote at roughly the same time that reports from MacArthur's headquarters in Tokyo spoke of ''Russian troops in Northern Korea . . . treating the inhabitants thereof with barbarous cruelty with the evident purpose of destroying their existing order and substituting a Bolshevist philosophy in its place. Korean and Japanese inhabitants are endeavoring to escape to American-controlled territory in search of safety.''[38]

The emerging cold war, of course, increasingly defined the reactions of American officials in Seoul, Tokyo, and Washington to the news from northern Korea. The London Foreign Ministers Conference had broken down on October 2 amidst bitter rhetoric and recrimination; American monopoly of the atomic bomb and aggressive Soviet diplomatic probes toward Japan, Iran, and Libya, along with brutal Russian behavior in Eastern Europe, had effectively destroyed what little remained of the uneasy spirit of Potsdam, to say nothing of the euphoric spirit of Yalta. Less than sixty days after the close of mankind's most terrible conflict the victors were obviously dividing in anger and mistrust.[39] To Washington the news out of Korea seemed part of an emerging pattern of tyrannical Soviet behavior that recalled some of the worst excesses of the Hitler gang. The peninsula was thus on the verge of becoming one more pawn in the developing ''East-West'' game of cold war when on November 3 the State Department at last decided to take a direct hand in seeking a solution to the Korean impasse.

Ambassador Harriman in Moscow was informed of Hodge's persistent reports of Soviet unwillingness to discuss and negotiate local problems arising from the zonal division of the peninsula. ''Consequently,'' Byrnes cabled, "the 38 degree parallel has become in reality a closed border with result that Korean national life has been greatly disrupted. Unless agreement is reached in near future on many vital issues, execution of commitments of this Government and U.S.S.R. that all Korea shall be independent in due course will be seriously jeopardized." Harriman was instructed to obtain from the Soviet government an agreement "in principle" assuring adequate and regular deliveries of coal and electric power from the Soviet zone to the American; resumption of railroad traffic and other means of communication between the two zones; adoption of uniform fiscal policies throughout the peninsula; resumption of coastwide shipping and normal trade in minimum commodities between the zones; and, finally, the orderly settlement of displaced persons, including the repatriation of Japanese soldiers and nationals to Japan.[40] Harriman replied on the eighth that the message had been delivered that day to Molotov, adding that his letter to the Soviet foreign minister "concluded with statement that we wished to learn whether Soviet Government will authorize Soviet Commander in Korea to negotiate with Hodge or whether it desires that these problems be discussed by two Governments."[41] Four days later Harriman cabled a somber message on Korea, stating that the Kremlin "has made it clear that historically it regards Korea in much same light as Finland, Poland and Rumania—a springboard for attack on USSR. Therefore USSR may be expected to seek predominant influence in Korea."[42] On November 23 Harriman told Washington that Vyshinski had just said to him that "competent Soviet authorities" were studying the American proposal concerning the possibility of direct, high-level negotiations on the future of Korea.[43]

Byrnes had already been induced by other events to consider calling another meeting of Soviet, American, and British foreign ministers. The London conference had technically broken down over a procedural matter: the right of the French and Chinese to share in the decision making process concerning Axis countries with which they had not been at war. A formal meeting of the Council of Foreign Ministers as established at Potsdam was clearly impossible. But a meeting of the "Big Three" foreign ministers seemed imperative to Byrnes by late November 1945. Problems of mutual accommodation faced the rapidly crumbling Grand Alliance all around the periphery of the Eurasian land mass from Stettin on the Baltic to Trieste in the Adriatic, from Libya on the Mediterranean and Turkey on the Bosporus to Japan and Korea in the Pacific. And over all these awesome problems dangled the terrible presence of the bomb. So Byrnes, sitting alone in the silence of a nearly-empty State Department on Thanksgiving Day, decided on his own initiative to make one final attempt to hammer out a series of agreements and arrangements with the Soviets. The bomb was on his mind; so were Iran, Bulgaria, and Rumania. And so was Korea.[44]

On November 29 Byrnes told Seoul that the State Department was giving "careful consideration" to abandoning the idea of a possible international trusteeship for Korea in favor of a governing commission composed of the two powers actually sharing the occupation burden. Seoul was also told that the Department "is aware of the difficult position which present conditions impose upon General Hodge and hopes that he will continue to use qualified Koreans to the maximum." However Syngman Rhee and his followers should not be delegated governing powers for southern Korea just yet, as "the Department believes that the USSR would react unfavorably to the creation by us" of an indigenous ruling commission "and if consulted, would not agree thereto." Still, the mounting pressures of emergent cold war had forced Byrnes to change his views sharply between the first and last week of November with regard to the potential political value of Syngman Rhee and his conservative allies.[45]

On December 14, as Byrnes prepared to leave for the hastily arranged Moscow conference of Soviet, British, and American foreign ministers, William R. Langdon, then acting political adviser in Seoul, reported that the first steps had been completed "in Korean independence." All Japanese troops were about to be repatriated, and the repatriation machinery was established and ready to run; local police and judiciary agencies had been created, "and order prevails." Exiled Korean leaders had been brought back, and "The Korean people have been told that the present division of Korea is a temporary measure. Now the Korean people wait for the next stage, which is independence." But no plans had been formulated. Once again, as in an earlier letter of November 20, Langdon pressed strongly for the creation by the American occupation authorities of a Korean governing commission, but his earlier enthusiasm for Kim Koo and Rhee and for direct American involvement in Korean politics had cooled perceptibly.

On November 20 Langdon had written: "In the light of actual conditions in Korea our policy of abstaining from any action which might interfere with the freedom of a liberated people to choose their own form of government seems inappropriate . . . the situation will remain static unless we take a hand in it. Our caution over becoming associated with the so-called Provisional Government in Chungking seems unwarranted now as Kim Koo's group has no rival for first government of liberated Korea, being regarded as quasi-legitimate by all elements and parties.'' Now, on December 14, Langdon reiterated his plea for the early creation of a governing commission but claimed that ''there is little apparent enthusiasm for either Kim Koo or Syngman Rhee, and likewise for the People's Republic which, for awhile, actively pretended to be a government.'' Very possibly the reason for Langdon's *volte face*, and that of Hodge's headquarters, was the appearance of a growing number of press accounts in both the United States and Great Britain, portraying the American occupation authorities in Korea and elsewhere as ''men of few parts, colonial-minded, and contemptuous of the Koreans.''

Langdon bitterly refuted these charges in a cable to the Department on November 26. He did admit, however, that the occupation authorities may have gone overboard in their support of ''plutocracy'' to the exclusion of ''popular left-wingers,'' but this situation was being rectified. A ''disproportionate number of rich and conservative persons'' had been favored. ''But how were we to know who was who among this unfamiliar people?'' Now, at any rate, ''the social base'' of the emergent Korean national ''structure'' was being ''broadened.'' Nonetheless, Langdon wrote on December 14, Korean political leaders, ''though friendly, are losing faith as they see the 38th parallel assume a permanent character which prohibits them from being useful or active. The masses themselves are impatient of legalistic and orderly procedures toward Japanese property and landlordism. Communistic agitators could find them good material to work as preachers of division of Japanese property and big estates and as critics of our occupation forces.'' Given these facts it was imperative to ''raise the curtain for the next act permitting the fulfillment of Korean aspirations as they feel them and not as we think they should be. . . .'' Should a governing commission prove impossible to obtain from the Russians at Moscow, Langdon added a further proposal for ''an exclusive trusteeship in our respective Zones for a 5-year maximum, followed by complete reciprocal withdrawal; free travel and the exchange of goods in the interim.'' If neither of these recommendations were acceptable to the Russians, then it was imperative to find out in Moscow just what the Soviet plans for Korea were.[46] Byrnes could be pardoned for experiencing a certain confusion in his impression of Korea in light of Langdon's reports. But one point seemed clear and consistent. The division of the peninsula into rival occupation zones could not be permitted to continue.

At Moscow Byrnes found Molotov and the Russians evasive. Harriman's letter of November 8 was still being studied, Molotov stated, and Byrnes's concrete proposal for a unified administration and trusteeship for Korea would require the presence of specialists and advisers on railways, finance, and commercial matters, "but time would not permit this."[47] Instead, the Soviets on December 20 proposed the establishment of a joint commission representing the Russian and American military commands in northern and southern Korea. This commission would assist in the creation of a *provisional* Korean government in consultation with various "Korean democratic parties and social organizations." The proposals for a provisional government worked out by the commission would then be submitted to the joint consideration of the United States, Russia, Britain, and China. In addition, the Soviets asked for a meeting within two weeks of representatives of the Soviet and American commands in Korea "to consider urgent questions which have relation both to southern and northern Korea" and to work out measures for permanent coordination between the American and Soviet commands.[48] If this was not all that Byrnes had hoped to get, it was a reasonable beginning. At the December 21 meeting with Bevin and Molotov, Byrnes told his Russian host that the Soviet proposals were acceptable to the U.S. government. With a few minor drafting changes, which the Soviets quickly accepted, the Russian proposal went into the final communiqué on the conference virtually intact.[49]

Byrnes returned from Moscow a happy man. Molotov and Stalin had apparently agreed to a wide range of American proposals regarding the future of Eastern Europe; the composition of a Far Eastern Commission to oversee the occupation of Japan; the presence of American troops in postwar China; the Korean problem; and, of possibly transcendant importance, a formula on the sharing of atomic information that would satisfy the Soviet leadership even as it mollified critics at home.[50]

But it quickly became evident that the Moscow conference had not arrested the awful drift into cold war but had accelerated it. The domestic critics of Byrnes's atomic policy proved far stronger and tenacious than he had believed, and he was soon forced to repudiate the Moscow atomic accord. The problem of continued Russian presence in the northern Iranian province of Azerbaijan had not been settled at Moscow, and ominous Soviet pressures both there and in Turkey during the early winter of 1946 generated great fears in the West. Then, too, it seems probable that American determination to practically exclude all other nations from a share in the occupation of Japan—no matter how justified it might have been in the case of Russia—generated great bitterness and anger in the

Kremlin, particularly in light of Anglo-American pressures on Stalin to relax the Communist grip on Bulgaria and the rest of Eastern Europe.

Whatever the precise reasons and motives—and they were many and various on both sides of Winston Churchill's "iron curtain"—it was clear by the spring of 1946 that Russia and the West were rapidly drifting into a new and dangerously tense relationship with one another. And Korea proved to be an early casualty of the burgeoning cold war.

On January 5, 1946, the Joint Chiefs of Staff directed MacArthur to arrange a conference with the Soviet commander in northern Korea under the Korean provisions of the Moscow Conference communiqué. "Political matters will not be discussed," the JCS warned, adding that the U.S. representatives should limit their discussion to economic and administrative matters.[51] On January 8 Hodge received a letter from General Chistiakov, commanding general of the 25th Soviet Army Forces in Korea, proposing a meeting at an early date, and by January 18 Soviet and American officials were deep in talks at Seoul.[52]

From the beginning, however, Soviet officials exhibited what seemed to the Americans a sinister determination to compress negotiations into the most mundane channels. The Russians quickly agreed to discuss the exchange of electric power, rice, raw materials, fuel, industrial equipment, and chemicals between the two zones. They also quickly agreed to discuss ways to expedite the resumption of rail and motor transportation and coastwise shipping between northern and southern Korea. They agreed to discuss ways of establishing uniform customs and commercial regulations and the free movement of Koreans from one zone to another. They even agreed to discuss the allocation of radio broadcast frequencies for the peninsula as a whole and to work out measures for the future coordination of economic administrative matters between the two commands. But the Soviets refused to discuss free newspaper circulation to all Korea or a prohibition on the further removal of capital goods. And they requested time to obtain authority to discuss the "adjustment" of the thirty-eighth parallel.[53]

Boundary adjustment soon proved to be the center of growing Soviet-American controversy. Between January 16 and February 5 fifteen formal meetings were held between members of the two commands. According to Benninghoff, who had returned to his post as political adviser at the turn of the year, it became apparent early in the discussions regarding an agenda

that the U.S. and Soviet delegations approached the solution of economic and administrative problems from widely divergent angles. The United States delegation based all its discussions and arguments on the desirability of removing the barrier of the 38th parallel and considering the country as an economic and administrative unit. The Russians, on the other hand, came to the conference with the idea of discussing economic and administrative matters from a very narrow viewpoint. . . . We talked in terms of opening up the country for the benefit of the nation as a whole, while the Russians talked in terms of negotiations between the two commands.

This basic divergence, Benninghoff concluded, "colored the whole proceedings, and was directly responsible for the failure of the conference to achieve any substantial results."[54]

Here was an increasingly familiar tale indeed: the imposition of yet another "iron curtain" wherever Soviet armed forces had come to rest at the close of World War II. Yet from the Russian perspective the Americans had just dropped an iron curtain of their own over Japan, had refused to consider Soviet desires for a trusteeship in Mussolini's former colony of Libya, and had reneged on an apparent promise to share at least some information on atomic matters with their wartime ally. No matter how generous its basic intentions, the United States could not expect to have it both ways with its former Russian ally; it could not demand a selectively open world without rousing the profoundest suspicions in the minds and hearts of a regime that had seized and maintained power by violence and duplicity and had elevated sleepless suspicion to the level of personal creed.

Not surprisingly Soviet-American negotiations in Korea quickly broke down. The immediate cause was Russian anger over the inability of the American command to supply sufficient quantities of rice to the northern areas. "It soon became evident," Benninghoff wrote in his February 15 cable to Washington, "that General Shtikov was sent to the conference with instructions to get as much rice as possible and to refuse to agree to any exchange of other commodities unless rice was forthcoming. It was explained to him and to other members of his delegation that South Korea was not in position to furnish rice, but the Russians did not see fit to accept the force of our arguments."

The Americans had not misled their Russian opponents. Benninghoff had cabled the State Department in late January that the "Principal administrative problem now confronting military government is distribution of rice, little headway having been made during period towards getting rice into hands of consumers at ceiling prices of 750 yen per koku.''[55] Hoarding had become widespread in recent weeks, and despite energetic recruitment and training programs there remained a shortage of qualified police and military personnel to enforce an antihoarding, antiinflationary program of rice consumption. But the Russians had not been satisfied with American explanations nor impressed by American problems. ''After considerable fruitless discussion on this point,'' Shtikov had submitted a statement on February 4 ''which virtually amounted to an ultimatum.'' Soviet representatives would not be able to continue discussions on commodity exchanges, including electric power from northern to southern Korea, until the American command was able to guarantee the delivery of a substantial quantity of rice to the Soviet command. When the American representative produced statistics to prove that on a per capita basis northern Korea should have been practically as self-sufficient as southern Korea in regard to food stuffs, the Soviet delegation refused to listen, and the conference broke up.[56]

In the meantime the American command at Seoul had come under another form of Soviet pressure. Native political leaders of all persuasions had greeted news of the Moscow interim agreements with unrestrained fury. They seemed the final act of American betrayal. Three months before, U.S. troops had been greeted as saviors as they trudged up the road from Inchon. To Koreans the end of the war had seemed a miracle. The long, dreadful night of Japanese occupation was suddenly gone. Thirty-five years of Japanese efforts to obliterate every vestige of Korean self-consciousness through enforced ''education,'' deportation, and physical torture were abruptly ended. ''Welcome apostles of freedom and justice,'' read one sign over a town gate as the Americans passed through. But the dawn had proved cold and bleak. The desperate hope of Korean intellectuals, students, and professional people that a free and unified Korean nation could be swiftly reconstituted in the hour of deliverance was shattered. The country would remain divided and occupied by aliens. For the first time the conservative element openly turned against Hodge and initiated general work sabotage while instigating mass demonstrations all over the southern half of the peninsula. Even the Korean employees of the American military government participated. ''Hodge had almost no backing. . . . The popularity of the United States reached its lowest ebb.''[57] On January 12 the National Mobilization Committee against trusteeship staged a large demonstration in Seoul demanding that a Korean government be immediately established to take over the affairs of the country "without further outside interference."⁵⁸

On the twenty-fifth the Russians intervened. The Soviet news agency, *Tass*, beamed a statement on the "Korean question" toward the restive nationalists at Seoul. Claiming that several newspapers published in southern Korea, "where control is in the hands of American military authorities," were spreading lies about the decision of the Moscow Foreign Ministers Conference, *Tass* determined to set the record straight. It had been the Americans who at Moscow had proposed for the peninsula a unified administration and four-power trusteeship, which would have effectively kept power out of native hands for years to come. It had been the Russians who had successfully pressed for a modification of these proposals to allow for an early creation of a "provisional Korean Democratic Government," which would act as the executive agent for any trusteeship, thereby insuring the protection of the "national interests of the Korean people."⁵⁹

The State Department's embarrassed verification of the Soviet charge in its covering dispatch of the *Tass* statement to Seoul and Tokyo brought a stinging rebuke from Hodge on February 2. The Department should have passed on such information "several weeks ago for guidance in planning, policies, and handling emergencies," Hodge told the JCS. The message was de facto proof that the State Department had paid little attention either to the information "painstakingly" sent in by those at Seoul "as to the psychology of the Korean people or to the repeated urgent recommendations of the commander and State Department political advisers." Washington's admission of the "full truth" of the *Tass* statement "comes as real news to me," Hodge continued, "particularly in view of my urgent recommendations beginning in October and the recent State Department attitude and broadcasts which shy away from the trusteeship idea and hold out hope that possibly it may not be necessary." The announcement of trusteeship had brought about revolt and riots but since they had been quelled, "our position here was the strongest since our arrival." But now all was once again in doubt. "Communist activity, on the wane for almost a month up until January 15, is locally again increasing materially both in boldness and effectiveness, while thinking and educated Koreans are again becoming sure they will now have to fight for their freedom and independence." The anxious and infuriated general closed with a bitter plea: "I hope that it can be impressed upon the Department that here we are not dealing with wealthy U.S. educated Koreans, but with early [*sic*], poorly trained, and poorly educated Orientals strongly affected by 40 years of Jap control, who stubbornly and fanatically hold to what they like and dislike, who are definitely influenced by direct propaganda and with whom it is almost impossible to reason. We are opposed by a strongly organized, ruthless political machinery designed to appeal to millions of this type.''[60]

Hodge's sense of betrayal by his superiors was thus matched by his contempt, fear, and ignorance for most of those over whom he ruled. The intelligent Illinois farm boy had revealed the limits of his political sophistication. Nor could the State Department be wholly blamed for the quandary in which Hodge felt himself by the first week of February. Admittedly, Washington had been criminally slow in sending detailed instructions to him, and he and his military and civil colleagues had been buffeted by press accounts that they were favoring a few rich natives at the expense of the masses. Nonetheless, the signals sent to Washington from Seoul in the early weeks of occupation clearly had been meant to discourage the State Department from assuming too active a supervisory role in Korean affairs. And when Hodge's headquarters began to grudgingly back down from this position the signals were often vague and contradictory. In his letter of November 20 Langdon had urged that the American command not scruple to interfere directly and decisively in Korean politics to bring about the kind of regime that could be dealt with easily. On December 14 Langdon had suddenly urged a hands-off policy at the same time that he asked for an early creation of a local provisional government. Harassed and distracted by a multitude of other policy problems at home and across the war-shattered world, Washington had simply not reacted with the speed, knowledge, and decisiveness that the Korean situation demanded. As late as May 22, 1946, in a regular meeting of the Secretaries of State, War, and Navy, the peripatetic Byrnes, briefly home between exhausting international meetings on European affairs, clearly revealed ignorance and essential disinterest of Korean developments.[61]

In these circumstances the policy making initiative remained in Seoul, and Hodge had two options: first, resumption of negotiations with the Soviets, looking toward the ultimate establishment of some instruments of economic and political unification for the country; or, second, the creation of some type of self-sufficient economic, social, and political life in southern Korea. Seoul chose initially to pursue the first option and hold the second in reserve.

The breakdown in Soviet-American talks on February 5 was not construed as permanent by either side. Discussions on an agenda were expected to continue.[62] In mid-February both sides decided to try again and soon agreed to establish a Joint Commission as provided by the Moscow communiqué.[63] But the accord was signed against an ominous background. For on February 12 the Russians announced the completion of an all-Korean Central Government of North Korea. According to Hodge, friendly sources in the south quickly pronounced all members of this "Government" and all members of the three major north Korean political parties to be "either violent Communists or unknown Koreans brought in from Russia or Manchuria."[64] Hodge told Washington that he planned to "keep up" the prestige of the Korean Representative Democratic Council, which he had recently established in the south under the chairmanship of Syngman Rhee. Moreover, Hodge would "make every effort to gain the full backing of the Korean people and discredit the Communists." "This will probably get liberal and pink press of US on my neck," he concluded, "but feel that any other local action would be fatal." Given such an attitude and the prevailing political atmosphere on the peninsula, the prospect of meaningful negotiations with the Russians grew dim.

Discussions with the Soviets dragged on until May 6, when the Joint Commission adjourned *sine die*. The Americans had certainly begun them in a hopeful spirit. In a mid-January radio broadcast from Washington (NBC's "University of the Air") John Carter Vincent, Edwin M. Martin, then chief of the Division of Japanese and Korean Economic Affairs, and Colonel Brainard E. Prescott of the Civil Affairs Division of the War Department all stated that the Joint Commission provided both Russia and the United States with, in Martin's words, "a made-to-order opportunity to show that we can free Korea without getting involved in any imperialistic adventures."[65]

Weeks of hard bargaining and constant American pressure, "including threat of full press release," at last forced the Russians in early April to accept a formula whereby all Korean parties agreeing to uphold the "aims" of the Moscow decision would, in cooperation with the Joint Commission, form a provisional Korean government. But the Soviets remained adamant "that the administrative and economic integration of the two zones of occupation must await the formation of the provisional government envisaged under the Moscow Agreement."[66] The American representatives believed the agreement was "sufficiently qualified" so that those southern Korean political parties opposed to trusteeship would have ample opportunity to express themselves when the commission began forming a provisional government. Hodge told Washington that at the time the April agreement was signed "the American Commander publicly stated that, no matter what form trusteeship might or might not take, southern Koreans were free to speak their minds on the subject.''[67]

The Russians, however, interpreted the April agreement quite differently. The Korean Communists in both north and south had not contested the Moscow agreement, and Soviet delegates on the Joint Commission were soon demanding the exclusion from any provisional Korean government of all parties and social organizations which in any way had opposed the Moscow decision. As heated discussions began, with the Americans upholding the right of unlimited free speech, the Soviets suddenly stated that all parties and organizations affiliated with Hodge's Representative Democratic Council of Southern Korea should be considered ineligible for consultation because acting chairman Syngman Rhee had stated the right of his group to oppose trusteeship after formation of the provisional government.[68]

The disheartened Americans believed that the Russians had deliberately created a situation which ''will inevitably involve considerable delay in forming a provisional government in addition to the 6 weeks already devoted to the question. . . .'' They therefore proposed that, pending clarification of the points raised by the Soviets, ''the Commission undertake to remove the 38 degree parallel boundary as an obstacle to the reunification of Korea.'' The Russians flatly refused to consider this proposal, and since there was no other task that the commission could profitably take up at this stage Hodge and his colleagues concluded there was ''no alternative'' but to ask for an adjournment of the commission, which was agreed to on May 6. Thereafter the Americans continued to insist that the Joint Commission meet with representatives of all Korean parties, but to no avail. Not until the Moscow conference in the spring of 1947 was Secretary of State George Marshall able to arrange for the Joint Commission to resume negotiations. But nothing came of them, and the Russians north of the thirty-eighth parallel and the Americans south of the line turned increasingly inward after the spring of 1946 to create rival native governments, to establish rival agencies of rule, and to nurture rival feelings of grievance and nationalism.[69]

Even before negotiations with the Russians broke down, both Seoul and Washington again had contemplated dealing with the Kim Koo-Syngman Rhee group in preference to the more leftish political elements in southern Korea. Soviet insistence that only those groups unreservedly supporting the Moscow agreement should be included in any Korean provisional government gave to the Korean Communist movement a prominence and power it in fact had not yet attained. Despite American anxiety over Communist strength and American assumptions that the Korean Communists were stooges of Moscow, a leading authority on the Korean Communist movement, Dae-Sook Suh, has argued vigorously and effectively that the Communists were not the only Korean group to support trusteeship, nor did they do so simply on orders from the Kremlin. The emerging Kim Il-sung and his followers were quite aware of the comparative weakness of their movement in the south relative to the Koo-Rhee faction. A five-year trusteeship would give them time to strengthen and discipline their ranks for the climactic battle with the nationalists at the moment when it was expected that both the Russians and Americans would quit the peninsula.[70]

Nonetheless Hodge and his lieutenants had exhibited a temperamental preference for the conservative nationalists ever since their arrival, and Washington, caught in the grip of early cold-war anti-Communism, was increasingly receptive to the idea of a monolithic movement directed from Moscow, which had to be contained wherever possible by whatever means.[71] Edwin Pauley, Truman's personal representative on reparations matters, visited both zones of Korea in May and June of 1946 and on June 22 reported grimly to the President of his great concern with the American position on the peninsula and the fact that Korea was "not receiving the attention and consideration that it should." Pauley feared not only an imminent communization of northern Korea but of the entire peninsula. "Communism in Korea could get off to a better start than practically anywhere else in the world," Pauley warned, since a sudden Communist takeover of all the railroads and public utilities, previously monopolized by the Japanese, would assume the character of a people's revenge. "This is one of the reasons why the United States should not waive its title or claim to Japanese external assets located in Korea until a democratic (capitalist) form of government is assured." In conclusion Pauley asserted that "the Soviet Army is obviously ensconcing itself for a long stay," presumably to protect its investment in the local Communist groups.[72]

Distasteful as the Koo-Rhee group continued to be to Washington, it seemed as time went on the only alternative to a Communist Korea. Washington's emerging mood was perfectly reflected in a proposed message to MacArthur drafted in the State Department on the last day of February 1946. It was obvious from recent cables from Seoul "that the Soviet authorities in Korea are applying the same tactics they have applied in Eastern Europe in order to gain control of the various governments through minority groups controlled by the Soviet Government." Accordingly, MacArthur was to "make clear in a strong public statement" the measures which the American command in Korea had put into effect "looking toward a free and independent Korea." In addition Hodge and his staff in Seoul were to make every effort to find political leaders in the American zone "who are neither associated with the Kim Koo group nor the Soviet dominated groups" and who could project "a firm progressive program for Korea." "Because of their background as exiles, the fact that they are apparently being supported by the Kuomintang, and the State Department's unsatisfactory experience with Rhee in dealings with him over a period of years," the State Department draft continued, "we should not show any favoritism to the Kim Koo and Syngman Rhee groups." However, the drafters admitted that it might be impossible to find "progressive leaders" who were not under the influence of either the Russians or the Koo-Rhee faction. Therefore "it might be necessary to make a strong effort to force the Kim Koo group to adopt and put into effect a progressive program" along lines favored by Washington.[73]

It is not clear whether this message was ever sent to Tokyo and Seoul, but it was, in any case, an ambiguous directive. And without further overt support from Hodge the Koo-Rhee "Nationalists" found it difficult to form a "single party of the right," to use Adviser Langdon's term.[74] However, Hodge had already given the nationalists a strong boost by permitting them to form the Korean Democratic Representative Council in mid-February and to utilize it for their own political ends. In reaction some forty leftish organizations in the south, including the Korean Communist party, formed a Korean Democratic People's Front on February 16.[75] Not until May 14, in the immediate wake of the breakdown of Soviet-American negotiations in the Joint Commission, did Langdon report from Seoul the partial success of Kim Koo in merging the various "Right Wing" parties into a single Korean Independence party.[76] At the same time the leftists in the Korean Democratic People's Front had tried without success to lure Kim Il-sung from Pyongyang to Seoul to take charge of the leftist movement.[77] The fragmentation of Korean politics into Communist North and right-wing South was accelerating markedly by mid-1946.

In these circumstances Hodge believed he had no choice but to court the conservatives in the south, Rhee and Koo in particular. In late May Langdon cabled Washington that if a satisfactory coalition of patriotic parties could be achieved "without Communist collaboration," Hodge proposed to increase "considerably" their participation in Korean affairs. The general would create a "Korean Nonadministrative Cabinet and

Legislative Body," which, under his overall direction, would enact regulations and laws for southern Korean prior to the establishment of a unified provisional government under the Moscow agreement.

> It will be made clear by adequate publicity that this step is not designed to postpone unification but, on the contrary, by giving the initiative to Koreans in the South to hasten its realization. In this connection there are indications that Korean puppets in the north are finding their position more and more difficult and might possibly be induced to enter private negotiations with a southern coalition to form a government slate which an American delegation might eventually put forward for consideration by the [Joint] Commission should it reconvene.

Langdon went on to deny the many stories from "home" that American authorities in Korea "are backing exclusively such conservative elements as Rhee and Koo. . . ." But he added that while Koo was becoming increasingly inept politically, "Rhee, on the other hand, has been cooperative in rallying all shades of opinion toward unification and has been helpful in preventing his following from excessive anti-Allied demonstrations." Hodge, Langdon concluded, did not necessarily feel that Rhee was essential or even desirable in a future provisional government, "but so long as he is one of the few nationally known leaders among democratic elements, his cooperation now can hardly be dispensed with."[78]

In early June the State Department's Office for Occupied Areas sent Hodge a new policy statement for Korea. It accepted and indeed called for an even greater emphasis upon the policy of utilizing qualified Koreans "in as many posts of responsibility as possible in the local and provincial administration and in the administration of the United States zone as a whole." Moreover, popular elections should be held as soon as practicable. The inclusion of Koreans "from all political groups" in the American administration of the south and the holding of elections to choose an advisory legislative body "should enable us to create a Korean leadership in the south which is more truly representative of all Korean political opinion" than was the leadership of the current Representative Democratic Council created by Hodge the previous February, which included "no leftists of any kind." Hodge was thus put on notice that Washington continued to view with concern, if not outright disfavor, Seoul's insistent support for Syngman Rhee and his fellow right-wing nationalists. Indeed, the directive went on to state baldly that "Agreement not only between the Soviet and United States authorities but also between the various factions in southern Korea would also be greatly facilitated if certain personalities who have been the storm centers of recent political controversy in Korea were to retire temporarily from the scene." Should Hodge miss the point, deliberately or otherwise, the Department defined these "certain personalities" as "a group of older *emigre* Koreans who have returned to Korea since the capitulation of Japan. They are not thought to be completely representative of Korean political opinion, nor are they felt to be essential to the establishment of Korean democracy or the attainment of United States objectives in Korea."[79]

The next day, however, Langdon sent Washington translations of various "documents of political action issued by local branches of the Communist Party in Korea for party members," in which Rhee, Koo, and their followers were singled out as "reactionary leaders who must be positively rejected."[80] Throughout the summer and autumn of 1946 the question of American support for the Rhee-Koo group remained unresolved as American headquarters in Seoul set about implementing the June policy directive and Hodge desultorily dispatched several letters to his Soviet opposite in Pyongyang asking for a resumption of negotiations. Langdon went up to Pyongyang in early October for "completely unofficial" talks with Soviet officials and assured them "that the United States had no intention of trying to establish a provisional government under the control of Syngman Rhee and Kim Koo and that we desired from the beginning to work with all Leftist elements in south Korea. . . ." Yet Langdon left his Soviet listeners with the distinct implication that Communist elements in the south had ruined such a generous policy by manipulating their fellow leftists into rigid opposition to American policies. For "up to recently these [leftists] groups had not only refused to work with us but had attacked our policies by underground means and a propaganda of lies."

In late 1946 a flurry of proposals and counterproposals for reconvening the Joint Commission flew between Pyongyang and Seoul, but nothing substantive developed. Meanwhile Hodge had become increasingly aware of the mischief which Rhee was prepared to make in order to realize his political aims. In response to the June directive Hodge in July 1946 had proposed that "a legislative body be established which would help determine the wishes of the Korean people in legislative matters." The proposed body ''would consist of members representing the major political parties and members elected to represent the various provinces.'' Since Rhee and his followers were rapidly consolidating their hold over the politics of the right, the American proposal presented them with their best opportunity to date to dominate native politics. Throughout the summer Rhee and Koo traveled the length and breadth of southern Korea whipping up support, and when the elections for the Korean Interim Legislative Assembly took place in October, thirty-one ''right wing candidates'' and twelve ''independents'' won forty-three of the forty-five seats up for election. The remaining forty-five representatives, it had been decided, would be chosen directly by the military government. Alliance between Rhee and Hodge became a practical, if not at that moment a permanent, reality. Hodge was uneasy. ''Rhee is a nuisance,'' he admitted in a cable to the Secretary of State on December 31, ''in that he wants everything done his own impractical way and wants to head separate Govt of South Korea. However, we cannot and must not overlook his potential to do irreparable damage unless carefully handled.''[81]

Hodge believed as late as the end of 1946 that he could ''handle'' Rhee. But 1947 proved to be the year of disillusionment. In January Hodge was forced to issue a condemnatory statement aimed directly at Rhee and his followers, euphemistically defined as ''certain elements,'' who ''through lack of knowledge of facts or through malicious intent to deceive the Korean people'' were seeking to create the impression that the United States ''now favors and is actively working toward a separate government in Southern Korea and that the Korean Interim Legislative Assembly is a completely independent body designed as the forerunner of that government.''[82] American officials went so far as to visit Kim Koo and Mrs. Rhee at Rhee's home and to plead with them ''to restrain and not incite the people.''[83] But it was all to no avail. Within a fortnight Hodge had to issue yet another statement against the Rhee party condemning ''extensive plans under way by certain Korean groups to instigate widespread demonstrations in South Korea against the Moscow decision, against the so-called trusteeship, coupled with attempts to discredit the American effort in Korea.''[84] By the end of January Secretary of War Patterson told his fellow Secretaries of State and Navy ''that the Korean problem was the single most urgent problem now facing the War Department. There was a lack of railroad, power, and fertilizer in the area and there seemed to be no leadership of political ability among the Koreans. There had been no cooperation at all between the Russian and U.S. Zones and all agreed that an approach to the U.S.S.R. by this government at this time would likely lead nowhere.''[85]

The political situation in Korea was rapidly slipping away from American control. The Russians had conducted elections in northern Korea during the autumn of 1946 in which 93 percent of the population went to the polls, forceably or not, to elect local ''People's Committees.'' American officials and Korean nationalists below the thirty-eighth parallel promptly viewed this development as the beginning of firm Communist control of the north.[86] The situation provided Rhee and his colleagues with both the motivation and rationale for pressing their own rule on the south. Throughout that fall there were disorders and demonstrations throughout the American zone, and in several instances Hodge's troops had to open fire on ''threatening mobs.''[87] By the time that the Joint Commission reconvened at American initiative in mid-summer 1947, Hodge was thoroughly disillusioned with Rhee. He cabled Secretary of State Marshall that Washington did not ''clearly visualize'' the political picture in Korea. ''Rhee and his gang are engaged in all-out opposition to the Russians, the Joint Commission, General Hodge and military government using the war cry of 'anti-trusteeship' and alleged high level promises to Rhee of a separate government for South Korea. His Washington lobby has recently tried to bog him down to no avail.''[88] Yet with the quick, immensely discouraging, reversion of Joint Commission negotiations to their impossible impasse of the spring of 1946, was there any alternative to the implacable Rhee?

By mid-1947 the cold war had taken firm direction of Soviet-American relations,[89] and in the State Department assistant chief of the Eastern European Affairs Division, Francis B. Stevens, wrote to Policy Planning Staff Director George Kennan of the immense danger should Korea slip completely from the American grasp.

> In the ideological struggle between East and West, between communism and Western political concepts, individual political acts may have an importance far beyond their local consequences. Korea is the one country in the world where Soviet and American forces are in direct contact and share between them the administration of the country. The United States is pledged to establish Korea as an independent nation. Korea consequently is a symbol to the watching world both of the East-West struggle for influence and power and of American sincerity in sponsoring the nationalistic aims of Asiatic

peoples. If we allow Korea to go by default and fall within the Soviet orbit, the world will feel that we have lost another round in our match with the Soviet Union. . . .[90]

Such sentiments also shaped the report which Lieutenant General Albert C. Wedemeyer sent to President Truman on September 9, 1947. Wedemeyer had been American chief of staff to Chiang Kai-shek from late 1944 to the end of the Marshall mission in early 1947, and he was ordered by Truman in July 1947 to proceed to China and Korea "for the purpose of making an appraisal of the political, economic, psychological and military situations—current and projected" in the two countries. At the very beginning of his report Wedemeyer sounded the cold war alarm. "Gradually it has become apparent," he wrote, "that the World War II objectives for which we and others made tremendous sacrifices are not being fully attained, and that there remains in the world a force presenting even greater dangers to world peace than did the Nazi militarists and the Japanese jingoists."

The major problem in Korea, Wedemeyer continued, was the implementation of the Moscow Agreement. The further deadlock in the Joint Commission meetings of May 1947 was due to Soviet unwillingness to abide by a formula embodied in the exchange of notes between Marshall and Molotov, which had promised "participation in consultation" of the "rightist groups" of southern Korea. The Korean problem was further complicated by the Soviet establishment of a Communist regime in the north "and by the machinations in South Korea of Communist groups, openly hostile to the United States." Under the circumstances Hodge and American officials in Washington had no choice but to do as they had done—"to carry out a policy of 'Koreanization' of the government in South Korea." In fulfillment of this policy it was clear to Wedemeyer that "The rightist groups are probably the best organized parties in South Korea. They command a majority of the Korean Interim Legislative Assembly and, if elections were held under present conditions, would gain control of any government established in South Korea by such elections."

America could not remove its political, military, economic, or moral support from South Korea precipitately, Wedemeyer stridently asserted. A continuation of present policies would give notice to Russia and other nations in the Far East that the United States would not abandon Korea in the face of Soviet intransigence and that the United States would continue to insist upon the fulfillment of the Moscow agreement. A continuation of present American policies would deny Russia direct or indirect control of all of Korea and foreclose free use of the entire peninsula as a military base of operations. Continued interim occupation by U.S. Army forces was mandatory until agreement could be reached with the Soviets for mutual withdrawal, and the United States must continue and expand its modestly budgeted programs for economic rehabilitation. At the same time Wedemeyer recommended continued arming of the national police and coast guard and the creation of an American-officered South Korean scout force to replace the current constabulary and serve as a bulwark against "the threat from the North."[91] Korea had become a forward outpost of the rapidly worsening cold war, and America slowly but inexorably became locked into a commitment to the strongest man available south of the thirty-eighth parallel. It was a situation perfectly suited to the guile, talent, and will of Syngman Rhee.

In late September 1947 the Soviets suddenly threw down a new challenge to their American opponents. The Russian delegation on the Joint Commission issued a statement suggesting a mutual and simultaneous withdrawal of forces in early 1948 and the organization by Koreans of their own government without outside assistance.[92] The Soviet motive seems clear enough now with the assistance of contemporary documents. Relations between Rhee and his American masters had become increasingly strained and now approached the breaking point. Yet the Americans were equally determined not to see a Communist Korea. If they could be removed, Rhee would stand alone with a recent history of strained relations with everyone, and the increasingly powerful and self-confident Korean Communists under Kim Il-sung might well be able to isolate and destroy him. Moreover, the Soviets were probably aware that domestic pressures upon the Truman administration were weakening the American military presence in southern Korea. Despite the pressures of cold war, Congress was in the midst of its postwar antispending crusade, in which the conflict with the Russians was to be contained by bombers, not soldiers. There was a strong urge in America to bring the troops home from the isolated outposts of containment that the cold war had created. Bending to these pressures, the Joint Chiefs of Staff had concluded by the autumn of 1947 that the forty thousand troops then in Korea constituted a "liability," should general hostilities break out in the Far East. The Truman administration, operating from a position of weakness, thus countered the Soviet proposal on troop withdrawals with one of its own, adopted by the UN General Assembly in November. A nine-nation UN commission would go to Korea and assist the Korean people in establishing their own government, and such a government would come into power through Korean-wide elections to be held no later than March 31, 1948.[93]

Events now conspired to produce the worst possible outcome for the Americans. Rhee and his followers vigorously sought to either discredit the UN commission or force it to recognize the nationalists of South Korea as the only rightful governing body for the peninsula as a whole. At the same time Rhee tried to set "Korean people against American authorities and administration by deliberately misrepresenting facts, U.S. aims, and relief operations" and portraying Hodge "as an absolute monarch or war lord . . ." Rhee knew well how to exploit the "nearly 2 years of discouragement and disappointment" of the Korean people, who had expected independence and self-government to come with their American, if not Soviet, saviors in September 1945.[94] At the end of December 1947, when it appeared that Canada might decline membership on the UN commission, Acting Secretary of State Robert Lovett wrote to Canadian Prime Minister MacKenzie King that if the Soviet proposal for mutual withdrawal in several months time were accepted it "would lead to the early establishment of a dictatorship in Korea."[95] The historian is justified in wondering whether Lovett meant a Communist dictatorship or one by Syngman Rhee.

The Communists provided the final conditions necessary to confirm Rhee's power and rule in South Korea. When the UN commission reached Korea at the end of 1947 the Soviet commander would not receive it. At a stroke the Russians had revived the issue of the Communist menace and had seemed to confirm all that Rhee had been asserting for years about Communist perfidy. The Korean Communists then gratuitously strengthened Rhee's posture as a patriot. On February 26, 1948, the United Nations had passed a resolution calling on its commission in Korea to observe elections throughout the country "or, if that were impossible, in as much of Korea as was accessible to the Commission." Hodge promptly issued instructions for elections to be held throughout the south during the month of May. The Communists just as promptly initiated an intensive campaign of overt terrorism and obstruction.[96] In April the North Korean People's Council approved a draft constitution for a Democratic People's Republic of Korea, and on May 31 the representatives elected by the people of South Korea convened as the National Assembly and elected Syngman Rhee as chairman. Although seats in proportion to the number of the population above the thirty-eighth parallel were arranged and left vacant as a symbolic invitation for later North Korean participation, the peninsula was firmly divided at last.[97]

The American Command at Seoul, to say nothing of Washington officialdom, were now tied to the one anti-Communist leader in all of South Korea whom they most feared and disliked. Nonetheless the situation had passed beyond the point of change or influence. As American forces slowly and grudgingly withdrew from the peninsula in 1948 and early 1949, following the Russian example, they turned over much of their arms and equipment to Rhee's fledgling Republic of Korea Army, which had emerged from the earlier constabulary forces. A Military Advisory Group remained behind to train ROK forces in the rudiments of modern war. The commitment to Rhee became binding.[98] It was not the first time, nor would it be the last, that the terrible imperatives of the cold war forced the American government and people to bed down with a very questionable political ally.

But even in 1948, to say nothing of the earlier years of the postwar era, the problems of Korea were overshadowed in American thinking by the vast drama of Asian nationalism which was working itself out amidst the hills and river valleys of China.

NOTES

1. Richard E. Lauterbach, *Danger from the East* (New York: Harper & Brothers Publishers, 1947), pp. 197-199. Lauterbach, along with Harold Isaacs, was an American correspondent in early postwar Asia, and his book is an account of what he saw and felt. Lauterbach claims that George H. McCune, chief of the State Department's Korea Division in 1945, told him that a draft directive *was* sent to Hodge before he left Okinawa for Korea, which " 'explicitly stated that he was to remove the Japanese administrators, though retaining for a time the general structure of government. An elementary political sense should have dictated the immediate removal of at least a token number of top-ranking Japanese officials, but apparently Hodge's advisers were too shortsighted to realize this.' " No such directive as McCune outlined has been found in State Department files.

2. U.S. Department of State, *Foreign Relations of the United States, 1945: Diplomatic Papers*, 9 vols. (Washington, D.C.: U.S. Government Printing Office, 1967-1969), 6:1041, 1043-1044 (hereinafter cited as *FR, 1945: Diplomatic Papers*); Robert K. Sawyer, *Military Advisers in Korea: KMAG in Peace and War* (Washington, D.C.: Office of the Chief of Military History, Department of the Army, 1962), p. 3.

3. *FR, 1945: Diplomatic Papers*, 6:1036, 1042.

4. Ibid., pp. 1045-1046, 1053n., 1053-1054.

5. The arrival of American forces in Korea was subsequently described by a participant during the course of a radio broadcast in early January 1946, entitled "Korea and the Far East," printed in U.S. Department of State *Bulletin* 14 (27 January 1946):104-109. See also the descriptions of Harold Isaacs and Richard Lauterbach, which stress that after decades of subjugation by the Japanese, the Korean people viewed the arriving Americans as knights in shining armor, as "demigods." Harold R. Isaacs, *No Peace for Asia* (New York: Macmillan Co., 1947), p. 81; Lauterbach, *Danger from the East*, pp. 184-185.

6. Isaacs, *No Peace for Asia*, pp. 7-34; Lauterbach, *Danger from the East*, pp. 223-224.

7. Sawyer, *Military Advisers in Korea*, p. 3; Gregory Henderson statement in *Conference of Scholars on the Administration of Occupied Areas, 1943-1955: April 10-11, 1970 at the Harry S. Truman Library* (Independence, Mo.: Harry S. Truman Library Institute, 1970), p. 10; Isaacs, *No Peace for Asia*, p. 93.

8. Draft Memorandum to the Joint Chiefs of Staff by Assistant Secretary of State James C. Dunn, Washington, D.C., n.d., *FR, 1945: Diplomatic Papers*, 6:1037-1038.

9. Robert A. Scalapino and Chong-Sik Lee, *Communism in Korea*, 2 parts (Berkeley: University of California Press, 1972), part 1, pp. 229-247; Gregory Henderson, *Korea: The Politics of the Vortex* (Cambridge, Mass.: Harvard University Press, 1968), pp. 116-117.

10. *Conference of Scholars on the Administration of Occupied Areas*, p. 35; Dae-Sook Suh, *Korean Communist Movement, 1918-1948* (Princeton, N.J.: Princeton University Press, 1967), pp. 297-299; Lauterbach, *Danger from the East*, pp. 197-201; E. Grant Meade, *American Military Government in Korea* (New York: King's Crown Press, 1951), p. 59. According to Meade, Hodge's instructions "clearly stipulated" that although he was to treat Korea as a " 'liberated country' he was not bound to recognize any situation challenging his duly constituted authority."

11. *FR, 1945: Diplomatic Papers*, 6:1049-1050. "Koreans made up for lost time talking and living politics. A disillusioned American officer in Seoul said, 'Everytime two Koreans sit down to eat they form a new political party.' In October, a month after the landings, all political parties were ordered to register with AMG. The national preoccupation with politics was such that by November 2, two hundred and five parties had presented claims for recognition. Among them were the Forlorn Hope Society, the Supporters' Union for All Korean Political Actors, the Getting Ready Committee for the Return of the Provisional Korean Republic Government, and the Boy Scouts. The Boy Scouts, incidentally, proved

so dangerous in their efforts to thwart law and order that they had to be disbanded.'' Lauterbach, *Danger from the East*, p. 203.

12. *FR, 1945: Diplomatic Papers*, 6:1049-1050.

13. Quoted in Harry S. Truman, *Memoirs*, 2 vols. (New York: Signet Books, 1962), vol. 2: *Years of Trial and Hope, 1946-1952*, p. 361.

14. Isaacs, *No Peace for Asia*, pp. 95-96.

15. Benninghoff cable, 15 September 1945, *FR, 1945: Diplomatic Papers*, 6:1049-1050; Isaacs, *No Peace for Asia*, pp. 95-96.

16. *FR, 1945: Diplomatic Papers*, 6:1049-1050; Henderson, *Korea: Politics of the Vortex*, p. 126; Sawyer, *Military Advisers in Korea*, p. 6.

17. *FR, 1945: Diplomatic Papers*, 6:1045, 1045n.

18. The "Basic Directive . . ." is printed in ibid., pp. 1073-1090.

19. Sawyer, *Military Advisors in Korea*, pp. 7-18.

20. Soon Sung Cho, *Korea in World Politics, 1940-1950: An Evaluation of American Responsibility* (Berkeley: University of California Press, 1967), p. 92; Lauterbach, *Danger from the East*, pp. 198, 218-220.

21. Lauterbach, *Danger from the East*, pp. 218-220; General Headquarters, Commander-in-Chief, United States Army Forces, Pacific, *Summation No. 6, United States Army Military Government Activities in Korea, for the Month of March 1946*, pp. 2, 8, 11 (hereinafter cited as *Military Government Activities in Korea*, number, month, and year); Meade, *American Military Government in Korea*, pp. 194-196. According to Meade, Dr. Arthur C. Bunce, economic adviser to General Hodge, declared in a press conference at Seoul on 4 September 1946: " 'I think we can admit frankly that we made a very grave mistake when we went into the free market for rice last year. We made that error partly because of the advice of Koreans.' " Dr. Bunce did not specify to which Koreans he went for the advice.

22. Meade, *American Military Government in Korea*, pp. 190-211; Lauterbach, *Danger from the East*, pp. 220-222.

23. Meade, *American Military Government in Korea*, pp. 205, 207, 212, 226, 230; Lauterbach, *Danger from the East*, pp. 222-225; *Military Government Activities in Korea, No. 6, March 1946*, p. 11, *No. 11, August 1946*, p. 4, *No. 12, September 1946*, p. 4, *No. 13, October 1946*, p. 5; Joyce and Gabriel Kolko, *The Limits of Power: The World and United States Foreign Policy, 1945-1954* (New York: Harper & Row Publishers, 1972), pp. 277-299.

24. *FR, 1945: Diplomatic Papers*, 6:1060.

25. Ibid., pp. 1061-1065.

26. Ibid., p. 1070.

27. Ibid., pp. 1091-1092.

28. Ibid., p. 1104.

29. Ibid., pp. 1113-1114, 1122-1124.

30. Ibid., p. 1112.

31. Acting Political Adviser in Japan (Atcheson) to the Secretary of State, 12 November 1945, ibid., pp. 1119-1120; Sawyer, *Military Advisers in Korea*, p. 8; Suh, *Korean Communist Movement*, p. 229.

32. *FR, 1945: Diplomatic Papers*, 6:1059-1068 passim, 1112-1113, 1118. Such rumors proved to be false. According to a report by special presidential envoy Edwin Pauley in June 1946, ''The Soviets are taking no substantial amount of capital equipment from Korea. . . .'' Truman, *Years of Trial and Hope*, pp. 366-367.

33. Henderson and Cho statements in *Conference of Scholars on the Administration of Occupied Areas*, pp. 34-35.   See also Scalapino and Lee, *Communism in Korea*, part 1, pp. 229-230; Suh, *Korean Communist Movement*, pp. 253-329 passim.

34. Henderson statement in *Conference of Scholars on the Administration of Occupied Areas*, p. 28.

35. *FR, 1945: Diplomatic Papers*, 6:1065-1066.

36. Ibid., pp. 1071-1073.

37. Walter Millis, ed., *The Forrestal Diaries* (New York: Viking Press, 1951), pp. 97-98.

38. Leahy Diary, 29 September 1945, William D. Leahy Papers, Library of Congress, Washington, D.C.

39. Lisle A. Rose, *After Yalta: America and the Origins of the Cold War* (New York: Charles Scribner's Sons, 1973), Chapter 5.

40. *FR, 1945: Diplomatic Papers*, 6:1106-1107.

41. Ibid., p. 1119.

42. Ibid., p. 1122.

43. Ibid., p. 1133.

44. Rose, *After Yalta*, Chapter 5.

45. *FR, 1945: Diplomatic Papers*, 6:1130-1133, 1137-1138.

46. Ibid., pp. 1130-1136, 1142-1143.

47. Ibid., 2:618-621.

48. Ibid., pp. 699-700.

49. Ibid., pp. 716-717, 721, 728, 820-821; Truman, *Years of Trial and Hope*, pp. 363-364.

50. James F. Byrnes, *Speaking Frankly* (New York: Harper & Brothers Publishers, 1947), pp. 110-122.

51. U.S. Department of State, *Foreign Relations of the United States, 1946*, 11 vols. (Washington, D.C.: U.S. Government Printing Office, 1969-1972), 8:607-608 (hereinafter cited as *FR, 1946*).

52. Ibid., pp. 608-609, 611-612.

53. Hodge to the War Department, 18 January 1946, ibid., pp. 611-612.

54. Benninghoff to Secretary of State, 15 February 1946, ibid., p. 634.

55. Ibid., p. 616.

56. Ibid., pp. 635-636.

57. Cho, *Korea in World Politics*, p. 79; Isaacs, *No Peace for Asia*, pp. 81-85.

58. Benninghoff to Secretary of State, 23 January 1946, *FR, 1946*, 8: 615.

59. The Chargé in the Soviet Union (Kennan) to the Secretary of State, 25 January 1946, ibid., pp. 617-619.

60. Ibid., pp. 628-630.

61. Ibid., pp. 681-682.

62. Benninghoff to Secretary of State, 15 February 1946, ibid., p. 636.

63. Benninghoff to Secretary of State, 20 February 1946, ibid., pp. 637-638.

64. Hodge to Secretary of State via General MacArthur, n.d. (received 24 February 1946), ibid., pp. 640-642.

65. "Korea and the Far East," U.S. Department of State *Bulletin* 14 (27 January 1946):104-110 passim.

66. Langdon to Secretary of State, n.d. (received 14 April 1946), *FR, 1946*, 8:660; U.S. Department of State Publication 3305, *Korea, 1945 to 1948* (Washington, 1948), p. 4.

67. Hodge to Secretary of State, n.d. (received 9 May 1946), *FR, 1946*, 8:665-666.

68. Ibid., p. 666.

69. Ibid., pp. 666-667; Byrnes, *Speaking Frankly*, pp. 222-223; U.S. Department of State Publication 7446, *A Historical Summary of United States-Korean Relations . . . 1834-1962* (Washington, D.C.: Historical Office, Bureau of Public Affairs, 1962), pp. 63-64 (hereinafter cited as *United States-Korean Relations*); *Military Government Activities in Korea, No. 8, April 1946*, pp. 5, 21.

70. Suh, *Korean Communist Movement*, pp. 305-306.

71. E. Grant Meade has argued that on the provincial level in some areas of southern Korea, American political, information, and agricultural officers "leaned over backwards in efforts to maintain an impartial attitude" toward various native political groups and movements during the first half-year of the occupation. But "this situation changed in the spring of 1946," after most of these officers had left the country. "Their replacements were conservatives, conditioned either by their experience in the companies or their briefing at the national level [i.e., at Seoul]." Leftist "terrorism was punished by fines and imprisonment, while the rightist goon squads were gently chided and warned not to repeat their offenses." *American Military Government in Korea*, pp. 164-165.

72. Truman, *Years of Trial and Hope*, pp. 365-367.

73. *FR, 1946*, 8:645-646.

74. Langdon to Secretary of State, 10 April 1946, ibid., pp. 658-659.

75. Suh, *Korean Communist Movement*, p. 307.

76. *FR, 1946*, 8:677.

77. Ibid.

78. Ibid., pp. 685-689.

79. Ibid., pp. 692-699.

80. Ibid., pp. 699-703.

81. Ibid., pp. 785-786; *United States-Korean Relations*, p. 64; *Military Government Activities in Korea, No. 10, July 1946*, p. 3, *No. 13, October 1946*, p. 3.

82. U.S. Department of State *Bulletin* 16 (19 January 1947):128-129; *Military Government Activities in Korea, No. 16, January 1947*, pp. 3, 4, 11-16.

83. U.S. Department of State, *Foreign Relations of the United States, 1947*, 8 vols. (Washington, D.C.: U.S. Government Printing Office, 1972-1973), 6:598-599 (hereinafter cited as *FR, 1947*). Rhee had left Korea for the United States in December to stir up support for his cause. *Military Government Activities in Korea, No. 15, December 1946*, pp. 3-4.

84. U.S. Department of State *Bulletin 16 (2 February 1947):210.*

85. Millis, ed., *Forrestal Diaries*, pp. 241-242.

86. Truman, *Years of Trial and Hope*, p. 367. Dae Sook-Suh has since argued that in the north "the Russians gave the governing power to the North Koreans, maintaining indirect control without a military governing body of their own." *Korean Communist Movement*, p. 311.

87. Truman, *Years of Trial and Hope*, p. 367.

88. Cable of 16 July 1947, *FR, 1947*, 6:703; Truman, *Years of Trial and Hope*, pp. 367-368.

89. As early as March 13, 1947, Dean Acheson stated in testimony before an executive session of the Senate Foreign Relations Committee studying aid to Greece and Turkey that "It is true that there are parts of the world to which we have no access. It would be silly to believe that we can do anything effective in Rumania, Bulgaria, or Poland. You cannot do that. That is within the Russian sphere of physical force. We are excluded from that. There are other places where we can be effective. One of them is Korea, and I think that is another place where the line has been clearly drawn between the Russians and ourselves." U.S. Congress, Senate, *Legislative Origins of the Truman Doctrine: Hearings Held in Executive Session before the Committee on Foreign Relations, March 13 and 28, and April 1, 2 and 3, 1947*, 80th Cong., 1st Sess. (Washington, D.C.: U.S. Government Printing Office, 1973), p. 22.

90. *FR, 1947*, 6:784-785.

91. *Report to the President, Submitted by Lt. Gen. A. C. Wedemeyer, September, 1947: Korea*, printed for the use of the Committee on Armed Services, United States Senate (Washington, D.C.: U.S. Government Printing Office, 1951).

92. *United States-Korean Relations*, p. 66; Truman, *Years of Trial and Hope*, p. 370.

93. *United States-Korean Relations*, pp. 66-67; Truman, *Years of Trial and Hope*, pp. 370-372; Millis, ed., *Forrestal Diaries*, p. 265.

94. *FR, 1947*, 6:862-867, 869-871.

95. Ibid., p. 883.

96. *United States-Korean Relations*, p. 68; Truman, *Years of Trial and Hope*, p. 373.

97. *United States-Korean Relations*, pp. 68-69.

98. Sawyer, *Military Advisers in Korea*, pp. 34-113 passim.

chapter 5

China: The Roots of Anti-Communism

During the second week of August 1945 all China tensely awaited news of Japan's surrender. Amidst the hills and caves of Yenan, Communist headquarters was in readiness for a series of military leaps into adjacent Japanese-controlled areas for the purpose of disarmament and occupation. In Chungking, nestled among the narrow river gorges of the Yangtse, the exhausted, graft-ridden Kuomintang government, facing the prospects of reconstructing a devastated land, ousting the million-man army of a defeated enemy, and dealing either militarily or diplomatically with a powerful and refractory rival, viewed the future with mingled hope and trepidation. Beset by a multitude of troubles, Chiang and his colleagues received news of the signing of the Sino-Soviet treaty in Moscow on August 14 with as great a relief as news the same day that Japan had at last capitulated. With luck and aid the Kuomintang might indeed survive to lead postwar China down the long and hard road toward that great power status which others had wished upon her.

But Yenan would have to be dealt with first. When the initial post-Hiroshima rumors had reached China of an impending Japanese surrender, Mao had ordered his forces "to launch a general offensive throughout the country" to disarm Japanese forces and to occupy areas hitherto held by the enemy and his "puppet forces." Chiang was not slow to respond. Should the Communists obtain the vast territories and prestige that would certainly accrue to them by their actions, the influence of the Kuomintang throughout most of north and northeast China might be forever obliterated.

On August 13, therefore, Chiang ordered Communist forces to remain in place and await further directives. He further admonished General Chu Teh, Commander of the Eighteenth Group Army "never again to take independent action."[1]

Chu Teh replied two days later. He would, he told Chungking, continue to fight the Japanese wherever they resisted and to accept surrenders where they did not. Continued Japanese military efforts in some areas nullified the stand and cease-fire order from Chungking, which did "not conform to the national interest. We consider that you have issued the wrong order, very wrong indeed, and we have to reject it resolutely."[2] In fact, there seems to have been very little Japanese willingness to resist the inevitable after the atomic blitz of Hiroshima and Nagasaki and the Soviet entry into the Pacific war. By August 20 the American embassy in Chungking began receiving reports of widespread surrenders by imperial forces to Chinese units, both Nationalist and Communist.[3] And in the ending of one war in China lay the beginnings of another. How would the Americans react? The answer was not long in coming.

As early as August 15 General Wedemeyer told Chinese reporters at Chungking that American officers would assist the Chinese takeover of Japanese-held areas in "advisory capacities." Wedemeyer was quoted by the Kuomintang newspaper *Ta Kung Pao* as saying that "Chinese troops will be moved as fast as possible to take over Japanese held points in China."[4] Since the country's only reasonably modern and efficient transportation network belonged to U.S. forces and since there were no American officers officially accredited to Communist headquarters, Wedemeyer was clearly reconfirming the existing commitment of his nation and government to the Kuomintang.[5]

On August 20 the Communists exacerbated tensions further. Chu Teh dispatched another cable to Chiang bluntly telling the Kuomintang leader that he "must act immediately to avert the 'grave threat' of civil war between Communist and Government forces in China." By this time clashes between Kuomintang and Maoist forces had steadily mounted in both numbers and intensity. From northern China alarming reports filtered down to Chungking and even into far off Washington that a "big Communist offensive" was moving toward Shanghai and Nanking, the latter city being the proposed future capital of the Kuomintang government. Against this somber background, Chu Teh's assertion "that 260,000,000 Chinese were 'dissatisfied' with General Chiang's regime" could only deepen the gloom and anxiety beginning to spread across Chungking after the first few euphoric hours following news of Japan's defeat. By August 25 the rival armies were openly seizing towns in preparation for what even then appeared to be a further protracted struggle for ultimate power in China.[6]

Ambassador Hurley's strenuous efforts to avoid civil war through negotiation were now doomed. But the former Oklahoma businessman and presidential crony was unwilling to face reality. On August 20 he had cabled Washington that the Japanese surrender had either "paved the way for final settlement between Chinese Communists and Central Government or an outbreak of large-scale hostilities between them in competition for regions to be given up by the Japanese." The recent exchange of proclamations between Chungking and Yenan indicated that hostilities were imminent, Hurley continued, unless a reconciliation could be effected "in immediate future." In the final week of August, after days of apparently intense diplomatic effort, Hurley flew to Yenan at Mao's invitation and with Chiang's blessing and convinced Mao and one of his chief political lieutenants, Chou En-lai, to return to Chungking for yet another round of talks. Some observers accused Hurley of deliberately employing diplomacy as a screen behind which Kuomintang forces could move into threatened areas of northern China—by means of American transportation—to thwart imminent Communist takeovers. Hurley vigorously denied the allegations, and by August 30 Chiang and Mao were dining with one another at Chungking, where the Communist leader continued to press for Kuomintang recognition of Yenan's right to disarm Japanese forces in all areas under Communist control.[7]

Direct and secret negotiations between Chiang and Mao began on September 2. Chiang made a number of specific proposals, all of which were directed at achieving the twin objectives of Communist inclusion and subordination in a postwar Chinese national government. Mao, while not yet insisting on a true coalition government, countered with proposals of his own based on existing but temporary military and diplomatic realities which would have given Yenan practical sovereignty over much of northern and eastern China.[8] Hurley was confident that the talks would ultimately achieve unity and harmony. In the words of his most recent biographer, the ambassador utterly failed to recognize the deadly division of purpose between the two sides; "they could come to no lasting accommodation—only an expedient one."[9] By mid-September discussions had become deadlocked, though neither side was willing to break them off, and they continued for another four weeks.

Hurley saw what he wanted to see. He felt, or claimed to feel, old and tired. He wanted out of China and at a moment when the general political atmosphere might be interpreted as promising. On September 11 he dispatched a lengthy cable to the Secretary of State, bluntly restating his conviction that U.S. Far Eastern policy had become supportive of European imperialisms. He then asked to accompany Wedemeyer back to Washington for discussions with Byrnes and Truman on "American-Asiatic policy."[10] Despite the disturbing tone of the telegram, Hurley's satisfaction with the course of Kuomintang-Communist negotiations was palpable. And when both sides asked him to delay his departure for the United States from September 18 to 22, "he did so, thinking that a little more work might bring agreement into sight." Such was not to be, but in the last telegram he ever sent from China, just before leaving for the Chungking airfield, Hurley praised the spirit with which both sides were negotiating and asserted that rapprochement was progressing and that fears of civil war were lessening daily. With that observation filed, he flew away.[11]

Throughout late September and October the possibility of an early end to hostilities steadily receded. Mao returned by plane to Yenan on October 11, leaving behind an ostensibly optimistic Chou En-lai, who informed an American embassy official that all differences had been resolved save agreement on the future status of those areas liberated by Communist forces. In the following weeks Kuomintang officials echoed Chou's sentiments, issuing statements on the satisfactory progress of the talks. But in fact there was no progress, and by the end of the month the always suspicious and impatient Communists had had enough of the charade. A member of Yenan's negotiating team bluntly informed the American embassy that the Kuomintang was stalling for time in order to invade and consolidate its hold over as much of northern China as possible. Recent negotiations between the government and the Communists, Wang Ping-man added, had gotten nowhere.[12]

Washington at last had to face the reality of China's plunge into civil war. The Communists might soon control the vast and rich areas of the country north and east of the Yellow River, including perhaps Manchuria; the possibility of an utter collapse of the Kuomintang could not be dismissed. Perpetually distracted and harassed by the problems of Europe and by the imminent dissolution of the wartime alliance with Russia, policy makers at the State, War and Navy Departments, to say nothing of the White House, were now faced with two terrible questions in Asia: to what extent did Yenan enjoy outright Soviet support and act as the outright executor of Kremlin policy in China? To what extent, if any, should American military aid and intervention be employed on behalf of the Kuomintang? Washington wrestled with these questions throughout the autumn.

During late September and October the lines between Chungking and Washington hummed with news of ever-increasing clashes between Kuomintang and Communist forces throughout northern China. Slowly but inexorably a "jagged Communist barrier" was built across much of the area and the routes north to Manchuria. The rural regions around Tientsin, Nanking, Shanghai, Hankow, Peking, the Shantung peninsula north up to the Great Wall, and even Canton were alive with well-disciplined Communist forces. Only the presence of Japanese troops guarding cities and rail lines in accordance with MacArthur's General Order No. 1 kept Mao's hordes from achieving the most spectacular political and military results throughout northern China. By the end of October the Communists were strongly concentrated in a triangle north and west of Peking and were active in a vast circle of northeast China, including the mountain, river, and coastal provinces of Shansi, Hopei, Chahar, and Shantung. Strong elements had even pushed south across the Yellow River into Honan while other groups were on the move northward out of the hills of Shansi across the plains of Jehol and into Manchuria. Yenan subsequently claimed that from August 11 to October 10 its forces accepted the surrender of 220,000 Japanese and puppet troops, killed or wounded another 10,000 and extended Communist rule over 18,717,000 people.[13] American policy makers were poignantly aware by the second week in November that the commitment to Kuomintang China was fast approaching a historic turning point. The "developments of the next few weeks," a high State Department official wrote on November 16, "will have a momentous bearing on the future of China, of the Far East and of the world."[14]

Despite such dramatic rhetoric, however, American officials remained divided over the dimensions, if not the depth, of China's tragedy. Were Mao, Chou, Chu Teh, and their colleagues and followers indigenous rebels waging civil war as Service, Atcheson, and Davies had argued and as John Carter Vincent continued to maintain implicitly as late as mid-November?[15] Or were the Chinese Communists simply stooges and tools of an international conspiracy directed from the Kremlin and aimed at the subversion of democratic and/or pro-Western governments everywhere on the Eurasian land mass? During the first feverish weeks and months of the postwar era, the views pressed by "experts," the reports of commanders in the field, and the behavior of the Soviets themselves apparently confirmed the latter supposition. The publication of the Sino-Soviet pact on August 14 had cheered a jittery American government and public. "The Chinese Communists can expect no aid or comfort from the Soviet Union in the threatened civil war in China," the *New York Times* observed late in the month. And in a similar story from Washington, James Reston reported that Soviet Russia had told Chungking it regarded the dispute between Nationalists and Communists as an internal matter and would "not interfere in it in any way." This categorical statement, Reston added, had been made by Molotov to Chinese Prime Minister T. V. Soong at the time that the pact had been signed.[16] On August 29 Harriman cabled from Moscow that Stalin had "said he believed an agreement would be reached between Chiang and the Communists since it was in the interest of both sides to do so. 'How stupid it would be,' " Stalin had said, " 'to have two governments in China.' "[17]

Harriman, however, refused to discard his long-standing suspicions of Soviet aspirations in both Europe and Asia. The Sino-Soviet pact, he told Washington in a typically gloomy telegram of September 4, settled nothing of substance. The Soviet Union had not required the agreement for achievement of any immediate objectives now being attained by the Red Army's advance into Korea and Manchuria in fulfillment of the August 8 declaration of war against Japan. Soviet readiness to admit a Chinese civil and military presence in Manchuria at an early date "does indeed reflect mature statesmanship on the part of Stalin and his Moscow advisers." But the initial Russian position as occupying power, together with the greater proximity and far greater scope and discipline of Soviet military strength, would make it easy for the Russians to remain masters of the situation in Northeast Asia even after the Red Army had pulled back within its traditional borders. As for China itself, Harriman continued, Soviet assurances of official noninterference in internal Chinese affairs simply constituted reaffirmation of a state of affairs which had existed since the late 1920s; and if the Kremlin was exerting control over Yenan, "it has probably been through the party apparatus and not through govt channels." Harriman admitted that Soviet assurances to Chiang undoubtedly prejudiced Mao's ability to bargain with the Kuomintang on the basis of implied Russian military support. On the other hand, the Sino-Soviet pact might well work to Mao's advantage in three ways. First, it would dispel considerably the suspicions of Soviet intentions that were then rampant in Kuomintang circles. Citizens and officials alike would be emotionally disarmed, and both the Kremlin and Yenan might well be able to exploit this weakness. Second, the pact had removed any excuse "for a Chung-king-American crusade against Yenan as a spearhead of Soviet penetration of China," thereby shielding Yenan from any possible clash with U.S. military units in their drive to wrest China from the Nationalists. And, third, the pact seemed to "place Soviet Govt policy in China on a disinterested and high moral plane." Meanwhile the Communist party in Russia through its agencies in the Soviet Union and elsewhere could "continue to give quiet but effective support to Yenan's program of 'democratization' and to exert political pressure on Chungking to compromise with Yenan."[18]

Harriman was not the only influential official to express profound concern about postwar Communist designs—both Soviet and Chinese—upon the Kuomintang. Wedemeyer "recognized that there would be grave difficulties involving the Communists" as soon as the war ended, and he felt vindicated by what he later claimed was a "stepped up program of propaganda emanating from Vladivostok, Yenan and Moscow" depicting the Americans as imperialistic conquerors and exploiters of the Far East and Chiang Kai-shek as a willing lackey of Washington and therefore an enemy of the people. Wedemeyer chafed under what he felt was the almost criminal vagueness of U.S. policy, "Hence my efforts to contain the Communists by interpreting my vague and contradictory instructions from Washington in the most elastic fashion possible." Wedemeyer was soon convinced "that the Soviet Government had no more intention of honoring the Sino-Russian Treaty of August 1945, than its pledges and agreements in Europe," and as the first days and weeks of specious peace wore on, he could point to the fact that the Kremlin had not only barred Nationalist forces from Manchuria, but was supporting Chinese Communist forces there and in northern China.[19]

In early October reports began reaching Chungking of active Soviet intervention in Manchuria and even in northern China on behalf of the Yenan Communists and of Yenan's growing bellicosity toward U.S. forces and objectives in northern China. On the sixth Chargé Walter S. Robertson cabled Washington that Soviet staff officers were present at Communist headquarters at Kalgan. The Russians were pledged to leave by November 15, but in the meantime they were serving as advisers to Liu Tien-chi, Yenan's designated political head of the Shansi-Hopei-Chahar region. Liu was characterized as an "indecisive person," and it was said that he had become "a Soviet pawn." Three days later Robertson sent another telegram to the State Department summarizing "significant although lowly evaluated" reports that Soviet military activity was increasing in Manchuria and northern China. "There appears to be little doubt," Robertson added, "that Chinese Communist forces identified up to the present as members of the Eighth Route Army are obtaining from Soviet forces in Manchuria considerable quantities of captured Jap military supplies."[20] Nor did Chinese Communist officials seek to hide an understandable dislike of American personnel whenever they were encountered in northern China. In his message of October 6 Robertson reported that the "indecisive" Liu Tien-chi had been spunky enough on September 16 to refuse several American officers permission to continue their investigatory mission to Peking. Not only had Liu chased the Americans away, he had disarmed them before dismissal. Robertson added a paragraph devoted to the disturbing evidence of extreme Communist "resentment" toward the Americans which derived from the flagrant and growing support which U.S. officials in China were extending to the Kuomintang. Robertson might have added that Wedemeyer's insulting behavior toward Mao during an interview on August 31 justified Communist antipathy.

The interview had taken place at Hurley's residence in Chungking just prior to the opening of talks between Mao and Chiang regarding peace between Yenan and the Kuomintang. Wedemeyer raised the issue of the recent killing of Captain John M. Birch during a clash between American and Communist units at the railroad station of Suchow, and he bluntly accused the Communists of murder. Mao replied that he had no knowledge of the incident, "but if the clash had taken place he hastened to apologize and to assure General Wedemeyer that the Communist Party High Command had taken precautions" to avoid such occurrences in the future. Wedemeyer was unappeased. He "insisted that the Communist High Command had not indicated a desire to prevent such clashes" and called attention to the fact that four OSS officers who had parachuted into a Communist area the previous May had been captured, disarmed, and held as prisoners of war. Moreover, Wedemeyer continued, Mao had never responded to his letters or dispatches regarding the incident. Mao again disclaimed any knowledge of the affair and asserted that the four Americans would be released promptly. A pleased Hurley reported that "Wedemeyer was firm and direct. He insisted that America had not participated in politics in China; that Americans were here as soldiers and as friends of China and that the killing of an American officer by Communists would be deeply resented by Americans both here and in America,'' a prediction whose total versimilitude not even Hurley or Wedemeyer could have then foreseen.[21]

As the armies of Yenan moved across northern and eastern China and into Manchuria, the Soviet Union dropped all pretense of support for the Kuomintang. Russian behavior in Manchuria had already excited the deepest American suspicions. During the last weeks of August the Soviet press had teemed with tales of grateful natives bowing low before their Soviet liberators, and Harriman had reported from Moscow during the first week. in September that ''democratic unions'' had sprung up to assume political control over all Manchurian provinces penetrated by the Red Army. There seemed an ominous parallel with Korea, to say nothing of Poland, and Harriman instinctively feared that these apparently Russian-spawned factions might combine with the northward moving bands of Chinese Communists so that Mao could simply use them to effect an easy takeover of Manchuria once the Red Army had departed.[22]

Meanwhile the Red Army was busily stripping Manchuria of its wealth of Japanese industrial equipment and property. Moscow defended such behavior in terms of the legitimate acquisition of ''war booty'' from a defeated foe—an argument with which Washington was already familiar with regard to Germany. Soviet behavior did not go unchallenged. The U.S. government formally objected on several occasions, claiming that disposition of Japanese assets should be decided by an Inter-Allied Reparations Commission for Japan. But the Kremlin rejected American assertions and continued to express resentment over exclusion from the military occupation of the Japanese home islands.[23]

Washington's very real concern for the future of Manchuria was based upon its equally profound concern for the future of Kuomintang China. It is true that when the Russians proposed to Nationalist China in early 1946 that the two countries exercise joint control over the former Japanese industries in Manchuria, the United States protested that such an agreement would violate the principle of the Open Door agreed to by Stalin at Potsdam and that American business interests should not be excluded from participation in the development of the postwar Manchurian economy. But Washington's overriding concern was to see Manchuria fall into the hands of Chungking. ''In regaining Manchuria,'' the State Department explained years later, ''China would inherit the extensive industrial complex built by the Japanese and a rich agricultural area capable of producing a substantial export surplus. With about one-fourth of the total area and one-ninth the population, Manchuria had come to possess an industry over four times as large as that of China proper and an electric generating capacity nearly three times as large.''[24] Should this tremendous economic prize fall naturally and legitimately to Chiang, further U.S. material and even military assistance to postwar China could be quickly curtailed even as the industrial base for a powerful postwar Chinese state would be assured.

But by mid-October Washington was unhappily aware that this vast prize was likely to remain Communist unless the United States was willing to resume war—this time against Yenan and/or Russia—to obtain it. On September 10 Chinese Foreign Minister T. V. Soong had presented the American government with a request from Chiang Kai-shek that the U.S. Navy transport Kuomintang troops from Canton to Dairen. The request had gone from Acting Secretary of State Acheson to Truman to the Joint Chiefs to Wedemeyer, all of whom acted on the assumption ''that it was our policy to help the Chinese government establish its troops in liberated areas, particularly Manchuria, as rapidly as possible.'' Kuomintang officials had in the meantime been in contact with General Malinovsky, the commander of the Soviet forces which had liberated Manchuria. The Chinese and Russians agreed, in conformity with a promise Stalin had made to Soong at Moscow during negotiations leading to the Sino-Soviet treaty, that Russian troops would begin a gradual withdrawal northward out of Manchuria starting in mid-October. Malinovsky told Kuomintang General Hsiung Shih-hui that by the end of November all elements of the Red Army would be back in the Soviet Union. Operating on this understanding, Kuomintang forces in American ships departed Canton for Dairen during the first days of October. But immediately the Russians objected. Chungking was told that under the Sino-Soviet Treaty Dairen had been defined as a commercial entrepôt, to be used for trade purposes only. Troop landings or garrisons in the city would violate the treaty provisions.[25]

For the next month, while an increasingly concerned Washington wisely refrained from intervention and reports grew in the American press of outright Soviet aid to Chinese Communist forces in northern China and Manchuria, Kuomintang and Soviet officials haggled over the fate of the Kuomintang expeditionary force ''jam-packed'' aboard U.S. Navy transports floating off the Manchurian coast. For the first two weeks the Chinese tried to pry Malinovsky away from his firm refusal to permit the soldiers to land at Dairen. At last the exhausted and disheartened Kuomintang negotiators agreed to a Russian suggestion that the troops be landed at another Manchurian port, perhaps Hulutao or Yingkow. Malinovsky had even offered to provide Soviet trucks to transport the Kuomintang troops from these ports to garrison areas. Chiang caved in and wired the American navy to take his troops to Hulutao and the navy agreed. But when the task force entered Hulutao harbor it discovered the city was controlled by the Chinese Communist Fourth Route Army, whose general told U.S. Admiral Daniel Barbey on October 27 that a Kuomintang landing would be resisted. After some fruitless maneuvering in Chungking, Chiang requested Barbey to take the force to Yingkow. There, during the first week in November, the same scene was enacted: Chinese Communist forces were discovered in control and busily throwing up defensive works; when appealed to by Chungking, Malinovsky innocently argued that this Chinese force had come up from the south through Jehol province and that he could not drive them out without compromising the earlier agreement with Chungking to withdraw from southern Manchuria; Communist guards refused to let anyone from American ships ashore, and the deputy mayor of the town stood on the dock shouting imprecations at the small grey fleet riding silently in the bay and vowed resistance to the death should any attempt be made to press a landing. Barbey, true to longstanding orders that no American units should become involved in any way in Chinese civil strife, refused to force the issue. The only solution was to land at the port of Chinwangtao down the Chinese coast, where the Kuomintang forces could begin a long march through the Shanhaikwan defile into Manchuria. It was a humiliating setback for Chiang and his American allies, yet conditions on the American transports after more than a month of crowded occupancy by Chinese troops left no alternative.[26]

Within a matter of days Malinovsky dealt the Kuomintang another blow. He permitted advancing Chinese Communist forces to surround the headquarters of the political mission which Chiang had sent to the city of Changchun for the purpose of establishing a civil government for Manchuria. After initial cordiality, the Russians had turned a cold eye on this mission, whose members gradually came to believe that the Soviets were actively discouraging the local population from cooperation. When thousands of Chinese Communists suddenly entered Changchun in early November, the Nationalist mission was quickly routed, while the Red Army turned its back and Moscow refused to listen to Chiang's subsequent expostulations.[27]

It was against this increasingly somber background that Washington had to measure the extent and nature of its longstanding commitment to the Chinese Nationalist government. Since the nature of the rapidly crystalliz- ing threat was entirely military and political, Washington had to gauge its response in military and political terms. It had indicated at the end of the war its willingness to aid Chiang militarily in his efforts to reoccupy and pacify all of China as swiftly as possible and in so doing had implicitly challenged Communist aspirations. Once Yenan—and apparently Mos- cow as well—accepted that challenge, American policy makers were faced with the simple, yet frightening problem of redefining the limits of their commitment to the Kuomintang in the face of an ever-expanding civil conflict. Specifically, how much military aid should Chiang be given in terms of arms and supplies for his own forces? To what extent and in what numbers should American troops be used to guarantee Chiang's objective of unilaterally controlling the disarmament and dispatch of Japanese forces from Chinese soil and the consequent occupation and pacification of all China?

Chungking had, of course, been a prime recipient of American military aid throughout the war. In May 1945, when Truman seemed about to cancel nearly all ordered lend lease aid, the United States postponed decisions concerning future military assistance for China. Goods and materiel would continue to flow down the pipeline until the end of the Pacific war, but questions of postwar aid were to be held in abeyance. In a sense this decision rescinded an earlier commitment made by Roosevelt to Chiang at the Cairo Conference in 1943 to equip a ninety- or one-hundred- division Chinese army. But the Americans believed that commitment had been ''loose'' and only pertained to the duration of the war. Chiang, however, had other ideas, and when Japan's surrender terminated the general lend lease program, the Generalissimo immediately brought forth what he conceived to be Roosevelt's one-hundred-divison commitment to China. Through both Hurley and Wedemeyer he importuned Washington not only for weapons to arm a ninety-division postwar army and a substan- tial air force but for the unlimited use of American advisory personnel so that his forces might employ American techniques and tactics as well as equipment. He asked for a permanent American military mission to be headed by Wedemeyer.[28]

Washington felt caught on the horns of an embarrassing dilemma. In purely military terms the War Department was convinced that Chiang would be much better off with a well-equipped and well-fed small army than a large one composed of half-starving conscripts. The White House and State Department were agonizingly mindful of the fact that virtual civil war had broken out across northern and eastern China and that American military aid to Chungking might be diverted to the prosecution of "fratricidal warfare" in support of an "undemocratic administration." These sentiments were forcefully conveyed by President Truman to T. V. Soong on September 14. This gratuitous condemnation of the Kuomintang was clearly meant to spur essential political, social, and economic reforms in Chungking; the Truman administration would retain the long-standing commitment to Nationalist China, but its patience and tolerance of Nationalist excesses and incompetence had passed the breaking point. Moreover, as Acheson had observed in an earlier memorandum, there existed the always thorny problem of obtaining further credit arrangements on short notice from an always parsimonious Congress made even more recalcitrant by the end of the war and the many demands to drastically cut public spending. Truman told Soong, therefore, that the U.S. government had decided to provide equipment and supplies for no more than a thirty-nine-division Chinese army and to support a Chinese navy and air force of commensurate size. For the moment nothing more would be done.[29]

But as the war ended, Chiang found his American allies eager to assist him in the race against Yenan for control of the vast Yellow River valley and the ancient cities on or near the coast. On August 10, the day on which Japan first indicated its willingness to accept surrender, the War Department had sent General Wedemeyer and all other theater commanders in Asia and the Pacific an order detailing interim plans and instructions to be followed to ensure the surrender of all Japanese armed forces. Wedemeyer was informed that additional troops were on their way to his command to be used in assisting and supporting Kuomintang efforts to reoccupy as swiftly as possible all areas of China then held by the Japanese. At the same time Wedemeyer was cautioned firmly that American ground forces were not to become involved "in a major land campaign in any part of the China Theater." They were there simply to expedite the disarmament and repatriation of Japanese forces, and once that task was completed they were to be withdrawn.[30]

Wedemeyer wasted little time carrying out his orders. By the first week of September aircraft of the U.S. Tenth Air Force were rushing Nationalist troops into key cities along or near the coast, including Nanking. Communist press and radio sources in both China and the Soviet Union reacted furiously and commenced "vitriolic" personal attacks upon Wedemeyer as an arch-imperialist flouting the popular will of China.[31] But neither

American nor Kuomintang forces were fully equal to the task of a quick and firm seizure of all northern China. The war had ended too abruptly to permit a careful plotting of reconquest. Instead of the contemplated flow of Nationalist and American forces gradually and inexorably north and eastward, Kuomintang units had to be hastily dropped into key urban points during the first days and weeks of "peace" with the hope that they could then, with the gradually increasing aid of American ground forces, slowly assume control over adjacent rural areas.[32]

Meanwhile, throughout September, as American transport planes were moving three large Kuomintang armies into vital sectors of eastern and northern China, including the crucial Shanghai-Nanking and, later, Peking areas, nearly fifty thousand U.S. Marines were landed along the coast to secure the ports and airfields of Tsingtao, Chinwangtao, and Peking. In the words of one authority, "It was planned to evacuate most of the Japanese through these ports, and deemed essential that they be strongly held, so that the deportation should be orderly." In addition, small marine detachments were sent to protect the railroad between Tangku and Chinwangtao and the coal mines and bridges of Tanshan. By mid-October at the latest it had become quite obvious to any interested observer that American ground and air forces had been instrumental in assuring the Kuomintang of a rapid resumption of control over the large cities and ports of central and eastern China, including the crucial Shanghai-Nanking region. The surrender of nearly all Japanese forces in this region was easily secured, and little Communist or local opposition was encountered south of the Yangtze. It would be found concentrated far to the north, in Honan and beyond the banks of the Yellow River. But for the moment American officials were gratified at the smoothness and rapidity of their operations. On October 4 General George E. Stratemeyer, who was in charge of the China theater during Wedemeyer's journey to Washington, cabled the War Department that all tasks then assigned to his command could be completed by the end of the year and that unless Washington gave new orders to American troops to remain in China for quasi-permanent occupation duties, U.S. forces should be sent home as soon as their duties were ended. At a news conference in Washington on October 22, Wedemeyer supported his subordinate's estimate. Unless new tasks should be imposed, the Chinese theater of operations could be deactivated as early as December 15, provided sufficient shipping was found to transport American army and air force personnel across the Pacific.[33]

But even as Wedemeyer spoke to reporters, his superiors were beginning to entertain grave doubts. The situation in northern China was rapidly getting completely out of hand, and in Manchuria even more ominous developments had occurred. Some reassessment of policies and priorities was obviously needed.

During October and well into November the State, War, and Navy Departments, the White House, and even some congressmen fretted over the China tangle. Several meetings of the State-War-Navy Coordinating Committee were devoted to the problem; position papers were drafted and recommendations tentatively made. State Department officials wrote memoranda filled with concern, and fearful congressmen drafted letters on the topic. In early November President Truman's special counsel, Samuel I. Rosenman, wrote a statement on China in which he defined the primary American objective as "a completion of the surrender, disarmament, and evacuation of the Japanese forces . . . with the assistance of the forces of Chiang Kai-shek." Rosenman bluntly added that the "Central Government of China under Generalissimo Chiang Kai-shek has been fully and helpfully involved in our common war against Japan" and enjoyed the formal recognition not only of the United States but also of Great Britain and the Soviet Union, "while the Chinese forces now in opposition to the Central Government contributed nothing to the war effort." Rosenman admitted that George Allen, a Truman crony soon to be appointed to the Reconstruction Finance Corporation, opposed this conventional argument as did presidential press secretary Matt Connelly. When a brief official statement on American assistance to China in expediting Japanese surrenders was issued some days later, Rosenman's definitions and arguments were conspicuously absent, though the message was suffused with the implication that the United States was routinely aiding a legitimately functioning Kuomintang government. With some exceptions, a rough consensus could be reached about China: Chiang, our traditional ally, was in deep trouble; the American commitment to him should probably continue but needed to be sharply redefined and circumscribed; American forces in China should fulfill their mission of disarmament and repatriation as rapidly as possible and then leave. But could these objectives be realized amidst the growing chaos and violence? Rosenman had bluntly stated: "There is no danger of our troops becoming involved in civil strife in China unless they are attacked by Chinese troops, in which event we may expect the American troops to react with vigor and success." But others, including John Carter Vincent and Congressman Mike Mansfield, were not so sure. Were not our troops a provocative presence? Should we not just get out and let both sides fight it out?[34] Consensus collapsed into confusion and contention whenever specific policy questions could no longer be avoided. Decision making was delayed and deferred. And as the weeks passed, Washington found itself faced with a fresh problem: morale had begun to plummet among the American forces already in China.

Throughout the summer of 1945 in officers' clubs and barracks and bars all over Europe, American soldiers had sung of their frustrations at being far from home after a long war to the tune of *Lili Marlene*:

> Please Mr. Truman, why can't we go home?
> We have conquered Paris, we have conquered Rome,
> We have defeated the Master Race,
> Oh, why is there no shipping space?
> Please Mr. Truman, why can't we go home?

And lest anyone miss the depth of their anguish:

> Oh, Mr. Truman, we have got our points,
> And we're tired of living in all these foreign joints.
> We just don't want the CBI.
> Please give it to some other guy.
> Oh, Mr. Truman, why can't we go home?

By late autumn, a similar restiveness had infected American troops all over Asia, and soon there would be "I wanna go home" riots in Manila and elsewhere. The men in China were no less restless than their brothers languishing in other parts of the Far East, and they too began asking why they should be where they were and what purpose they were serving. As early as mid-October marine train guards were exchanging gunfire with Communist troops along the rail lines from Peking to Tientsin and Mukden; Communist troops also fired upon marine fighter aircraft patrolling out of Tientsin. Those Americans less exposed to combat had more time to dwell upon the meaning of events swirling about them.

A corporal from the Sixth Marine Division at Tsingtao—always a relatively quiet area—wrote Senate Foreign Relations Committee Chairman Tom Connally at the end of November that "There is much speculation concerning our future, and I'm enclosing a few questions I would appreciate your answering. . . ." Why had the marines been sent to China, "and why are we kept here while army troops are being steadily removed?'' ''Are we going to fight Communism in China and if so why don't we pitch in and get it over?'' And could not enough men be found in the States ''to take our place if it is necessary . . . ?'' Another young marine had written on November 5 of the prevalent confusion concerning the role American forces were to play. On their way to Tsingtao, Sergeant S. C. McKay wrote,

> We were told . . . that we were to assist in the disarming of Japanese troops in this area. Before we arrived, the Chinese had the situation well in hand, and have since gone so far as to re-arm some Japanese units for added protection against Chinese Communist forces. Recently we have been told that the reason for our prolonged visit is to hold the area in lieu of the arrival of General Chiang Kai-shek's Nationalist forces. . . . Everything we do here points directly or indirectly toward keeping the Chinese Communists subdued.

McKay added that he was no Communist; he was a democrat who believed in the republican form of government. But was it not true that America's foreign policy was predicated on the self-determination of peoples? ''Who are we (U.S.) to say what form of government the Chinese people have? Why should we influence them in any manner? How do we know what form of government is best for China?'' ''We sit here waving a loaded gun in the face of Chinese Communists and Communism in general,'' McKay continued, while 55 percent of the enlisted men in his squadron had amassed scores of points toward discharge. And ''From what I have observed in Tsingtao, communism might not be such a bad idea for these people.''

McKay was not alone in either the vigor of his complaint or the astuteness of his observation. A persistent theme ran through the scores of letters which Connally received from young Americans in China during November and December: the suspicion that American soldiers ''are intervening in the Chinese Civil War'' in order to protect the interests of a questionable ally. In response, Connally sent out a form letter simply asserting that the marines would be withdrawn ''when they are no longer required for the purpose for which they were sent,'' which was to hold vital urban and port areas in northeast China until ''they can be relieved by Chinese Government forces.''[35]

But when could American policy makers be satisfied that their armed forces had fulfilled the commitment to Nationalist China? When

Wedemeyer had gone back to Chungking at the end of October, he had asked when the American mission might end. He had been told that the answer would be forthcoming shortly. On November 1 he was informed that neither the War Department nor the Joint Chiefs had as yet been able to set a firm date for the deactivation of the China theater. On November 3 he was bluntly asked whether the Chinese Nationalists could maintain control of areas currently guarded by American forces should those forces be withdrawn. On November 9 he was told that the Joint Chiefs considered it "undesirable" to deactivate the China theater until a military advisory group for China could be established.[36] Throughout the following weeks various agencies and individuals in Washington continued to fitfully probe and puzzle over China and America's role there while remaining distracted and harassed by the apparently greater drama of emerging cold war with Russia that centered around the future of Europe and that had been symbolized by the abrupt and frightening collapse of the London Foreign Ministers Conference in early October. Suddenly in the last days of November Patrick Hurley dramatically brought the whole cluster of problems to an embarrassing and well-publicized climax.

There had been signs even before he left China that angry frustration was assuming mastery of Hurley's mind and domination of his temper. There had been the September 11 cable, in which he had prefaced his request to return home with a long jeremiad on the fall of American diplomacy from the grace of democracy and free trade to outright support of European imperialism. There had been another cable sent on the twentieth, even as Hurley was winging his way toward Washington, complaining rather bitterly about the sudden appearance of such old political enemies as George Atcheson and John Service on the newly created Far Eastern Advisory Group under MacArthur. The telegram had been sent by Chiang, but no one then or now could doubt that Hurley's hand lay heavily upon it.[37]

In the little more than eight weeks between his arrival home and his abrupt and dramatic resignation, Hurley's spirit was broken by a succession of blows. First, of course, there was the increasingly bad news out of China, which the ambassador could read in the newspapers or in the messages sent to the State and War Departments—and occasionally to him personally—by the diplomatic and military personnel in Chungking. Second, the appointment of George Atcheson to the Far Eastern Advisory Group and of John Carter Vincent to the State Department's Far Eastern desk seemed to confirm not only to Hurley, but to his allies—both Chinese and American—in Chungking that Washington was on the verge of selling out the Kuomintang. Third, discussions with Truman and other high officials certainly did nothing to dispel Hurley's mounting depression. In an extended discussion at the White House in early October the President made it quite clear to both the ambassador and Wedemeyer "that it would be our policy to support Chiang Kai-shek but that we would not be driven into fighting Chiang's battles for him." Yet as the weeks went by it seemed that American military intervention might be the only way of fulfilling the existing commitment in China.

Hurley was shaken and wearied enough during his October 13 talks with Truman to ask for relief from duty. The President would not hear of it and told his ambassador to go back to New Mexico and "take the cure" that sunshine and relaxation could afford. He flattered Hurley with expressions of confidence, and the ambassador wavered sufficiently for Byrnes to announce after the interview that Hurley would indeed be returning to Chungking. But news of the ever-worsening situation in China plagued Hurley, seeming to darken the bright New Mexico sun under which he rested. He also found himself criticized in the American press for being too uncritical a supporter of the Nationalist cause. His erratic temper again swung toward disillusion and angry dismay. But the decisive factor that sent him careening down the road toward what his most recent biographer rightly labels the "Politics of Frustration and Revenge" seems to have been the final collapse of negotiations between the Communists and the Kuomintang during the third week of November. A "Political Consultative Conference," representing all Chinese political parties and designed to consider and make recommendations on a draft national constitution, had been agreed to by Mao and Chiang during the promising days of early October; but deadlock, rancor, and combat had eroded hope to the vanishing point. November 20, the day the conference was to have convened, came and went without Communist and Kuomintang negotiators having been able to clarify the final point concerning the ultimate political disposition of those areas overrun and occupied by the Communists. At last on November 25 Chou En-lai, Yenan's chief political negotiator at Chungking, withdrew from negotiations and flew back to northern China. The next day his first deputy followed him, and Hurley walked into Byrnes's office ten thousand miles away in Washington and handed the Secretary of State a letter of resignation.[38]

Byrnes refused to accept either the letter or Hurley's charge that it was his spiteful former enemies among the young foreign service crowd at

Chungking—Atcheson or Ludden or Davies or Service or someone—who had gotten the American press, including the *Daily Worker*, to charge him with being too close to Chiang and too unsympathetic toward Yenan. Byrnes said further that he would not pass the letter on to Truman. Writing years later, Dean Acheson stated that Byrnes dealt with Hurley "tactfully and soothingly as only he could do," and it seemed by the next day that all was well; Hurley saw Truman early that morning at the Oval Office, went over the most recent telegrams with his President, and agreed that it would be best if he returned to Chungking without delay. Two hours later, in the midst of a cabinet luncheon, Truman was called to the phone and told by a White House correspondent that Hurley was at the National Press Club talking to newsmen, attacking "the administration, the State Department, our foreign policy, and me personally." Hurley had, in fact, changed his mind once again and had released his undelivered letter of resignation to Truman to the press just as the President was sitting down to his luncheon. What had caused Hurley to change his mind yet again? Apparently it was a speech by Congressman Hugh DeLacy of Washington, which Hurley read upon returning to his office following the interview with Truman. DeLacy had reiterated the tiresome charges that Hurley was guilty of " 'full scale' support of the 'reactionary' regime of Chiang Kai-shek" and that American aid was being used by the Kuomintang to stifle the legitimate aspirations of the Chinese people. DeLacy also charged Hurley with a deliberate and brutal " 'purge' " of the able China hands, including Atcheson, Service, and Davies. To Hurley this was the last straw. Within the hour he had contacted the press and read the letter of resignation.[39]

It was not so much what Hurley did, but rather what he said in justification for what he did, that was to have such a baleful effect upon so much of American foreign policy in following years. For as he left the American foreign service, Hurley planted the seeds of a bitter fruit.

So dramatic was the ambassador's exit, and so sensational were the charges he made in justification for quitting his post, that he was given two opportunities to expound his grievances and substantiate his charges. The first opportunity lay, of course, in the very letter of resignation which he had unsuccessfully sought to deliver to Byrnes and Truman before eventually turning to the press. What comes through this longish, often rambling essay, filled with unsubstantiated charges of personal and institutional sabotage by a malevolent State Department and its young officers, is an embittered confession of failure on the part of an old-line, dedicated, middle-American isolationist. The world that emerges from the distraught sentences and paragraphs of Hurley's letter is a Manichean world of good and evil, black and white, divided sharply and clearly between democracy and free trade on the one hand and "colonial imperialism and communist imperialism" on the other. The Chinese Communists, with whom Atcheson, Service, Ludden, Davies, and the rest had all chosen to ally, were but the agents and instruments of an imperialism no less malevolent and sleepless than that of the prewar European colonial powers; and both groups of imperialists, colonial and Communist, were endeavoring in every manner possible to "keep China divided against herself." The only alternative to their designs, the only bulwark against their early success, was America's old and trusted ally, Chiang Kai-shek. In his own efforts to support and sustain this quasi-democratic champion of China, Hurley wrote, he had excused the young foreign service officers working against both him and the better world outlined by Roosevelt in the Atlantic Charter. But what had happened? "These professional diplomats were returned to Washington and placed in the Chinese and Far Eastern Division of the State Department as my supervisors. Some of these same career men whom I relieved have been assigned as advisors to the Supreme Commander in Asia. In such positions most of them have continued to side with the Communist armed party and at times with the imperialist bloc against American policy." As a result of this conspiracy—and although Hurley never was bold enough to use the term, the idea suffused his entire letter—America's international policy was hopelessly "confused," the desires of the good and decent men at the top of government being constantly frustrated by the machinations of dangerous and irresponsible subordinates. Disaster was now imminent, for "make no mistake, Mr. President, America has been excluded economically from every part of the world controlled by colonial imperialism and Communist imperialism. America's economic strengh has been used all over the world to defeat American policies and interests. This is chargeable to weak American Foreign Service."[40]

Here was an interpretation of current history that was as untrue and dangerously simplistic as it was forceful and attractive. For if Hurley's charges were to be believed, then that minimal public trust without which no government can long endure would be gravely compromised.

And some did choose to believe and to accept what Hurley had to say. Whether their defense of the ambassador stemmed from conviction or expediency was of little consequence. As Arthur Krock quickly observed, the pot would be kept boiling, the blast would become a roar. Hurley's earliest champion was Senator Kenneth S. Wherry, a former mortician and used-car salesman from the Nebraska heartland, whose most famous remark to date had been the pledge to "lift Shanghai up, up, ever upward until it's just like Kansas City." Even as Truman and Byrnes were discussing a new assignment for George C. Marshall at the White House on November 29, Wherry took the Senate floor to demand an investigation of the charges against the young foreign service officers whose reported conduct Wherry characterized as skirting the edge of treason. Wherry knew that he enjoyed some backing in the House. Representative Carl T. Curtis, also of Nebraska, and Robert F. Jones of Ohio, both Republicans, demanded, according to one authoritative source, "that the State Department 'discharge all Communists from the payroll,' that the entire field of U.S. foreign policy be investigated and that General Hurley be invited to address a joint session of Congress in recess." The suggestion that Hurley come to the Hill and explain himself proved to be the only point on which his defenders and detractors could agree. A furious Tom Connally had followed Wherry on the Senate floor in demanding that Hurley appear. " 'I'd like to have General Hurley come up here and look us in the eye and tell us what some of the terrible things are,' " the Texas Democrat had shouted, and his sentiments were echoed more quietly in the House by Republican Edith Nourse Rogers of Massachusetts. Hurley himself had titilated congressional sensibilities by his long-scheduled appearance before the National Press Club the previous day in which he was reported to have said "that he hoped those who took issue with his resignation blast would not push him too far 'because I know the names, the numbers and the places where we have supported ideologies that are in conflict with those we asked our men to fight for and to die.' "[41]

And then there was the *Amerasia* case. *Amerasia* was a monthly magazine edited by Philip Jacob Jaffe, apparently a close friend of American Communist leader Earl Browder. By the spring of 1945 the FBI had become convinced that Jaffe had masterminded the thievery of over six hundred highly classified government documents, chiefly from the files of the State Department and the Office of Naval Intelligence. The FBI began a nine-week investigation of the magazine and placed its personnel and offices under surveillance. It was during this period that John Stewart Service, who had returned to Washington in April after being relieved by Hurley, came in contact with Jaffe. According to a hostile study released in 1970 by the Senate Judiciary Committee, Service was warned by Harold Isaacs, a "former Communist," to stay away from Jaffe, who was characterized as " 'bad medicine.' " But Service ignored the caution and turned over to Jaffe some of his own private journals and reports on his recent meetings with Mao Tse-tung in Yenan. Service also told Jaffe of plans ostensibly being drawn up in Wedemeyer's headquarters to utilize the Chinese Communists in any possible U.S. invasion of Japanese-held areas in China. The planning for this effort had not crystallized, and so Service was able to give Jaffe little information of real value. Shortly after the Jaffe-Service interview, on June 6, the FBI moved in and arrested six suspects, including Jaffe, Emmanuel Larsen of the Far Eastern Section of the State Department, and Lieutenant Andrew Roth of the Office of Naval Intelligence and charged them with espionage. Service, whose journals and diaries were still in the *Amerasia* office, along with a record of his conversations with Jaffe, was also among the six arrested and charged.

Two days later Acting Secretary of State Joseph C. Grew publicly announced that " 'a comprehensive security program' would be pursued 'unrelentingly' in the Department of State in order 'to stop completely the illegal and disloyal conveyance of confidential and other secret information to unauthorized persons.' " The rest, insofar as Service was concerned, was anticlimactic. On August 10 a grand jury indicted Jaffe, Larsen, and Roth on espionage charges, but granted Service a " 'sweeping exoneration.' " In light of known facts, even as presented by a hostile congressional committee years later, the grand jury's action was eminently just. One could argue on the basis of available evidence that Larsen and Roth had been deliberately leaking highly classified information over a long period of time to an active Communist agent for deliberately subversive reasons and purposes; Service, however, a political babe-in-the-woods, had merely tried to get a scarcely known source sympathetic to his perspective to openly publish some of his ideas and observations. But the end of the case seemed highly suspicious to many politically excitable Americans: on September 29 the government for all practical purposes dropped the case against Jaffe without even introducing as evidence the six hundred or more documents he had pilfered. Jaffe was allowed to pay a stiff fine and go free without a full-fledged trial. In early November Larsen was also let off with the payment of only a nominal fine. Suspicious politicians and citizens then and later would ask why, in the words of Michigan Senator Homer Ferguson, the government had been so "timid" in pursuing the *Amerasia* affair. Had there been a deliberate cover-up by Communist sympathizers or agents who had wormed their way into even higher levels of government than those occupied by Larsen, Roth, and

Service? Naive and innocent as he undoubtedly was, Service did unwittingly help precipitate his own eventual persecution and the emergence of an emotional, uncritical, and highly dangerous "witch-hunt" and "red baiting" environment in early postwar America. And, of course, his behavior lent greater credence than otherwise would have been the case to Hurley's reckless and irresponsible charges of November and December 1945.[42]

Hurley appeared before Connally's Senate Foreign Relations Committee on Wednesday morning, December 5, 1945, and spent all of that day and the following morning in testimony. He was at once truculent and evasive in his efforts to stipulate more precisely the charges against State Department officials. He stuck to his contention that these men had not only sabotaged his mission to China, but were in fact deliberately jeopardizing American foreign policy all around the world. But when the senators asked point-blank for specifics, he came up with little of substance: under direct questioning he admitted that the top-ranking State Department officials had resolved his conflict with George Atcheson in his favor at all points; that the Atcheson telegram of February 28 had not led Washington to seek a major change in China policy; that in fact Atcheson and his young allies may very well have been speaking in the context of a more vigorous and effective prosecution of the war against Japan rather than the downfall of the Kuomintang when they urged more direct aid for Yenan; and that there seemed no evidence at that time (the first week of December 1945) of direct and active Soviet aid to the Chinese Communists—an assessment which, in fact, was quite untrue. Hurley did try to drag in Service and *Amerasia*, but a majority of the senators became so quickly irritated, frustrated, and finally angered by his voluble evasiveness and his frequent allusions to personal fatigue when pressed on controversial points that they chose not to pursue the matter.

Byrnes and Dean Acheson were magnificent in rebuttal. "What it all amounts to," the Secretary of State told the Senate committee during a long and devastating counter-testimony on December 7, "is that within proper channels they [Atcheson, Ludden, Service, Davies, and the others] expressed to those under whom they served certain views which differed to a greater or less degree from the policies of the Government as then defined."

Of course, it is the duty of every officer of the United States to abide by and to administer the declared policy of his Government. But

conditions change, and often change quickly in the affairs of governments. Whenever an official honestly believes that changed conditions require it, he should not hesitate to express his views to his
superior officers.

I should be profoundly unhappy to learn that an officer of the
Department of State, within or without the Foreign Service, might
feel bound to refrain from submitting through proper channels an
honest report or recommendation for fear of offending me or anyone
else in the Department. If that day should arrive, I will have lost the
very essence of the assistance and guidance I require for the successful discharge of the heavy responsibilities of my office.[43]

Hurley's own performance and the testimony of his superiors in the State
Department should have ended the incident then and there. But it did not.
The credulous, the naive, the ambitious, and the seekers after expediency
are always drawn to sensation, and Hurley's case proved no exception.
Connally's mail, it is true, ran about five-to-one in favor of the quick
decision of the Foreign Relations Committee to study Hurley's charges in
executive session, thereby practically dismissing the ambassador's argument, and Connally himself wrote one supporter on December 17 that ''the
Hurley fiasco conferred no credit upon him. His charges were so wholly
exploded that it was unnecessary to pursue the inquiry further.'' Very
probably most of the senators, and much of the country, were also impressed by the testimony at the very close of the hearings of a vigorous and
tough-minded young foreign correspondent, speaking for himself and
several colleagues who together comprised a veritable Who's Who of the
very ablest young American reporters on wartime China. ''I know of no
attempt whatsoever to sabotage General Hurley's policies in China by any
career officer of the State Department,'' Theodore H. White bluntly told
the committee on December 10, and he then produced telegrams and letters
from Jack Belden, Annalee Jacoby, Richard Watts, and Eric Sevareid,
fully supporting his contention. ''I have,'' White concluded, ''an aversion
for seeing my friends falsely slandered,'' and he added once again that he
spoke not just for himself, but for Belden, Watts, Jacoby, and Sevareid as
well.[44]

Others were not willing to dismiss either Hurley or his charges so
rapidly. Radio commentator Raymond Gram Swing, surely no naive
rabble-rouser, noted in his broadcast of December 11 that Hurley at least
had enjoyed the comfort of airing his grievances, ''and the State Depart-

ment has two elements of discomfiture.'' One was that in the wake of such sensational condemnation of government personnel the Senate committee decision to hold no more public hearings ''does not quite clear the air.'' The State Department ''has been unjustly injured,'' Swing continued, and could really do little more about it. The second element was quite simply that Hurley had probably damaged American relations with both Britain and Russia, to say nothing of China itself. And as he pursued his theme, Swing discovered yet a third element of danger. ''The outstanding mystery of the Hurley case is why Secretary Byrnes, until the very end, tried to persuade the General to return to his post in China.'' Byrnes had done a splendid, forthright job in defending his department; ''but this mystery neither he nor anyone else has explained.''[45] This unease over Hurley's rapid dismissal would fester and grow in less sophisticated and more suggestive minds during the coming years of frustration until it hardened into the conviction of a deliberately contrived cover-up, a whitewash of very legitimate and serious charges.

But even at the time there were those who argued that Hurley had made his point, and one such individual was crusty and conservative Styles Bridges, the New Hampshire Republican member of Connally's Foreign Relations Committee. Bridges grilled Byrnes at some length during the Secretary's testimony and caught him in what would soon prove to be some embarrassing elisions and cover-ups. Had there been any deal made at Yalta involving China, Bridges asked. Byrnes, who, of course, had been taken by Roosevelt to the Crimea and who knew perfectly well of the existence of the Far Eastern Accords and their impact and influence upon postwar China, was evasive; he would have to look up the official communiqué and see what had been said. Bridges pressed on: it was very important to know whether there was an agreement made at Yalta between the Big Three regarding China—an agreement obviously made in China's absence. Pinned to the wall, Byrnes chose to keep the existence of the accords a secret, as Roosevelt had always wished. Not for another two months—on the first anniversary of the Yalta Conference and amidst rapidly deteriorating relations with the Soviets—would the Secretary of State come clean. Now he simply told Bridges that he did not remember all the agreements that had been entered into at the Crimea. ''It is entirely possible that some of the agreements arrived at at Yalta affected China in some way or other, and I have told you that I would gladly furnish you the communiqué and then you can determine whether or not they affect China.'' The Secretary, too clever by half, would go no further than this.

He invited that suspicion of sinister behavior by high national officials which would all too soon infect public debate throughout the country.

But Bridges was not finished. He quickly turned to the question of loyalty in the State Department. Had Byrnes yet fired anyone for disloyalty? Had he instigated loyalty investigations within the State Department? Connally suddenly interjected himself: would not Byrnes immediately fire anyone found to be disloyal? To this drumfire of questions, Byrnes gave the appropriate answers. Bridges moved ponderously to Service and *Amerasia*; why had Service been reinstated? Because, Byrnes replied, he ''was told the prosecutor had submitted everything else he had against him [Service] to the grand jury and in the opinion of the Assistant Attorney General there was no reason why that man should not be reinstated in the service.'' Bridges immediately raised the specter of a ''secret telephone call from a very high-up in this Nation to a Department of Justice official telling him to lay off Service.'' Byrnes vigorously denied the allegation, and Bridges, admitting he had no firm evidence of who such ''a very high-up'' might be, retreated. But he continued to hammer at Byrnes over the Service affair; had there been a proper and sufficient investigation? And, finally, Bridges asked about the establishment of a system of loyalty checks; did the Department have such a system, and when told it did and that every prospective employee was properly screened by the personnel office, Bridges asked about the loyalty of the investigators themselves; were they absolutely free from the taint of insubordination or disloyalty? Thus did the issue of America's China policy effortlessly generate an obsession with political ''loyalty'' and a passion for national ''security.''[46]

For Bridges was not alone in his concern that national policy objectives in the Far East had been subtly but unmistakably sabotaged by diplomats whose loyalty lay not with their government and country, but with the tide of ''international communism.'' According to his biographer, Hurley was ''inundated'' with letters as soon as he resigned commending him for his behavior. ''Moderate critics of New Deal domestic and foreign policy vented their pent-up frustrations. . . . Right-wing groups saw in his action proof of their paranoic suspicions, thought of him as an obvious spokesman for their views, and sought to win him to their side.'' Russell D. Buhite adds that these ''right-wing'' elements ''misinterpreted'' Hurley's remarks and obviously did not understand the situation in China. The latter observation is surely incontestable, but one can legitimately take issue with the former. It is true that during his testimony the former ambassador had admitted that Kuomintang China was not purely democratic and probably could not become so for some time. But the tenor and thrust of his remarks about the vacuity of America's China policy and the behavior of young State Department officials were certainly clear enough to invite the kind of excited and irrational interpretation placed upon them by those whom Dean Acheson years later would scathingly refer to as political "primitives."[47] And Hurley himself, angry and baffled by failure and defeat, his bridges to the Washington political establishment now forever burned by intemperate behavior, embraced his new allies and their paranoid view of the world. In coming years, as the cold war with Russian and later Chinese Communism became ever more pronounced and bitter, Hurley and his fellow "primitives" would come to preach an increasingly hysterical brand of "anti-Communism" which all too often equated dispassionate political analysis with internal subversion and irresistible political change in Asia with national defeat.

The roots of virulent anti-Communism in America were thus firmly laid by Patrick Hurley and his supporters during the first uncertain months of the postwar era. And the initial source and focus of this dangerous public mood was China and the American foreign service, not the Soviet Union. Hurley managed, wittingly or not, to give form and substance to the developing yet often uncertain fears of millions that "an international Communist conspiracy"—capable, it was believed, of illimitable guile and of the assumption of many forms—posed as great a threat to the United States as had Hitlerian fascism. To countless citizens who had never become emotionally or ideologically reconciled to the wartime alliance with Stalin and the Soviet Union, Hurley's simplistic view of a world divided between democracy and predatory Communism, in which the Communists could count on the active aid of dupes or traitors within the democratic camp, seemed as comforting as it was cogent. Paranoia seemed confirmed by events, or at least one's interpretation of events. Hurley and his sour or fearful colleagues all too soon obtained enthusiastic support among a public steeped in all the delusions and simple idealisms of an isolationist past.

The true meaning of the great revolt of Asia against the old order—not just in China, but in Indochina and Indonesia, and even in Korea—thus became tragically obscured and distorted in the American mind. For Hurley and his allies depicted the great revolt as something utterly alien to American traditions and interests. Any success which the revolt might obtain would have to be equated with the defeat of American global objectives and triumph of a treasonous American foreign service, many of whose members, it was argued, must be in active collusion with the nation's enemies. And as the cold war between Russia and the West inexorably grew throughout the late forties to become the prime fact of international life, it became convenient and then inevitable to assume that the revolutionaries of Asia—many of whom admittedly professed and indeed were deeply tinged by their own peculiar brands of Marxism—were merely the willing agents and pawns of an international Communist conspiracy emanating from and directed by the Kremlin. During the hysterical days of the Korean War, when McCarthyism rode high, and for long years thereafter, it seemed impossible for Americans to appreciate the fact that in politics and diplomacy alliances are at best tense and delicate balances of mutual exploitation masking mutual grievances and that their fragile fabric can be exploded at any moment by nearly any issue, great or small. Long ago an English statesman observed that Britain had no eternal friends nor eternal enemies, only eternal interests. This was equally true of the Asian revolutionaries of the mid- and late-twentieth century. But Americans of the late forties, caught in the grip of an anti-Communist hysteria generated as much by the decline and "fall" of China as by the behavior of the Kremlin in Iran and Eastern Europe and Berlin, refused to walk the hard road of dispassionate inquiry and evaluation. And so they alienated themselves from, and indeed finally came to oppose by force, Asia's great revolt. The result, as is all too well known, was unmitigated tragedy for all.

It was not clear, of course, that at the end of November 1945 the United States stood on the brink of tragedy in Asia. The situation in China was very bad, to be sure, but there still seemed time to salvage our interests from the spreading wreckage of civil war, to impose if not our will at least our wishes on the contending forces. What was needed was a good man. Harry Truman knew that he could count on the services of a great one—George Catlett Marshall. And so the call went out from the White House to the quiet countryside of Virginia where Marshall was preparing, he thought, to begin a richly-earned retirement after a lifetime of superbly effective service to his country. The soldier responded to the demands of duty and returned to the capital to prepare himself for possibly the most important assignment he had ever accepted.

NOTES

1. *New York Times*, 13 August 1945, p. 1; Tang Tsou, *America's Failure in China, 1941-1950* (Chicago: University of Chicago Press, 1963), p. 303; Lionel Max Chassin, *The Communist Conquest of China: A History of the Civil War, 1945-1949*, trans. from the French by Timothy Osato and Louis Gelas (Cambridge, Mass.: Harvard University Press, 1965), p. 57.

2. Quoted in *New York Times*, 15 August 1945, p. 6; see also Chassin, *Communist Conquest of China*, p. 57, which translates Chu Teh's remarks somewhat less vociferously.

3. U.S. Department of State, *Foreign Relations of the United States, 1945: Diplomatic Papers*, 9 vols. (Washington, D.C.: U.S. Government Printing Office, 1967-1969), 8:535 (hereinafter cited as *FR, 1945: Diplomatic Papers*).

4. Quoted in *New York Times*, 15 August 1945, p. 6.

5. Tang Tsou stresses this point with satisfaction. *America's Failure in China*, pp. 305-308.

6. *New York Times*, 20 August 1945, p. 1. The Swiss consul general at Shanghai reported in late August that Communist "elements" were already "seeping into" the city. *FR, 1945: Diplomatic Papers*, 7:537. See also Hurley's cable to Washington of 20 August, ibid., pp. 534-535.

7. Ibid., pp. 453-454, 534-535. See also *New York Times*, 28 August 1945, p. 1; 30 August 1945, p. 4; and Herbert Feis, *The China Tangle: The American Effort in China from Pearl Harbor to the Marshall Mission* (New York: Atheneum Press, 1965), pp. 360-361.

8. Russell D. Buhite, *Patrick J. Hurley and American Foreign Policy* (Ithaca, N.Y.: Cornell University Press, 1973), p. 234; Tang Tsou, *America's Failure in China*, pp. 317-320.

9. Buhite, *Hurley*, p. 234.

10. *FR, 1945: Diplomatic Papers*, 7:555-557; Buhite, *Hurley*, pp. 239-252.

11. U.S. Department of State, *United States Relations with China with Special Reference to the Period 1944-1949*, reprinted and cited hereafter as *China White Paper*, 2 vols. (Stanford, Calif.: Stanford University Press, 1967), 1:106-107; Feis, *China Tangle*, p. 362.

12. *China White Paper*, 1:108-109, 135; *FR, 1945: Diplomatic Papers*, 7:472-476, 482; Chassin, *Communist Conquest of China*, pp. 54-55; Feis, *China Tangle*, p. 407n.

13. *FR, 1945: Diplomatic Papers*, 7:567-568, 572-573, 575-577, 601-602; Chassin, *Communist Conquest of China*, p. 53; Tang Tsou, *America's Failure in China*, pp. 301, 311. Tang Tsou emphasizes that in the early postwar weeks Mao could not have been at all certain of Soviet aid in light of Stalin's treaty with Chiang. Ibid., pp. 304, 320, 325-326. See also Feis, *China Tangle*, pp. 362-363.

14. Memorandum by the Chief of the Division of Chinese Affairs (Drumright), 16 November 1945, *FR, 1945: Diplomatic Papers*, 7:629.

15. See, for example, Vincent's memorandum to Secretary of State Byrnes, 12 November 1945, in ibid., pp. 614-617.

16. Quoted in *New York Times*, 27 August 1945, p. 1.

17. *FR, 1945: Diplomatic Papers*, 7:454.

18. Ibid., pp. 982-984.

19. Albert C. Wedemeyer, *Wedemeyer Reports!* (New York: Henry Holt & Company, 1958), pp. 344, 348.

20. *FR, 1945: Diplomatic Papers*, 7:576, 578.

21. The Mao-Wedemeyer interview and Hurley's comments thereon are printed in ibid., pp. 542-543.

22. Feis, *China Tangle*, pp. 380-381.

23. *China White Paper*, 1:123; Lisle A. Rose, *After Yalta: America and the Origins of the Cold War* (New York: Charles Scribner's Sons, 1973), p. 149; Freda Utley, *The China Story* (Chicago: Henry Regnery Company, 1951), p. 7.

24. *China White Paper*, 1:123-124, 128; see also Chassin, *Communist Conquest of China*, pp. 61-62.

25. Tang Tsou, *America's Failure in China*, p. 328; Feis, *China Tangle*, pp. 383-384; *FR, 1945: Diplomatic Papers*, 7:565.

26. Tang Tsou, *America's Failure in China*, pp. 329-330; Chassin, *Communist Conquest of China*, pp. 63-65. Chassin's contention that the Russians "carefully kept out of the conflict" is simply false. Feis, *China Tangle*, pp. 384-386; Utley, *China Story*, p. 7; *FR, 1945: Diplomatic Papers*, 7:577, 602-603; and *New York Times*, 29 October 1945, p. 1; 30 October 1945, p. 1.

27. Feis, *China Tangle*, pp. 387-388. Tang Tsou claims that the Kuomintang mission was actually "surrounded and disarmed," not by the Chinese Communist forces, but by units of the Red Army. *America's Failure in China*, p. 330.

28. Feis, *China Tangle*, pp. 368-370; *FR, 1945: Diplomatic Papers*, 7:545-554.

29. Feis, *China Tangle*, pp. 371-372; *FR, 1945: Diplomatic Papers*, 7:547-548, 559-562.

30. Feis, *China Tangle*, pp. 337-338; *FR, 1945: Diplomatic Papers*, 7:527-528.

31. *New York Times*, 6 September 1945, p. 3; Wedemeyer, *Wedemeyer Reports!*, p. 345.

32. Feis, *China Tangle*, pp. 335-339; Chassin, *Communist Conquest of China*, p. 60.

33. Chassin, *Communist Conquest of China*, p. 59; Feis, *China Tangle*, pp. 362-363, 373; *FR, 1945: Diplomatic Papers*, 7:566-567, 579, 599; Wedemeyer, *Wedemeyer Reports!*, p. 348; *History of U.S. Marine Corps Operations in World War II*, 5 vols. (Washington, D.C.: Historical Branch, G-3 Division, Headquar-

ters, U.S. Marine Corps, 1968), vol. 5: *Victory and Occupation*, by Bemis M. Frank and Henry I. Shaw, Jr., pp. 543-565.

34. Feis, *China Tangle*, pp. 387-389; *FR, 1945: Diplomatic Papers*, 7:566-617 passim; Samuel I. Rosenman, "Preliminary Draft Statement," 9 November 1945, Samuel I. Rosenman Papers, 1945, Box 1, Harry S. Truman Library, Independence, Mo.; U.S. Department of State *Bulletin* 13 (18 November 1945):812.

35. The many letters to Connally during November and December and Connally's reply to them all may be found in the China folder in the Tom Connally Papers, Box 103, Library of Congress, Washington, D.C. The dullness of comparatively quiet garrison duty at Tsingtao is recounted in Frank and Shaw, *Victory and Occupation*, p. 536; accounts of armed clashes between marine and Communist elements from October on are in ibid., pp. 566-567.

36. Feis, *China Tangle*, pp. 367, 388; *FR, 1945: Diplomatic Papers*, 7:611.

37. *FR, 1945: Diplomatic Papers*, 7:565-566. Within a week of his arrival in the States, Hurley told Forrestal over lunch that "a good many of the professional staff of the State Department . . . had not been merely of no help but a definite hindrance to him. He said that many of the American correspondents . . . were communistically inclined, as well as many people in the State Department." Walter Millis, ed., *The Forrestal Diaries* (New York: Viking Press, 1951), pp. 98-99.

38. Buhite, *Hurley*, pp. 253-266; Tang Tsou, *America's Failure in China*, p. 341; Harry S. Truman, *Memoirs*, 2 vols. (New York: Signet Books, 1965), vol. 2: *Years of Trial and Hope, 1946-1952*, pp. 81-86.

39. Congressman De Lacy's speech is partially quoted in Buhite, *Hurley*, pp. 266-268. See also Truman, *Years of Trial and Hope*, p. 85; Dean Acheson, *Present at the Creation: My Years in the State Department* (New York: W. W. Norton & Co., 1969), pp. 133-135; Millis ed., *Forrestal Diaries*, p. 113. Byrnes's contemporary account is in U.S. Congress, Senate, *United States-China Relations: Hearing before the Committee on Foreign Relations*, 92d Cong., 1st Sess. (Washington, D.C.: U.S. Government Printing Office, 1971), pp. 153-155 (hereinafter cited as *United States-China Relations*).

40. The Hurley letter was initially published in the *New York Times*, 28 November 1945, p. 3, and later in *China White Paper*, 2:581-584.

41. Wherry's pledge to the citizens of Shanghai is quoted in Eric F. Goldman, *The Crucial Decade—And After: America, 1945-1960* (New York: Vintage Books, 1960), p. 116. The comments of Curtis, Jones, Connally, and Hurley are quoted in *New York Times*, 29 November 1945, p. 1. These remarks do not appear in the "Excerpts from an Address by Patrick Hurley before the National Press Club at Washington, Nov. 28, 1945," which was inserted into the record of the Hurley hearings before Congress the following week at Hurley's own insistence. *United States-China Relations*, pp. 69-71.

42. Buhite, *Hurley*, p. 283. Quotations regarding the *Amerasia* case are taken from U.S. Congress, Senate, Committee on the Judiciary, *The Amerasia Papers: A Clue to the Catastrophe of China*, 91st Cong., 2d Sess. 2 vols. (Washington, D.C.: U.S. Government Printing Office, 1970), 1:36-62 passim.

43. The Hurley, Byrnes, and Acheson testimonies are reprinted in *United States-China Relations*, pp. 59-208 passim. Byrnes had first challenged Hurley's charges and assumptions during a press conference on 28 November, the transcript of which may be found in U.S. Department of State *Bulletin* 13 (2 December 1945):882-883.

44. *United States-China Relations*, pp. 200-208; Tom Connally to Lewis M. Herrman, Editor, *New Jersey Labor Herald*, 17 December 1945, Connally Papers, Box 103.

45. Transcript copy of Raymond Swing radio broadcast over WMAL (ABC), Tuesday, 11 December 1945, in Rosenman Papers, 1945, Box 1.

46. *United States-China Relations*, pp. 165-174.

47. Buhite, *Hurley*, pp. 282-283; Acheson, *Present at the Creation*, pp. 354-361.

chapter 6

China: Failure
of a Mission

George Catlett Marshall was little more than a month away from his sixty-fifth birthday when entrusted with possibly the most important, certainly the most frustrating mission of his career. Possessed of a strong soldierly body capped by an austere, yet not unkindly face, Marshall was, in the words of his most recent and best biographer, "conservative in habits and thoughts. Born in an era which spoke often of responsibility, duty, character, integrity, he was marked by those so-called 'Victorian' virtues. A natural reserve, simplicity of living, aloofness of manner were strengthened by the austerity of Army life." Yet such a portrait does not quite define the man. He could be selfless and was steeped in the American military tradition of personal rectitude. But on more than one occasion during his career he abandoned caution when he believed he was right and became outspoken to the point of committing professional suicide if not outright insubordination. His behavior earned him the enmity of Douglas MacArthur during the late thirties, and he worked his way back from limbo and into the highest position in the U.S. Army by some astute and persistent, if low-key politicking. If this quasi-Victorian gentleman-soldier could not be expected to be temperamentally in tune with the great revolt, he might well prove to be politically cognizant of its scope and force.[1]

Marshall was in Washington by November 30, three days after announcement of his appointment. He immediately plunged into a round of hastily called meetings at the White House and State Department, interspersed with long hours in congressional hearings. Shortly after his arrival in China he complained to a friend at home that he had left Washington "with a minimum of preparation" because of the crushing burden of business.[2] The record confounds the complaint. Unfolding events in China and Hurley's explosive departure had defined Washington's dilemma with a brutal clarity that Marshall could not miss. The overriding question was simple. How far did the American commitment to Chiang Kai-shek extend? The chief task remained the political and military unification of China under the Kuomintang. A formula would have to be devised by which Chiang would agree to abandon "one party government" and enter into dominant coalition with Yenan.[3] But what if one side or the other refused to cooperate, refused to accede to American designs?

These questions were at last confronted at a White House conference between Truman, Marshall, Byrnes, and Admiral Leahy on the afternoon of December 11, just days before the general's departure for the new Kuomintang capital at Nanking. According to Marshall's own account of the meeting, Truman began by stating "that he wished to have a clear and complete understanding among us as to just what was the basis on which I was to operate in China in representing him." Byrnes replied that the primary task of American military and naval forces currently in the country was to transport units of the Kuomintang army north to Manchuria for the purpose of disarming and repatriating the remaining Japanese. Byrnes added that there were also plans to move some of Chiang's men into northern China for the same reason, but that "this was to be maintained in a status of secrecy, for the present" in order to keep both the Kuomintang and Communists guessing as to the scope of American intentions. Marshall could then "utilize" the uncertainty in Yenan and Nanking "for the purpose of bringing influence to bear both on the Generalissimo and the Communist leaders towards concluding a successful negotiation for the termination of hostilities and the development of a broad unified Chinese government."

This sounded good to Truman, who promised Marshall that he would be supported in his efforts "whatever they might be to bring about the desired result." Marshall then took the floor. It was his understanding, he said, that he would do his best to influence Chiang to make reasonable concessions in his negotiations with the Communist leaders, "holding in abeyance the information that this Government was actually preparing shipping to assist the Generalissimo in moving his troops into north China. . . ." The Communists would also be kept in the dark so as to bring their leaders "to the point of making reasonable concessions in order to bring about desirable political unification." Should Mao and his lieutenants refuse to make such concessions, then Chiang would receive unhesitating and unconditional support.

But suppose Chiang proved obdurate? And suppose "this resulted in the breakdown of the efforts to secure a political unification, and the U.S. abandoned continued support of the Generalissimo"? This would surely lead to "the tragic consequences of a divided China and of a probable Russian resumption of power in Manchuria." The "combined effect" of these tragic but inexorable developments would be "the defeat or loss of the major purpose of our war in the Pacific." Was there not but one way out of this awful dilemma? "Under these circumstances, General Marshall inquired whether or not it was intended for him, in that unfortunate eventuality, to go ahead and assist the Generalissimo in the movement of troops into North China." Marshall had no illusions about the course he was advocating. "This would mean," he continued, "that this Government would have to swallow its pride and much of its policy in doing so." But there seemed no other choice. The preservation of a united and "free" China under Chiang Kai-shek had indeed been one of the "major" purposes "of our war in the Pacific," and it seemed either too late or too early to abandon the Kuomintang leader. Thus "The President and Mr. Byrnes concurred in this view of the matter; that is, that we would have to back the Generalissimo to the extent of assisting him to move troops into North China in order that the evacuation of the Japanese might be completed." After some further discussion, in which it was unanimously agreed that the United States should not extend its commitment to include the further dispatch of its own troops, and after Marshall was assured that he had the authority to offer more economic and financial assistance as a bribe to keep the wheels of negotiation spinning, the meeting ended.[4]

Within a week the general was on his way to China, apparently having had no other extensive discussions with either the President or the Secretary of State. But on December 15 Truman did release a formal letter of instruction to General Marshall entitled, "U.S. Policy towards China," which for the most part faithfully adhered to the decisions taken in private discussion and to the essentially conservative atmosphere in which those discussions had taken place. American support of the Kuomintang as the official national government of China was firmly reiterated. Strong advocation of a national conference of representatives of all political parties was advanced as the best means of broadening China's admittedly undemocratic "one-party government" and of achieving true national unity. At the same time "the existence of autonomous armies such as that of the Communist army is inconsistent with, and actually makes impossible, political unity in China." Finally, resolution of China's internal strife properly belonged to the Chinese people and political leadership; "intervention by any foreign government in these matters would be inappropriate." However, the letter advanced, for one of the first times in the early postwar period, the hint of an oncoming American universalism to justify the Marshall mission. "The U.S. Government has long subscribed to the principle that the management of internal affairs is the responsibility of the peoples of the sovereign nations. Events of this century, however, would indicate that a breach of peace anywhere in the world threatens the peace of the entire world. It is thus in the most vital interest of the U.S. and all the United Nations that the people of China overlook no opportunity to adjust their internal differences promptly by methods of peaceful negotiation." George Marshall was being sent to Nanking to assure that Nationalists and Communists should overlook no opportunity to end their bitter struggle for China.[5]

Given the nature and orientation of the Marshall mission, the reaction of the two chief protagonists was singular indeed. Chiang and his highly influential wife received news of the general's coming rather sulkily. Chiang told Wedemeyer on November 27 that he was "highly gratified" that Marshall had been selected and was "keenly interested" in the date of Marshall's arrival. But he then spoke at some length of his fondness for Hurley and of his strong endorsement of Hurley's letter of resignation. Wedemeyer later wrote that it was his impression "that Chiang was not certain of Marshall's attitude in light of Stilwell's earlier removal from China." Madame Chiang made little comment "except to express her personal regret that Ambassador Hurley would not return." Although Chiang subsequently praised Truman's December 15 policy statement, terming it a document which "showed clearly the President's understanding of [the] China situation," Marshall could still expect Hurley's shadow to dog his negotiations with a suspicious Kuomintang.[6] The Communists, on the other hand, projected a curious blend of euphoria and anxiety. On December 20 Chu Teh told Colonel Ivan D. Yeaton, who commanded the American observer group at Yenan, that " 'the U.S. China policy has changed' (to the better)." Chu Teh promised complete cooperation with American troops in disarming and repatriating Japanese forces throughout northern China, and it was Yeaton's reported belief that a "Slight hint in

U.S. policy has quickly brought out a desperate cry to stop the civil war earliest and successfully conclude negotiations. I detect a new low in assurance and believe Communists ready to make greater concessions than ever before and at same time if General Marshall's reactions favorable to throw themselves in the lap of United States.''[7]

Even as Yeaton and Chu Teh spoke at Yenan, Marshall's plane touched down in Shanghai after hours of tedious flight across America and the Pacific. The general alighted to be met by an elaborate reception including a Chinese and American guard of honor. Wedemeyer was on hand also, and after the two men drove to Marshall's hotel, a disturbing incident took place. Marshall showed Wedemeyer his directive from the President, and Wedemeyer bluntly replied that it would be impossible ever to effect a working relationship between Chiang and the Communists. Marshall turned furiously and replied, ''I am going to accomplish my mission and you are going to help me.'' Wedemeyer made the appropriate reply of support, but he was unhappy at Marshall's morose demeanor both then and later. The war, he decided, ''had exacted a heavy toll both on [Marshall's] physical condition and his nerves,'' and the long air trip from the States had exacerbated the condition.[8] The next day Marshall flew to Nanking and plunged into the first of what would prove to be hundreds of conferences over a long and increasingly unhappy year.

Despite his fatigue Marshall began his mission in subtle, almost feline fashion. Adopting the manner of an innocent, he told both Chiang and Mao's envoy, Chou En-lai, that he wished to listen and learn before passing judgment or making recommendations. The American people, he told both men, had just concluded a long and costly war in the Pacific—a war that had originated in Manchuria a decade and a half before when a weak and divided China had invited Japanese depredation. China's weakness must never again tempt would-be aggressors. The United States was eager to help China work out her own solution to the present chaos and was prepared to extend lavish economic aid in the bargain. But there was little time. A war weary and traditionally volatile American public had little patience. A just and durable answer to China's agony must be found quickly or the Truman administration might be forced by an intemperate citizenry to abandon China to ceaseless strife.

Having established his role and issued his warning, Marshall sat back and watched Chiang and Chou talk themselves into firm commitments to serious negotiation. Both protagonists were on the horns of a dilemma. American troops were still in their country; perhaps more would come in an effort to force a solution should American impatience manifest itself in bellicosity rather than despair. Alternatively, the prospect of American aid was most attractive, particularly should it be possible during the course of negotiation for one side or the other to convince Marshall and his distant superiors that the opposition was faithless and utterly self-seeking. The wisest course for both the Kuomintang and the Communists at the end of 1945 was to abandon violence, embrace diplomacy, and seek to exploit the new situation as best they could. None of this was said or hinted to Marshall, of course, but it clearly underlay the suspiciously generous remarks of both Chiang and Chou, who sought to outdo each other in benign protestation. Yes, they both said, they wished to follow the American way, to abandon conflict and ''one party government'' and embrace democracy, to create a true coalition government and a national army that would embody the collective purpose of the Chinese people. Chou, meeting Marshall at Chungking on December 21, was particularly effusive. He conjured up the liberal ideological images of Washington and Lincoln and FDR to support repeated claims of good will and intent.[9]

Marshall was properly skeptical of all this. On the twenty-ninth he wrote Truman in a sardonic vein that he had now held lengthy interviews with all the protagonists—Kuomintang and Communist as well as the small fringe groups such as the Democratic League and the Youth Movement.

> All agree to leadership of Generalissimo [Chiang] and to high sounding principles or desires for more democratic government, a coalition government, a reorganized and completely nationalized Army. But the practical procedure to secure these ends, especially as to the nationalization of Army and selection of senior provincial officials are [*sic*] almost completely lacking. This I have plainly and emphatically indicated in my repeated questioning and blunt statements. I think I have made this point glaringly clear to all and now they appear to be struggling towards a more realistic point of view.

Marshall added that he had his own ideas of procedure in some of these matters, notably the nationalization of the Chinese army, ''but have not yet thought the moment had arrived to state them.'' The following day Communist representatives presented their first firm truce proposals and Chiang followed suit by announcing that the long delayed Political Consultative Conference would convene at Chungking within a fortnight. Significant bargaining over China's destiny had begun.[10]

In the meantime Byrnes had met with Molotov and Bevin in Moscow. All were conscious that the wartime web of cooperation and wary amity was rapidly unraveling. The United States held exclusive control of the atomic bomb, that most horrendous weapon of destruction yet devised by man; the Soviets had openly and brutally repudiated what the Western powers thought were generous European settlements arrived at in the Crimea; and the Kremlin had so far refused to evacuate either the northern Iranian province of Azerbaijan or Manchuria. In the latter case Molotov could and did point to a November 15 request by Chiang that Red Army units remain until Kuomintang military and civil forces could arrive and hold the area. Now the Kremlin had taken "under consideration" a February 1 target date for total withdrawal from the former Japanese province. But what of American forces in northern China, Molotov asked Byrnes on December 16. How soon would they be leaving? For the next week the American Secretary of State and the Soviet Foreign Minister sparred over this question. The American position, as outlined by Byrnes both verbally and in writing, was simple if profoundly disquieting to the ever-suspicious minds in the Kremlin.

The United States was committed to aiding the common ally, Chiang Kai-shek, in his efforts to disarm and remove all Japanese units currently in northern China. Chiang was at the moment too weak to carry out such a task unaided. As soon as American aid in the form of air and sea transportation and marine guard units was no longer required for Chiang's assistance, it would be withdrawn. The Russians countered with charges that were brushed aside and with contempt that was ignored: Japanese troops, Molotov noted, were not being disarmed but were in fact being employed against the Communists, whose strength, Stalin told Byrnes on the twenty-third, was undoubtedly being exaggerated by the always boastful Chinese. On the twenty-first Molotov had handed Byrnes a stiff note which stressed Soviet adherence to a policy of noninterference in Chinese affairs and which stated bluntly "that the interference of foreign troops in the internal affairs of China is leading to an aggravation of the internal-political struggle and complicates the situation in China." Since the issue came down to the "question of Japanese troops in a zone where the disarming of these troops, according to General MacArthur's order no. 1, approved by the four powers, should be carried out by the troops of the Chinese Government," the Kremlin note insisted "that the Chinese Government urgently take appropriate measures." And the note closed by reasserting that with respect to the internal problems of China "the Soviet Government believes that these tasks should be decided by the Chinese people itself and its Government without interference from other states.''[11]

How sincere was the Russian demand for total disengagement of all the powers from China? The evidence strongly suggests that it was probably most sincere. Stalin had been on record for months as contemptuous and suspicious of the power and pretensions of Yenan. It is quite true that the Red Army had facilitated Chinese Communist penetration of Manchuria and of broad areas of northern China and on occasion had actually hindered the meager efforts of the Kuomintang to assert early control over these regions. But Stalin did comply with Chiang's November 15 request to remain in Manchuria, and thereafter the Red Army departed reasonably on time. It may well be that Red Army commanders had instructions from the Kremlin to make extensive contact with Yenanese forces in order to assess their strength and ability, and that having done so, the word went back to Moscow that Mao and his men were of doubtful value to Soviet interests. Certainly, as we shall see, Stalin finally calmed any fears Byrnes may have had that the Soviet Union was about to repudiate or abandon its recent treaty alignment with the National Government of China. And there existed various and good reasons for the Soviet dictator to stay completely out of Chinese affairs at this time. For he had once before dipped into the cauldron of Chinese politics, only to be badly burned.

This had been in the mid-twenties, when a young Stalin had dispatched the ill-fated Borodin mission to Chiang only to see it come to grief when the Generalissimo, having exploited Soviet organizational and administrative expertise to the hilt, ruthlessly drove the Russian mission and all its followers and suspected followers from Kuomintang China. It would be far better now to wait and see if Chiang could impose his rule on all China before repudiating him and the recent Sino-Soviet treaty. Should this strong man fail completely, then would be time enough to deal with Mao or whoever might emerge. But should Chiang succeed, enormous benefit would accrue from a history of steadfast alliance to this waspish schemer. Why should Stalin, preoccupied at this moment with securing his East European flank against any future thrust from the West while probing for soft spots around the Eurasian land mass from Libya, Turkey, and Iran to Japan, take on a fresh and possibly fatal burden in China? It was best to wait and let chaos crystallize into a recognizable and manageable pattern.

By the same token, however, it was essential to remove the American military presence from China at the earliest possible moment. The United States must not be allowed to impose its will on China with impunity;

China must not be permitted to become a slavish client of the United States. Fluidity and conflict, not American will, must define China's ultimate fate.

Such are the musings of the observer, not the indubitable facts of history which are shrouded in the minds of men long gone and in archives shut tight against inquiry. But such musings do seem to correspond satisfactorily with what we now know of the tangled story of Sino-Soviet relations from 1925 to 1960. The always smoldering animosity between Mao and the Kremlin after 1946 which broke into outright contention after 1956 argues too strongly against an active Soviet interest in promoting the fortunes of Chinese communism during the violent days and years of the late forties.

In the event, at Moscow, Molotov pursued a skillfully retreating Byrnes, pressing the American for a firm withdrawal date, which Byrnes tenaciously refused to name. At last the exasperated Secretary "said that he believed that Mr. Molotov was asking these questions merely because he liked the sound of his (Mr. Byrnes') voice." Molotov riposted "that he found Mr. Byrnes' voice very pleasant but even more pleasant would be an agreement for the simultaneous withdrawal of [Soviet and American] troops."[12] Some hours after this exchange the perturbed Byrnes went to the Kremlin to talk with Stalin, who proved pleasantly accommodating. The Generalissimo was airily contemptuous of the Chinese plight, it is true, "laughing heartily" at Kuomintang estimates of Communist strength. But finally Stalin "expressed the greatest confidence that if any man could settle the situation it would be General Marshall whom he regarded as one of the few military men who was both statesman as well as soldier."[13] Recounting this conversation to Marshall some days later, Byrnes concluded that in his estimation Stalin "at this time intends living up to his treaty with [Kuomintang] China and will not intentionally do anything to destroy our efforts for a unified China."[14]

So the focus of interest and activity swung again to Chungking, where at the close of the year Marshall made his first decisive intervention in the negotiations. When Chiang seemed about to reject the initial Communist proposals for a cease fire, Marshall countered with an unspecified "suggestion of the moment," which Chiang obviously took as a rebuke. The Kuomintang quickly submitted a counterproposal centering on an immediate cease fire, appointment of a Kuomintang-Communist commission to consult with Marshall on terms and methods of enforcing an armistice, and appointment by the Political Consultative Conference of a fact-finding commission to visit areas of disputed control. Ten days later, after intensive bargaining between Communist and Kuomintang officials, Marshall got his cease fire and more. Both Chinese factions had been forced to retreat. On January 4 Chou En-lai had capitulated to Marshall's insistent assertion that the United States was committed to the movement of Nationalist troops into Manchuria. On the other hand, Marshall disputed Nationalist insistence upon the right to continue troop movements into the northern China provinces of Jehol and Chahar in order to secure important rail junctures. Not until late in the evening of January 9 did Marshall at last secure Chiang's agreement to drop all reference in the armistice arrangements to the situation in northern China. Nationalist troop movements were to cease in those provinces, and the issue would be left to later political negotiations.

Beyond an immediate cease fire, Marshall achieved another cherished goal: the establishment of an "Executive Headquarters" at Peking to police the truce agreement. "I am quite certain that no other method will give genuine effect to the cessation of hostilities, reopening of rail lines, acceptance of Jap surrenders and repatriation of Japanese," Marshall had cabled Truman on New Year's Day. "There must be an impartial source of direction and authority on the ground." The directive for guiding the executive headquarters was drawn up by Marshall "and the two hostile representatives" from proposals drafted by Marshall's staff, and then it was approved by Chiang and Mao.

The arrangement of a truce and the establishment of an enforcement agency did not exhaust the list of Marshall's achievements. The cease-fire agreement enabled the Political Consultative Conference to meet between January 10 and 31 in an atmosphere of comparative calm, an essential element in the creation of any durable peace structure. Moreover, the truce also emboldened the hard-pressed Chiang to ask Marshall to participate directly in a Kuomintang-Communist conference on the reorganization and consolidation of the respective armies. The Communists supported the request and Marshall agreed. On January 10 Chiang formally announced formation of the military committee, which held its first meeting on February 14.

Here was a diplomatic triumph of truly astounding proportions. In less than three weeks Marshall had brought the contending parties together and had secured agreement to a cease fire and the machinery to implement it. Mao and Chiang had also agreed to convene a political conference to rewrite the national constitution and to blend their respective military units into a national army. Great relief was expressed in both China and Washington. The conditions and atmosphere for meaningful negotiation had at last been created. Now would come the crucible of debate and compromise.[15]

Peacemaking depended, of course, upon peacekeeping. From the outset both sides accused each other of gross and flagrant truce violations. The State Department later intimated that a majority of the real violations were probably instigated by the Kuomintang. ''The indication of strong resentment against'' the People's Consultative Conference ''on the part of powerful groups within the Kuomintang and the opposition by a powerful group of National Government Army generals to any reorganization of the armies which would threaten their position were seen as obstacles, on the Kuomintang side, to successful implementation'' of the truce agreements. ''Disquieting incidents'' came to light of alleged attacks by Kuomintang plainclothes men on a mass meeting in Chungking held to celebrate the initial success of the Political Consultative Conference; police interference with minority party delegates to the conference was reported; and an attack on the Communist party newspaper premises at Chungking became widely known.[16] As early as January 13 there were allegations from Yenan ''of Kuomintang attacks on all fronts,'' and a month later Communist headquarters was broadcasting widely collected reports of Nationalist disruption of the armistice, including Kuomintang attacks on Communist forces in Manchuria and the apparent movement of Nationalist units from Manchuria into the disputed province of Jehol in flagrant violation of Chiang's promise of January 9 to Marshall.[17] By late February Moscow, too, was voicing fury over ''reactionary elements in China,'' whose disruptive activities in Manchuria and ''slander campaign'' in the Chinese press threatened the Sino-Soviet alliance. Reports from Consul General Clubb at Mukden in late March seemed to confirm Kremlin charges at least in part. Russian citizens had been ''assassinated . . . shortly after Soviet withdrawal'' from several Manchurian cities, and the remaining Soviet citizens in Manchuria were petitioning Moscow for protection.[18] Such incidents, if indeed staged by Kuomintang diehards, were counterproductive, for the Russians were encouraged to delay their departure from Manchuria until the end of April, and some local Soviet commanders were doubtless tempted to give further aid to Chinese Communist forces in the province.[19]

In such an umpromising environment the work of Marshall's executive headquarters was obviously of critical importance. Its function ''was to bring the rival Chinese face-to-face, to thrash out problems and send three man 'truce teams' into warring areas to enforce or at least report on—the cease fire.'' But in typical American fashion the austere headquarters began to expand. The modest radio network and fleet of C-46 military planes quickly swelled with the influx of a new and controversial group of American officers. Marshall, ever the diplomat, knew that the Chinese revered age, and so he cabled Washington to send out senior colonels as U.S. members of the truce teams. According to Benjamin Welles, who covered the Marshall mission for the *New York Times*, the War Department proceeded to ''fob off'' on Marshall many of its self-styled misfits, and irreverent Chinese soon began nicknaming the Peking Union Medical College, which housed executive headquarters, the ''Temple of Ten Thousand Sleeping Colonels.''

In fact, there were ultimately about three hundred U.S. colonels attached to executive headquarters, and Welles has argued that many, though not all, were as active and as effective as they could be in their difficult and confusing posts. Executive headquarters worked well when the rival Chinese factions allowed it to. In the early months of 1946 its truce teams fanned out across China and Inner Mongolia to patrol areas often the size of Pennsylvania, ''moving by jeep, truck, horse or whatever other local transport could be scrounged.'' Welles argues that the colonels and their Chinese colleagues halted much fighting and that because of their accurate radio reports to Marshall in Chungking or Nanking, the American negotiator had accurate information on which to base his latest estimates and efforts. ''The teams roughed it, usually in rude mud homes in tiny, isolated villages. The arrival of the C-46's with mail, reading matter, supplies—and sometimes with newsmen—every few days was eagerly anticipated. The work of the truce teams was hard, lonely and often dangerous; yet the Americans, Chinese Nationalists and Communists got along surprisingly well.'' In an inspection visit to Peking late in February Marshall paid warm tribute to the teams, praising them for having ''made an inestimable contribution to the peace and future prosperity of East Asia.''[20]

Marshall himself was no laggard. ''It was hard to remember how many conferences he attended,'' but it was somewhere in the upper hundreds and often involved flying from city to city. In the first week of March he flew nearly four thousand miles over northern China with Chou En-lai and Kuomintang General Chih-chung, visiting a dozen urban areas. Banners greeted his tall, austere figure everywhere, cheering him as the savior of China and the God of peace. "If sheer activity or the enthusiasm of his initial reception could have ensured success," Robert H. Ferrell has noted sadly, "Marshall would have become the savior of China."[21]

But in Asia, American enthusiasm, hard work, and good will have seldom been sufficient, in and of themselves, to assure success; this was the hard lesson that Stilwell had learned, that Marshall would in turn learn, and that Americans of a later generation would have to learn, to their sorrow and heartbreak, all over again in Indochina. At first, however, events unfolded in a most pleasing fashion for Marshall and the American mission. At the opening session of the Political Consultative Conference on January 10 Chiang had announced his decision to grant immediately certain fundamental democratic rights to his people, including freedom of speech, assembly and association, equal legal status for all political parties, and the like. At its final session on January 31 the Political Consultative Conference released the text of a series of agreed resolutions which were designed to carry the political unification of China one step further. A national assembly was to convene in early May to adopt wide-ranging reforms in the existing draft constitution of 1936. Pending convocation of the national assembly, the Political Consultative Conference resolutions provided for a thorough reorganization of the Nationalist government. The existing but largely impotent state council was to become the supreme organ in charge of national affairs. The revised council was to be comprised of forty members, half of whom would be members of the Kuomintang and all of whom would be chosen by Chiang. General resolutions of the state council would require a majority vote of councilors present, but any resolutions involving changes in administrative policy would require a two-thirds vote of the members present for approval. The Communists promptly began pressing for control of at least fourteen of the twenty non-Kuomintang seats in the council so as to veto possible changes in the Political Consultative Conference resolutions by the state council. The ever-suspicious men of Yenan had pinned the recent enemy to firm agreement; the enemy should not be permitted to wring sudden and unexpected advantages out of further change.

The PCC resolutions also provided for the legal equality of all political parties, who in turn were pledged to recognize the leadership of Chiang Kai-shek. The status quo was to be maintained in all liberated areas until the final national political settlement was achieved by the forthcoming national assembly. The reorganization, reduction, and unification of China's armed forces was also demanded. All in all the PCC had managed to achieve agreement on a striking range of problems in a very short time. As Tang Tsou has noted, it had adopted a political program basically unfavorable to the Kuomintang. But at the end of January it seemed that men of good will could hope that China was at last on the road to peace.[22]

Three weeks later Marshall reported another triumph. On February 22 the Committee on Demobilization, Reorganization, and Integration of the Chinese armies reached final agreement on all points. Within a day both Mao and Chiang had given their blessings to the plan, which was formally signed on February 26 and transmitted by Marshall to Washington on March 4 as "Basis for Military Reorganization and for the Integration of the Communist Forces into the National Army."[23] At the close of his cable to Truman on the formal signing of the military agreement, Marshall requested permission to go home for a brief period. There were, he told his President, "a number of aspects of the situation I would wish to discuss with you and the Secretary of State, but I am particularly anxious to go directly into the details of certain matters regarding transfer of surplus property and shipping and with regard to loans." Then Marshall casually revealed how far his head had been turned by dramatic success: "I should be back in China in time to balance differences that are bound to rise over the major adjustments that will then be getting under way, political as well as military."[24]

Truman by this time was euphoric over Marshall's performance; it was the one bright spot in an otherwise dismal political atmosphere which saw the administration buffeted by strikes and the threat of strikes, a rapidly burgeoning cold war in Europe with the Soviet Union, and internal demoralization, incompetence, and infighting. "His praise of your achievements was glowing," a former aide cabled Marshall on the last day of February. "He indicates a strong desire to leave China to you and is interested largely in determining what, if any, further support he can give you." Surely if Marshall wished to return for consultation, Harry Truman was not going to say "no." And it did seem a propitious time to leave China, to catch one's breath, report one's successes, and talk over the problems that remained with a sympathetic Commander-in-Chief. Just a week before his departure Marshall saw Mao at Yenan and was assured "that the Chinese Communist Party would abide wholeheartedly by the terms of the Agreement for the Cessation of Hostilities, the Resolutions of the Political Consultative Council, and the Basis for the . . . Integration of Communist Forces into the National Army, and that under the leadership of Generalissimo Chiang Kai-shek, and the encouragement and assistance of American friends, all Agreements would no doubt be translated into positive action which was *sine qua non* in China's program of reconstruction.'' Or at least this is what the American notes of the conversation report that Mao said. Marshall later remarked that he could never "penetrate" Mao, never knew what Mao was really thinking. "That is a real iron curtain when you get there." Still the words looked good, even if the inflection was somewhat puzzling. Marshall was at the apex of achievement, and he told Mao in reply "that he was gratified with the spirit of the Chinese Communist Party and was particularly appreciative of the fine show of cooperation, straightforwardness, and friendliness of General Chou En-lai during the entire course of negotiations."[25] Marshall saw Chiang just before his departure for Washington, and his message betrayed no sense of unease.[26]

Perhaps Marshall first sensed impending disaster on the day he left, March 11, when Chou came to him and related Yenan's fears concerning the future of Manchuria. The military and political aspects of Manchuria's future should not be separated. Should Chiang be allowed to reimpose his leadership over the region just as the Communist armed forces there were disbanded and reintegrated, then, Chou said, all of Manchuria would fall under one-party rule, and this would be "difficult for us to accept, and particularly difficult in convincing our armed forces in the Northeast [Manchuria]."[27] We do not know what Marshall's reaction was to this suddenly looming threat; it was too late to cancel his flight and he would be back shortly. Probably the weary man added the Communist warning to his list of important tasks to be accomplished upon his return and then gratefully cast his eyes eastward across the Pacific.

His determination to leave China at a critical juncture has earned Marshall some bitter criticism. Benjamin Welles has called Marshall's decision to "turn his back on the contending forces," no matter how briefly, a "fatal mistake." Possibly, but was there not a limit to what one man could do, no matter how commanding in presence and persistent in negotiation he was? Both sides talked of peace while continually preparing for war. Tang Tsou has noted that "On their part, the Communists never failed to take actions in the field to occupy new territory, to expand their armies, and to increase their influence. These actions were taken by them when they were clamoring for peace and were justified by them as measures to prepare themselves for a breakdown of the negotiations or a collapse of the settlement.''[28]

By March of 1946 Chiang and Mao had gone as far with Marshall as they possibly could short of surrendering their lifetime hopes and dreams of power. Marshall's trip, however brief, provided the pretext for a renewal of battle, but it is extremely doubtful if another pretext for war might not have been found had he been tied to the negotiating table in Chungking for all the days of his absence. The truth was that neither Marshall nor those who had dispatched him to Asia really knew anything about China, her people, or her politics. The national government and the Communist insurgents had been locked in deadly conflict for nearly two decades, ever since Mao's expulsion from the Kuomintang coalition in the late twenties. At one point Mao's followers had been reduced to a harried, semi-starving cadre; since then Mao had staged an astounding revival of power and prestige. Now the very dynamics of the situation made showdown unavoidable. To paraphrase Lincoln in another context: there were those who would make war in order that their fortunes might continue to prosper, and there were those who would accept war in order that their fortunes might not flag. To think that Mao and Chiang could be deterred from a climactic test of strength and that the situation which they had created could be defused by means of formula and procedure and compromise and accommodation imposed by a stranger from without was to indulge in the rankest folly. Unfortunately this was what Truman and Byrnes and Marshall—all ignorant men—had believed, and the inevitable failure of their hopes was to breed the bitterest disillusion and the meanest suspicions among the people whom they led.

When Marshall returned on April 18 the war had all but come. The two immediate causes were apparent Kuomintang repudiation of the PCC resolutions and Manchuria. The Central Executive Committee of the Kuomintang met from March 1 to March 17 to pass on the PCC resolutions. It was clear from the beginning that the reactionary cliques within the party, which had crippled every attempt at necessary internal and external reform for the past three years, were in an implacable mood. Bitter speech followed bitter speech: the presidential system of power was extolled, the prospective drain of power to the provinces deplored. In the end the Central Committee ratified the proposals in ostensible unanimity. But it was evident that powerful forces within the Kuomintang would fight ceaselessly for drastic revision of the PCC effort. The Communists quickly countered with the demand that any proposed revisions have the agreement of all parties, and they refused to nominate members to serve in a reorganized government until the Kuomintang mood crystallized favorably. At the end of March Yenan canceled the meeting of its Central Committee which was to ratify the proposals, and Mao's agents refused to submit a complete list of their units to the military committee as required by the agreement of February 26. By the last weeks of April, shortly after Marshall's return, "discussions on political matters reached a complete deadlock." At the same time fighting in Manchuria was nearing a climax.[29]

As early as November 14, 1945, Wedemeyer had cabled Washington that, in the words of the official State Department history, "the National Government was completely unprepared for occupation of Manchuria in the face of Communist opposition." Six days later Wedemeyer amplified his views: "Chinese Communist guerillas and saboteurs can and probably will, if present activities are a reliable indication, restrict and harass the movements of National Government forces to such an extent that the result will be a costly and extended campaign. . . . Logistical support for National Governmental forces and measures for their security in the heart of Manchuria have not been fully appreciated by the Generalissimo or his Chinese staff."[30] Wedemeyer begged Chiang to concentrate all his efforts at reconquest south of Mukden—in northern China—until he was sufficiently strong both militarily and morally to mount a powerful offensive into Manchuria. But it was no use; Chiang was as much or more a captive of events as anyone else. He *was* China, or so he and his American allies claimed; he dared not risk deferring recapture of an area that not only was potentially the richest in all his realm but had also been the scene of his earliest disgrace in the long and debilitating war with the just-defeated Japanese. What physical and spiritual authority might accrue to Mao if his hold over the province was not immediately contested no one could say, and Chiang dared not discover.

So the Generalissimo committed forces to Manchuria as best he could and with predictable results. At the end of February the embassy at Chungking was telling Washington that if recent statements from Yenan were at all accurate, "there exists in Manchuria a local force of approximately 300,000 men, styled the Manchurian Joint Democratic Army, which is said to have been organized by cadres from the Communist Eighth

Route and New Fourth Armies. . . . If the statement in the release with regard to numerical strength can be relied upon, it would indicate truly remarkable Communist expansion in Manchuria since the collapse of Japan.''[31] The importance of such news was initially obscured by the apparent dimensions of Marshall's achievement. But things began to come unstuck at the beginning of April. On the sixth the Red Army at last began its final withdrawal from the province, and the Kuomintang commander promptly endeavored to extend his military control as far as possible. With only 137,000 troops at his disposal and limited railroad rolling stock, he soon found himself greatly overextended, while Communist forces flooded into the broad territorial interstices between Nationalist garrisons. Soon the hinterland between the Nationalist lines of communication, previously bare of troops, was filled by the men of Yenan; the countryside was now in a position to strangle the cities and all within them.[32]

It was at this point that Chiang and his commanders committed one of the first of many blunders that were to eventually cost them China. The situation in Manchuria was tailor-made for executive headquarters field teams to create and enforce a truce. Instead the Nationalists ''offered obstructions to the functioning of the teams, first by the refusal of the Commanding General in Manchuria to permit the teams to enter Manchuria and later by the refusal of the National Government members of the teams to take any action on the basis that they had no authority.'' Not until April 8, ten days after a Communist commissioner had requested that executive headquarters take action on the ''excessive movement'' of Nationalist armies into Manchuria did the first teams even proceed into the province.[33] The Nationalist blunder was promptly followed by an American error of equally grave proportions. For some weeks Yenan had been mounting frequent propaganda attacks against the transportation of Nationalist troops to Manchuria by American facilities. On March 31 Chou himself protested the transportation of Nationalist forces in American vessels on the ground that the February 26 agreement had restricted the number of Nationalist troops in Manchuria to five armies. The Americans responded coolly. Chou was reminded that the troop limitation clause of the agreement was not to be effective for a year and that authorization for the movement of Nationalist troops into Manchuria had been written into the original cessation of hostilities agreement of January 10.[34] This was true, but at this moment in China's history apparent American disinterest in Communist grievances proved nothing short of disastrous. Communist forces were well entrenched throughout Manchuria; the Kuomintang position was tenuous, perilous in the extreme. To assume a high-handed attitude toward Communist pretensions was to goad Yenan into an open trial of strength with Kuomintang garrisons.

On April 15, three days before Marshall's return, the blow fell. Twenty-four hours after Russian withdrawal from Changchun, Chinese Communist forces attacked the city and seized it within three days. The incident immediately aroused heated passions on both sides. To the Kuomintang reactionaries it was at once a humiliation that must be avenged and a confirmation of all they had preached about the evils of coalition with political opponents; to Communist generals and soldiers in the field it was a heady triumph whose repetition proved irresistible. Compromise with a demoralized and corrupt foe was no longer necessary or desirable. "At the time of General Marshall's return to China on April 18, the impasse [in Manchuria] was complete except that the Chinese Communists were willing to submit the future military dispositions and local political reorganization to negotiations if the fighting were terminated."[35] This Chiang was initially unwilling to do. He adamantly demanded fulfillment of the cease-fire agreement, which permitted Nationalist troops to move anywhere they wished in Manchuria, and he bluntly informed Marshall that he was of a mind to occupy Changchun and overpower Communist forces in the area. Not for some days was Chiang prevailed upon to propose a cease fire and negotiations. But it was too late. Communist commanders in the Changchun region had strengthened their forces immeasurably by the capture of Japanese equipment and stores, including artillery and tanks, while the Nationalist commander rashly continued his policy of garrisoning remote areas with small detachments, thus ensuring the steady erosion of his power.[36]

The Nationalists did manage to retake Changchun on May 23, while Chiang was in Mukden personally supervising military operations, but the Communists had offered no resistance, choosing instead to melt away into the countryside to wait and watch. On May 10 Marshall had dispatched a remarkably cool and judicious cable to Truman.

The Communists have clearly broken the plain terms of the cease firing agreement of January 10 last regarding the freedom of action to be accorded the Government in the establishment of sovereignty in Manchuria. On the other hand the Government itself, up to the time of my return to the States, did not proceed in strict accordance with the terms of the agreement in that it did not admit teams to control the sporadic and I think unnecessary fighting during the northern advance of Government armies, which fighting finally developed into success-ful Communist opposition.

"I am in the midst of the problem," Marshall concluded. "At this moment I submit no recommendations. . . . I am going ahead in the hope that I can resolve the difficulties without troubling you and while I am taking many diplomatic liberties I am trying to do so in a manner that will keep the skirts of the U.S. Government clear and leave charges of errors of judgment to my account."[37]

This was to prove a chimerical hope. Marshall was able to arrange a brief Manchurian truce in June, but subsequent negotiations simply emphasized the intransigence of both sides. Nationalist proposals that Yenan evacuate all provinces and cities under its control in northern China and permit entry of Nationalist troops aroused bitter Communist resentment. Frequent demands by prominent Kuomintang spokesmen to settle all issues by force intensified tensions, as did mounting Communist attacks upon American policy in China and protests that American military and financial aid to the Kuomintang encouraged a civil-war policy by the Nationalist government. At the end of June the Manchurian truce collapsed. "During July there began a gradual worsening of the military situation with the spread of hostilities to various points in China proper," and the situation finally passed from Marshall's control.[38]

Possibly, just possibly, the United States could have avoided attracting Yenan's hostility and mistrust as China fell into full-scale, irresolvable civil war in mid-1946. But the continued presence of American troops guarding key supply and transportation points precluded even this faint hope. In early April Wedemeyer had announced that the U.S. Army in the China theater was to be disbanded. At roughly the same time the marine units were ordered to be greatly reduced in strength. But marine field commanders successfully pleaded with Wedemeyer to slow withdrawal appreciably; the official U.S. Marine Corps history is quite explicit in stating the preference of senior field commanders for the Kuomintang and their mounting antipathy for the Communists, no matter what their men might have felt.[39] Clashes between Communist forces and marine detach-ments throughout northern China were inevitable. As Frank and Shaw note, local Communist commanders, flushed with ambition and arrogance, claimed as "liberated areas" all ground under their jurisdiction right up to the marine and Kuomintang perimeter defenses along the key rail and road lines from the port cities inland to Peking and elsewhere.

The first incident occurred on July 13, a hot summer day, along the Peking-Mukden railroad. A Communist detachment suddenly seized seven marines illegally searching for ice in a village beyond their compound. Marine units promptly gave chase, but instead wound up negotiating for eleven long days, during the course of which "Communist officials hammered away at one theme—the Marines were actively aiding the Chinese Nationalist Army."[40] The men were ultimately returned on July 24, but five days later came the incident at Anping, a village astride the Peking-Tientsin road. A marine-escorted motor convoy ran into a Communist force, and after someone had fired a shot both sides opened up and a firefight ensued, during which three Americans were killed and a dozen wounded. Both Communist and American spokesmen claimed that their troops had been ambushed by the other side, but the true significance of the event lay in the fact that a furious Marshall at last lost his self-control.[41] First learning of the incident as he was preparing to draft a cable to Washington, Marshall told Truman on July 30 that the incident "is undoubtedly the result of violent Communist propaganda against so-called American military support of the National Government and the present confusion of military action all over North China."[42]

Marshall was not at all happy with the American military presence in China, but he gave no indication of this attitude to Chou in an "icy" interview on August 1 at Nanking. Marshall branded Yenan's charges of a Kuomintang-American ambush at Anping "a complete, and I think deliberate, misrepresentation."[43] Both men managed to maintain a semblance of civility as they worked out an agreement to appoint a fact-finding group. But the winds of war had now driven Marshall and Chou far apart; there could no longer be ease or trust between them, and this brute fact practically destroyed Marshall's effectiveness as a disinterested negotiator. The fact-finding mission itself "encountered great, although anticipated, difficulties. The Communists employed delaying tactics and vicious propaganda," according to the official American account.[44] Marshall lingered in China until the end of the year, watching the civil war grow and spread until eventually it became one of the greatest of wars in a century of great wars. But before that happened he had gone, recalled to Washington in

January 1947 by a disappointed Truman to become Secretary of State. Thereafter, for better or for worse, in uncertainty and concern and mounting despair, the United States aligned itself politically and financially with Chiang's failing effort.[45]

NOTES

1. Forrest C. Pogue, *George C. Marshall: Education of a General* (New York: Viking Press, 1963); Robert H. Ferrell, *George C. Marshall as Secretary of State, 1947-1949* (New York: Cooper Square Publishers, 1966), pp. 3-20.

2. Rose Page Wilson, *General Marshall Remembered* (Englewood Cliffs, N.J.: Prentice-Hall, 1968), p. 314.

3. See the various memoranda and the statements drafted by War and State Department planners during late November and early December 1945 in U.S. Department of State, *Foreign Relations of the United States, 1945: Diplomatic Papers*, 9 vols. (Washington, D.C.: U.S. Government Printing Office, 1967-1969), 7:745-766 (hereinafter cited as *FR, 1945: Diplomatic Papers*).

4. Ibid., pp. 767-769.

5. "U.S. Policy towards China" is printed in many places. The public text is in *Public Papers of the Presidents: Harry S. Truman, April 12 to December 31, 1945* (Washington, D.C.: U.S. Government Printing Office, 1961), pp. 543-545; and U.S. Department of State, *United States Relations with China with Special Reference to the Period 1944-1949*, reprinted and hereinafter cited as *China White Paper*, 2 vols. (Stanford, Calif.: Stanford University Press, 1967), 2:607-609. The complete text is in *FR, 1945: Diplomatic Papers*, 7:770-773.

6. *FR, 1945: Diplomatic Papers*, 7:752, 785; Albert C. Wedemeyer, *Wedemeyer Reports!* (New York: Henry Holt & Co., 1958), p. 362.

7. *FR, 1945: Diplomatic Papers*, 7:793-794.

8. Quoted in *Wedemeyer Reports!*, pp. 363-364.

9. Marshall's initial conversations with Chiang and Chou are printed in *FR, 1945: Diplomatic Papers*, 7:794-804.

10. Ibid., pp. 825-827; *China White Paper*, 1:136.

11. *FR, 1945: Diplomatic Papers*, 7:837-840.

12. Ibid., p. 841.

13. Ibid., p. 850.

14. The Secretary of State to General Marshall, 4 January 1946, in U.S. Department of State, *Foreign Relations of the United States, 1946*, 11 vols. (Washington, D.C.: U.S. Government Printing Office, 1969-1972), 9:17-18 (hereinafter cited as *FR, 1946*).

15. The record of Marshall's mission in China during the first ten days of January 1946 is in ibid., pp. 1-130 and *China White Paper*, 1:136-143, which also

contains some observations on Chinese public opinion. Robert L. Smyth, Counselor of Embassy at Chungking charged with monitoring radio broadcasts from Yenan, reported to the Secretary of State on 21 January that "there were reports of great public demonstrations in Yenan to celebrate" the cease-fire order. File 893.00/1-2146, Records of the Department of State, National Archives, Washington, D.C.

16. *China White Paper*, 1:143-144.

17. General Chou En-lai to General Marshall, 13 January 1946, *FR, 1946*, 9:342. See also Counselor of Embassy in China (Smyth) to the Secretary of State from Chungking, 26 January and 4 March 1946, in files 893.00/1-2646 and 893.00/3-446, Records of the Department of State, National Archives, Washington, D.C.

18. The Chargé in the Soviet Union (Kennan) to the Secretary of State, 25 February and 25 March 1946, in files 740.00119 PW/2-2546 and 740.00119 PW/3-2546, Records of the Department of State, National Archives, Washington, D.C.; Consul General at Mukden (Clubb) to the Secretary of State, 24 March 1946, file 740.00119 PW/3-2446, ibid.

19. The Chargé in the Soviet Union (Kennan) to the Secretary of State, 24 March 1946, file 740.00119 PW/3-2446, ibid.

20. Benjamin Welles, "Recollections of an Asian Truce," *Washington Post*, 10 February 1973, p. A14; "Remarks by General Marshall at Meeting of the Committee of Three with Commissioners and Officers of Executive Headquarters," Peiping, 28 February 1946, in *FR, 1946*, 9:463-464; General Marshall to President Truman, 6 March 1946, ibid., pp. 510-511.

21. Ferrell, *Marshall*, pp. 29-30; General Marshall to President Truman, 6 March 1946, *FR, 1946*, 9:510-511.

22. *China White Paper*, 1:138-140; Tang Tsou, *America's Failure in China, 1941-1950* (Chicago: University of Chicago Press, 1963), p. 407.

23. *FR, 1946*, 9:290, 295-300, 444.

24. Ibid., p. 446.

25. Ibid., p. 501; Ferrell, *Marshall*, p. 30.

26. *FR, 1946*, 9:510-511.

27. Ibid., pp. 535-536.

28. Tang Tsou, *America's Failure in China*, p. 413.

29. Ibid., pp. 416-418; *China White Paper*, 1:144.

30. Quoted in *China White Paper*, 1:131.

31. *FR, 1946*, 9:448.

32. *China White Paper*, 1:147.

33. Ibid., p. 148; *FR, 1946*, 9:713.

34. *China White Paper*, 1:149.

35. Ibid.

36. Ibid., pp. 149-150.

37. *FR, 1946*, 9:815-818.

38. *China White Paper*, 1:158-170.

39. Tang Tsou, *America's Failure in China,* p. 411; *History of U.S. Marine Corps Operations in World War II*, 5 vols. (Washington, D.C.: Historical Branch, G-3 Division, Headquarters, U.S. Marine Corps, 1968), vol. 5: *Victory and Occupation*, by Bemis M. Frank and Henry I. Shaw, Jr., pp. 604-605.

40. Frank and Shaw, *Victory and Occupation*, p. 610.

41. Ibid., pp. 610-612; *China White Paper*, 1:172; Welles, ''Recollections of an Asian Truce.''

42. *FR, 1946*, 9:1421.

43. Ibid., pp. 1427-1437; Welles, ''Recollections of an Asian Truce.''

44. *China White Paper*, 1:172n.

45. Identification with Chiang, of course, meant not only a practical severance of ties to the Communists but also outright opposition to them. In a policy statement of 27 September 1948, the State Department flatly asserted, ''In striving to achieve our fundamental objectives [in China] we support and extend assistance to the present National Government as the only instrument now available which has any capability of bringing about an independent stable China friendly toward the US.'' U.S. Department of State, *Foreign Relations of the United States, 1948*, 9 vols. (Washington, D.C.: U.S. Government Printing Office, 1972-), 7:612.

chapter 7

China: The Revolt Triumphant

For two years, while the Truman Doctrine, the Marshall Plan, the Berlin airlift, the Czechoslovak tragedy, NATO, and the Hiss case all focused popular concern upon Europe and the fully developed cold war between Russia and the West, Americans from time to time shifted their gaze to Asia and the awful agony that was unfolding in China. During this time George Marshall seemed transfixed by the tragedy he had unwillingly helped bring into being. By mid-1947 "the Chinese situation" was clearly "disintegrating" and the new Secretary of State was "searching for a positive and constructive formula," but none could be found. The Kuomintang was now rent with open factionalism, and Chiang was forcing his ablest commanders into retirement. American military officials, led by Secretary of Defense James Forrestal, were now convinced that a Nationalist collapse would mean "that the Russians will come in as we go out." Given the realities of the cold war with the Soviet Union, continued support of Chiang seemed mandatory. By February 1948 Marshall had reached the conclusion "that we regard the China problem under present conditions of disorder, of corruption, inefficiency and impotence of the Central government as being practically unsolvable," yet "we cannot afford to withdraw entirely from our support of the Chiang Kai-shek government and . . . neither can we afford to be drawn in on an unending drain upon our resources."[1] Continued economic and military aid on a scale which was minuscule in comparison to that currently being offered Western Europe seemed the only solution.

The United States was at last confronted with the fruits of its China policy. Chiang had won some spectacular victories in late 1946 following the complete breakdown of meaningful negotiations that summer. In July he had commenced a great offensive to clear Communist forces out of the Yangtse valley area. The drive had developed its own momentum until by autumn the Communists also had been ousted from a number of cities in both Manchuria and northern China. As a result of comparatively easy victories, Chiang had become intoxicated with overconfidence. The Kolkos have charged that Chiang would not have dared to move so boldly against his opponents without the assurance of continuing American aid and the presence of American troops in northern China. While this is a typically harsh judgment, it stands the test of fact.[2] For the crucial truth about China between 1943 and 1949 is that Chiang always assumed he could finally count on American support against the Communist enemy. Ultimately that support proved insufficient to overcome his own follies and those of his nominal subordinates. Certainly he was forced to endure humiliating lectures on good government and proper military tactics from a succession of American officials including Stilwell, Wedemeyer, Marshall, and after July 1946 U.S. Ambassador John Leighton Stuart, a hand-picked Marshall appointee. But the support was there, and it was constant, if grudging.[3]

When the Communists unexpectedly counterattacked in early 1947, penning up Kuomintang forces in the cities of northern China and Manchuria through control of the countryside and thus of the rail and transportation networks, American troops were withdrawn in large numbers from the unhappy land. Those comparative few who remained were transferred from the battlefields of the hinterland to a few coastal enclaves, most notably Tsingtao, abandoning in the process some sixty-five hundred tons of equipment to the Nationalists.[4] By September the withdrawal was completed, and for the next year and one-half Tsingtao became the last and greatest center of American military power in China. Collected there were the last marine garrisons, and there also the U.S. Navy based its now minute western Pacific fleet, generally consisting of an undermanned aircraft carrier and a handful of support ships.[5]

Nineteen forty-eight proved to be the year of disaster for Nationalist China. Chiang had permitted the finest of his troops to be starved into surrender in the northern cities, and thereafter demoralization and defection spread like malignant plagues through his remaining armies. Never outmanned, never outgunned until the last, the armies of Nationalist China melted away as the increasingly confident and competent Communist forces began their massive sweep to the south. By the end of 1948 Mao's forces controlled Manchuria and most of China north of the Yangtse and had surrounded Tsingtao. Desperate Defense Department officials in Washington informally discussed the possibility of a carrier strike against the port in order to support the marine garrison, which in December was reinforced by twelve hundred men sent in from Guam. Perceptive observers of all political persuasions were now convinced that, as Manfred Gottfried, chief correspondent for *Time-Life* put it, "China is very nearly lost."[6]

But Washington stubbornly refused to abandon its commitment. At the end of November Marshall rejected a State Department proposal to go to the American public "now to explain the inadequacies of the Chiang Kai-shek government." Marshall told his colleagues in cabinet session "that this would administer the final *coup de grâce* to Chiang's government, and this, he felt, we could not do."[7] On December 30 Acting Secretary of State Robert Lovett cabled Ambassador Stuart in China that the U.S. government "recognizes and continues extend aid Chi Govt accordance China Aid Act 1948." Lovett added that Washington completely rejected the notion of promising aid to a non-Communist succession government in China in order to force Chiang's retirement, as had been recently suggested by Carsun Chang and other nonaligned political figures in China.[8] On January 20, 1949, however, Marshall turned over his office to Dean Acheson. That same day Chiang resigned his, turning over the presidency of the Chinese Republic to General Li Tsung-jen, whom he ultimately left in the lurch by transferring all of China's foreign exchange and monetary reserves, along with himself, to Formosa. Chiang had already requested the United States to ship military equipment destined for China to the island. Twelve years of intermittent civil war and twenty-two years of Nationalist rule in China were practically at an end.[9]

The decline and fall of Kuomintang China deeply affected American public opinion, and strident cries that China's "loss" would constitute a strategic and emotional disaster for the "free world" doubtless exerted great influence on American policy makers during the melancholy years of the late forties. By 1947 a China bloc had emerged in Congress and a China lobby appeared to give it vociferous support across the country. Interestingly enough, Patrick Hurley was never an active member of the China lobby. But he supported it and provided some of its members with material.[10] The standard bearers were Senator Pat McCarran of Nevada, Representative Walter Judd of Minnesota, Alfred Kohlenberg, and, possibly as chief pamphleteer, General Claire Chennault, the former leader of the "Flying Tigers" of wartime China fame.

Chennault trenchantly presented the views of the China lobby and bloc in a short article first printed in the *New York World Telegram*, then republished in condensed form in the April 1948 issue of the *Reader's Digest*. China had to be helped, Chennault argued, because Franklin Roosevelt had given Manchuria away to the Russians at Yalta, and the Soviets had subsequently begun to press China while exploiting Manchuria. Should Russia be allowed to continue her Manchuria-China policies, she would feel free and secure to move in Europe, threatening an immediate outbreak of World War III. But should the United States do its duty in China, should it help Chiang—not with men, for the Generalissimo had plenty of those—but with massive amounts of arms and goods and training, then Chiang could resist Russian encroachments, eventually reconquer Manchuria from the Kremlin puppets who currently controlled it, and, it was implied, save the world from the horrors of a third planetary holocaust. During the course of his argument Chennault also proposed that General Wedemeyer be dispatched to China once more, not on an essentially futile fact-finding mission as had been the case in mid-1947, but as Commander-in-Chief of all Chinese armies as he had been in 1945. With Wedemeyer leading the way, a victorious crusade against Communism in China and Manchuria would be assured, along with the "consolidation and recovery of a great nation that could be the eastern bastion of the only kind of world we want to live in."[11]

The truly remarkable aspect of the Chennault essay is its total ignorance of the Chinese Communists, who are never once mentioned by name. Chennault was obviously convinced beyond question that Mao, Chou, Chu Teh, and their millions of followers were simply "puppets" of the Kremlin, slavish doers of Soviet bidding. It is even questionable if Chennault knew who Mao was. Regrettably, the general was not alone in his assumptions. In mid-December 1948 someone in the Pentagon, State Department, or, more likely, on MacArthur's staff in Tokyo, apparently leaked the contents of an "urgent" sixteen-page message from MacArthur to the Joint Chiefs of Staff "which gave our top military men a historic shock." Reportedly, MacArthur told the JCS "that the Communist victories in China have gravely jeopardized U.S. security." MacArthur claimed that "the Soviet Union will soon be in a position to seize Okinawa and Japan and to sweep the U.S. from the western Pacific." MacArthur allegedly then asked for immediate naval, air, and ground reinforcements in Japan. He then backed down somewhat. He "did not say that a Soviet attack on the U.S. in the western Pacific is either likely or imminent. He simply said that the loss of most of China to the Communists will create the strategic conditions for such an attack, and that in the present state of our defenses, Okinawa, Japan and the rest of our offshore line cannot be long held."[12]

Whether or not MacArthur ever dispatched the sixteen-page message attributed to him cannot be determined at this time. It has not appeared in any government publications so far as this writer can ascertain. However, there appears to be no indication of any repudiation by MacArthur or his staff of the remarks attributed to him by the Luce publication. Taken together, the remarks of MacArthur and Chennault conveniently fitted either explicitly or implicitly into the emerging myth of America's postwar predicament which would be embraced and propounded by an articulate and vociferous minority of political primitives, not the least of whom eventually would be Senator Joseph R. McCarthy of Wisconsin. This myth presumed that all the nation's troubles in the world could be traced to Yalta, where a dying and intrinsically woolly-headed Franklin Roosevelt had turned over much of Europe and Asia to Joseph Stalin in a feckless effort to meld democracy and Communist tyranny into a postwar partnership. Now in China, as in Poland and Czechoslovakia, Roosevelt's rancid chickens were coming home to roost. The slavish minions of an international Communist conspiracy directed by Joseph Stalin from his Kremlin office were flooding over much of Europe and Asia, obliterating democratic governments—or at least the allies of the greatest democratic government in the world. Soon Russia, through control of her minions, would bestride the Eurasian land mass from the Elbe to the China Sea, forcing a militarily weak United States either to use her ultimate, horrifying weapon in desperate retaliation, or to withdraw in total surrender across the Pacific and the English Channel leaving three-quarters of the earth's habitable surface and 90 percent of the world's peoples in abject bondage to Communism.

So discredited has this world view become in recent times that it is now fashionable to assume that serious men and women never subscribed to it or propounded it as intelligent dogma. It now seems a relic of an older and frighteningly simpler time and the personal targets of this world view— Truman, Acheson, John Carter Vincent, to name but three—appear heroic and ennobled by their martyrdom. The extent to which Truman and Acheson perhaps unwittingly subscribed to this view will be examined in due course. But it is important to note here that the demonology of the Chennaults and MacArthurs was more widely and publicly accepted than we would now wish to believe. To take but two examples, Thomas E. Dewey, then leader of the "liberal Eastern-establishment, internationalist" wing of the Republican party, and young Congressman John F. Kennedy of Massachusetts, who all too soon would be projected as the clearest and coolest liberal Democratic thinker of his time, openly espoused the views set forth so firmly by Chennault and MacArthur, McCarran and Judd. Whether from conviction or expediency, Dewey felt impelled as early as November 1947 to state that the civil war then raging in China was unlike all the others that had periodically wracked the land. "The previous civil wars in China have been primarily internal affairs. The present struggle is a war of conquest under the leadership of a small group of avowed Chinese Communists who are serving the purposes of Soviet imperialism."[13]

Young Kennedy preferred to pitch his remarks on a somewhat different plane, one that would soon become all too familiar and enticing to the public. Speaking in the House of Representatives in January 1949, the representative bitterly condemned "the Lattimores and the Fairbanks" who were so preoccupied with "the imperfection of the democratic system in China after 20 years of war" that they "lost sight of our tremendous stake in a non-Communist China."[14] Kennedy's motives are obscure. Probably he believed what he was saying. Certainly, recent and critical scholarship on the Kennedy career has indicated that the man was often not what he appeared. Possibly, however, he was speaking from a kind of mischievous expediency which was an outstanding aspect of his political character in the prepresidential years.[15] If so, he, like Dewey, was responding to a powerful political current that could not be compressed within one philosophy or one political party.

By early 1949, however, with Nationalist forces suffering reverses everywhere on the mainland and with Chiang ensconced on Formosa, the State Department, under its new leader, Dean Acheson, had had enough. Acheson and his colleagues had become completely disenchanted and disgusted with the Kuomintang. At a Senate hearing in March, Acheson stated flatly, "We have got to the point where in fact there is nothing more constructive that is coming out of this government." Continuing aid for Nationalist China, which was what the hearings were about, would be folly, Acheson implied.[16] In further testimony the Secretary advocated "a wait, look, see policy" toward China, and while he emphasized that for the foreseeable future the triumphant Communists would bind themselves tightly to Moscow, he did not preclude the possibility that at some future point, as the inevitable problems emerged of ruling a vast land and a turbulent people, Mao and his cohorts might for some reason break with the Kremlin. After all, Tito's apostasy was still fresh in many minds. Six months later this suggestion had become National Security Council doctrine.[17] Such an attitude was anathema, of course, to the China lobby.

When at last the end neared in China and the final marine detachments were leaving Tsingtao, the State Department decided to issue a White Paper in an effort to counter and, if possible, still the persistent agitation of the China lobbyists. But Acheson's hope that this lengthy document might appease or quiet Chiang's American supporters was doomed to swift and bitter disappointment. The White Paper "evoked bellows of pain and rage from the China bloc in Congress and the China lobby in the country" when it appeared in August 1949.[18] Two months later China—America's China—formally "fell to Communism."

With the formal proclamation of the People's Republic of China in October 1949 the U.S. government and the world were at last faced with the reality of Asia's great revolt.[19] In 1947 and 1948 Washington had felt a deep moral obligation to continue support of the established Kuomintang government of Chiang Kai-shek. This had not meant either a suspension of criticism or armed intervention to tip the scales decisively in favor of the Nationalists. In one of his last discussions with Chiang, on December 1, 1946, Marshall had "briefly, but firmly restated his view that this large Communist group could not be ignored and that the National Government was not capable of destroying it before the country would be faced with complete economic collapse." In his final report, made public shortly after his return from China in January 1947, Marshall asserted, "The salvation of the situation would be the assumption of leadership by the liberals in the Government and in the minority parties and successful action on their part under the leadership of the Generalissimo would lead to unity through good government." Nonetheless, the thrust of this "frank statement" was "to give some guidance to misinformed people both in China and in the United States" about "Chinese Communist misrepresentations and vicious propaganda against the United States."[20]

Thereafter the United States had extended just enough military and economic aid to Chiang to ensure on the one hand the continuing enmity of the Communists and on the other the growing suspicion of domestic critics that not enough was being done to save "democracy" in the Far East.

Marshall, then Secretary of State, and his colleagues understood the dilemma with agonizing clarity. At a meeting of the Secretaries of State, War, and Navy in mid-1947, Marshall stated the problem lucidly: the "immediate and urgent problem to be decided is what are we to do about rearming the Chinese Nationalist Army. He said that the Army is beginning to run out of ammunition and it appears that we have a moral obligation to provide it inasmuch as we aided in equipping it with American arms. He said that action in this case poses a real dilemma because we will be taking an indirect part in the civil war if we continue to rearm the National Army; on the other hand, we will be favoring the Communists if we do not provide the equipment to the Nationalists." Beyond the ethical problem lay considerations of possible Soviet responses if the United States continued military aid to Chiang. Forrestal and Patterson were adamant, however, in stating the "obligation to support the government in China which we have recognized and have previously supported."[21] Not for another twenty months did Washington at last conclude that it had gone as far as humanly possible to sustain Chiang's ever-weakening hold on the Chinese mainland.

Mao's triumph posed obvious problems, the most important of which was the fact that domestic pressures made it "clearly politically impossible in 1949 and 1950 for the Administration to make significant positive overtures to the new Communist regime." There is now incontrovertible evidence that as they completed their victory the Communists were quite anxious that Washington break totally with Chiang and recognize the new regime in Peking.

The first sign of Communist desires came in June and July of 1949 when John Leighton Stuart, our last ambassador to China, held veiled conversations with various Communist officials who made it clear that Mao showed some interest in establishing formal diplomatic ties. But then congressional opinion and President Truman's own inclination to remain "tough" with Mao became decisive. A possible ambassadorial trip to Peking to see Chou and Mao was firmly vetoed by Acheson after he received a congressional petition demanding nonrecognition of the Chinese Communists and after members of the congressional China bloc visited the White House. The Stuart-Huang Hao conversations soon lapsed.

A far more dramatic gesture came from Peking in October. At nine o'clock on the evening of October 1, 1949, Consul-General O. Edmund Clubb in Peking received a letter in official note form as follows:

Sir: Mao Tse-tung, Chairman of the Central People's Government of
the People's Republic of China, on this date issued a public statement.
I am sending this public statement to you, Sir, with the hope that you
will transmit it to your country's Government. I consider that it is
necessary that there be established normal diplomatic relations between the People's Republic of China and all countries of the world.
Chou En-lai (signature and seal), Minister of Foreign Affairs of the
Central People's Government of the People's Republic of China,
Peking, October 1, 1949.

Here was the clearest expression imaginable for an end to alienation and
hatred, if not suspicion, and a reasonable normalization of relations between a Communist and capitalist power—indeed between a Communist
power and all capitalist nations. The Peking request was prominently
featured in Europe and the Soviet Union (though no other nation publicly
admitted—if it knew—that Peking had included the United States in its
gesture), and suspicions that the United States itself might have been
approached surfaced in press reports from various spots around the world.
The British almost immediately responded favorably, and it was clear that
London's recognition of Peking was but a matter of time. France and the
United States responded with expressions that ranged from guarded to
hostile. The first response from Washington did not occur until October 6,
when Acting Secretary of State Webb cabled Clubb that "you shld take
advantage of Chou letter to incorporate in reply reiteration our anxiety re
position Mukden staff." Washington was determined to wring every
advantage from the situation in which it found itself.

But it would be wrong to assume that the diplomats in Washington and in
various posts abroad were prepared to reject the Chinese Communist
gesture out of hand. Ambassador Kirk, for example, cabled from Moscow on October 7 that Communist China's eagerness to take the China
seat at the United Nations and its pressing need for foreign trade to ease
economic and social problems provided the United States with "two trump
cards." Formal recognition, Kirk added, would allow Washington to
counter "USSR imperialism" in Manchuria and China and would permit
encouragement of pro-United States elements remaining on the mainland.

Acheson, however, was determined to move slowly, to wait and assess
the emerging power relationships not only in Asia but also in Congress. A

circular telegram of October 12 to the chief diplomatic posts around the world reiterated Washington's views on recognition expressed as early as the previous May and June. Announcement of the establishment of a Chinese Communist "government" had been a long anticipated development and did not lend any special urgency to a consideration of the question of recognition by non-Communist countries. "To this end US Govt emphasizes need for full exchange views prior any definitive or independent steps looking toward recog[nition] by other interested friendly govts."

But time proved an enemy, not an ally, of Acheson's efforts to master the course of events in the Far East. British insistence on early recognition of the Peking regime was matched by an equal insistence on the part of China lobbyists in Congress that America set its face firmly against the anti-Christs who had wrested control of mainland China. On November 1 the British government dispatched a cruelly logical note to the State Department. The Communists had taken complete control of the mainland and had pressed to the very borders of Hong Kong; the Nationalist regime had completely collapsed and had been swept away to Formosa; long-standing British trading and commercial interests in China had to be maintained and protected. Therefore, every consideration of logic, law, politics, and self-interest dictated early recognition, which would, it was implied, be extended at the conclusion of the forthcoming conference of United Kingdom representatives at Singapore.

Even before the British note reached Washington, Acheson had held a series of meetings with his Far Eastern advisers during which the question of recognition was implicitly buried. As a result of searching discussions on October 26-27, it was agreed that extension of further military aid to the Nationalists on Formosa would be foolish; that with respect to the Communists on the mainland, great strains could be expected to develop between Peking and Moscow and within the Chinese Communist regime itself as the burdens of rule increased. The United States should not actively seek to drive a wedge between the two leading Communist powers, for this would be counterproductive; rather it should wait upon events. Thus, when Acheson and British Ambassador Sir Oliver Franks sat down on December 8, 1949, to discuss China policy, Acheson said bluntly:

> It seemed to us that the inclinations of the Chinese Communists were to follow the Russian example of considering themselves not an evolutionary regime which had sprung from the previous one which,

therefore, entailed that they assume both the rights and the obligations of the former regime, but a revolutionary one which would seek to assume all the rights and only those obligations they choose to undertake. It was important to know what the real situation was and, if possible, to prevent such a development. Secondly, it was important to have evidence of how they proposed to conduct themselves with respect to the outer world: whether it would be in conformity with international law and usage as a civilized power, or as an uncivilized or semi-civilized entity. Thirdly, we did not believe that hasty recognition would confer any permanent benefits on those who undertook it. Fourthly, as respects the U.S., it was important for us to bring Congress into our deliberations so that, at any rate, the problem would be fully talked out and the issues clarified. Therefore, regardless of the action taken by other powers, we would not act hastily.

On January 10, 1950, a month after his talk with Franks and three weeks after His Majesty's government had decided to extend recognition to Peking, Acheson publicly outlined the U.S. position with respect to recognition of Communist China. The People's Republic would have to meet ''necessary 'international obligations' '' before obtaining recognition. These obligations, as defined, meant the practical assumption by Peking of all the treaty commitments of imperial and Kuomintang China with regard to protection of American property interests and the rights of diplomats and diplomatic property. ''If the Communists had met these obligations,'' a recent Senate staff study concludes, ''their actions would have been interpreted in the American press and in the Administration as a signal that the Communists were going to be more responsible, less anti-American, and less extreme in their Communism.'' In other words, they would have been expected to surrender at the very moment of triumph that revolutionary, anti-Western fervor which had brought them victory in the first place. Given the situation in China at the moment, this was arrogance of the rankest sort.[22]

Peking's response was immediate. Four days after Acheson's statement the Communists seized buildings in Peking that the State Department considered to be American diplomatic property. In retaliation Washington withdrew its last remaining personnel in China.[23] One final effort was made to heal the breach. During the course of a speech at San Francisco's Commonwealth Club on March 15 Acheson reduced to one the stipulations for possible U.S. recognition of Peking. Should the People's Republic guarantee ''the proper treatment of American diplomats,'' then possibly the grounds for dialogue and recognition could be prepared. Several weeks later Ambassador to India Loy Henderson made roughly the same offer in a speech at New Delhi, which was subsequently printed in the Department of State *Bulletin*.[24] But Peking, busy with more pressing matters, remained silent. On December 18, 1949, Mao had arrived in Moscow for prolonged discussions with Stalin, which culminated in a Sino-Soviet Treaty of Friendship, Alliance, and Mutual Assistance, signed on February 15, 1950. In exchange for Mao's public acknowledgment that the Chinese Communists were ''Marshal Stalin's zealous disciples'' the Soviet Union renounced its Far East claims upon China drawn up, with American aid and support, at Yalta precisely five years before and extended lavish economic aid to the Peking regime.[25] Thereafter America's China policy was reduced to reluctant support of the Taiwan regime and forlorn hope that somehow, some way, some day a ''wedge'' could be driven between Peking and Moscow. Within the year even that hope was dashed as Americans and Chinese began killing one another amidst the bitter snows of Korea.

Four months after Mao had proclaimed the establishment of the People's Republic of China, an obscure junior senator from Wisconsin stood before a gathering of Republican women in Wheeling, West Virginia, and in a sentence crystallized and focused all of the frustrations and bitterness that had been festering in so many hearts and minds over the past half-decade of mounting affluence and anxiety. ''While I cannot take the time to name all of the men in the State Department who have been named as members of the Communist Party and members of a spy ring,'' Joseph R. McCarthy intoned in that thick, nasal voice that was soon to become notorious, ''I have here in my hand a list of 205 that were known to the Secretary of State as being members of the Communist Party and who, nevertheless, are still working and shaping the policy in the State Department.''[26] Within days a slightly bewildered but highly pleased McCarthy discovered that he had embroiled the country in divisive debate over the issue of ''Communists in government.'' Passions were to boil for the next four years until at last they consumed their creator.

The sources of McCarthyism were many and varied. The dynamics of partisan politics surely played a major role: the problem of Communists in federal employment had been with the government for over a decade, as the Hiss case demonstrated, and the issue had become closely linked with the often venomous reactions of many conservatives within and beyond the Republican party to the New and Fair Deals. Nelson Polsby has demonstrated rather convincingly that ''election returns bear out the thesis that

McCarthy ran best where the Republican Party was strongest . . . the McCarthy vote was concentrated in areas of Republican strength, and was neither scattered, nor distributed in some pattern unique to McCarthy, nor particularly strong.''[27] Then, too, there was McCarthy's own prior unpopularity with the Washington press corps and many of the voters back home: the man was desperately searching for a viable partisan issue that long-ago night in West Virginia.

There is also the thesis advanced by historians and social scientists during the late fifties and early sixties that McCarthyism was a reflection of deep-seated status anxieties on the part of certain Americans—generally assumed to be midwestern Republicans and/or ''ethnic isolationists'' such as Germans, Irish, and Poles—who felt their political, social, and personal power draining away to the great urban centers of the East where dwelled not only liberal Democrats but Republican ''internationalists'' who had capitulated totally to Wendell Willkie's ostensibly muddle-headed view of ''one world.''[28] Richard Rovere at the very end of the 1950s advanced his own somewhat unique hypothesis that McCarthy was simply the creation of the Washington press corps, and that as this segment of the media created him, so another—television—ultimately destroyed him.[29] And, finally, there is the recent theory of certain self-styled revisionists that McCarthyism was not a product of Republican conservatism, but of phony Democratic liberalism. According to these writers McCarthyism was fostered by a Truman administration which after 1946 deliberately sought to whip up anti-Communist hysteria in America through emphasis on loyalty programs in order to enlist popular support for policies and programs designed to secure global dominance for American capitalistic interests.[30] The fatal weakness of this argument is that it must presuppose a comparatively weak and defensive postwar Soviet Union. But a generation steeped in the memories and lessons of Adolf Hitler and appeasement could not be expected to receive with equanimity creditable tales of mass arrests, gunfire in the night, and ruthless suppression of civil liberties everywhere that the Red Army was to be found. Nor could it ignore the evidence of Soviet probes into Iran and Turkey only months after the close of the greatest war in history. In dismissing the apparent, if not real dimensions of the Soviet threat to the West in the late forties, the revisionists have inevitably distorted the American response.

But this is not to say that by early 1950 the political climate in the United States was anything but poisonous. ''There was an atmosphere throughout the land that year of suspicion, intolerance and fear that puzzled me,''

William Shirer later recalled. People seemed afraid of becoming involved in controversy, of getting in trouble with dozens of self-styled vigilante groups which seemingly had gotten control of government agencies, the press, university boards of trustees, and almost every other kind of agency, public and private, that the individual could imagine. It seemed to Shirer that the avoidance of free speech and its inevitable concomitance, controversy, had become the highest goal to which Americans aspired at midcentury.[31] McCarthy thus exploited a situation; he did not create it. The extent to which it had been created by the "fall" of China is difficult to measure. So much had happened to fashion this fetid environment before Chiang at last fled to Formosa. There was the accelerating erosion of trust and friendship for Russia in this country in 1946 and 1947 that had swiftly turned to bitter fear and hatred; there were Hiss and Judith Coplon; there was Masaryk's mysterious death in Prague and the brutal obliteration of at least a partially functioning democratic government in Czechoslavakia; there was always, it seemed in those years, Berlin. And, above all, there was the Soviet atomic explosion in August 1949 and the arrest of Klaus Fuchs the following February. Yet China—Chiang's China—had meant so much to Americans during the war years; we had projected so much of our best hopes and aspirations onto that tired, overburdened regime that when at last it fell—and to the anti-Christ—the blow was doubly appalling. Granted that the Hiss case had involved the State Department and the foreign policy establishment in general, it is striking, though not really surprising, that McCarthy opened his long crusade against "Communists in government" by attacking the same institution which Patrick Hurley had assaulted some years before for allegedly defeating America's purpose in Asia.[32] Thus once again Asia impinged, perhaps decisively, on the American imagination. Soon some of its leaders and people would give shape to an entire decade of U.S. foreign policy.

But even before the outbreak of war in Korea, American civil and military officials had begun to adjust their policies and perspectives on Asia to conform to the new realities of power. The formal Communist seizure of rule on the Chinese mainland late in 1949 had galvanized the National Security Council, and the result was NSC 48/2, an exposition of America's new Asian policy considered and approved by the National Security Council, President Truman presiding, on December 30, 1949.

An introductory report by the NSC, dated December 23, opened with a sensitive and sensible appraisal of the Asian scene: Asians shared a common experience of "poverty, nationalism, and revolution." The U.S. position with respect to Asia was therefore that of "a rich and powerful country dealing with a have-not and sensitively nationalistic area . . ." But such promising wisdom swiftly collapsed into the rhetorical perspective of the newly-minted cold war. America was in "competition together with friendly countries [presumably including France in Indochina and Britain in Malaya, as well as Japan] against the USSR for influence on the form and direction of the Asiatic revolutions." Asia would not be permitted to work out its destiny in peace. Washington no less than Moscow was determined that henceforth Asia would become a battleground of the ·rapidly globalizing struggle between Russia and the West. The NSC report was frank to the point of brutality:

> Our over-all objective with respect to Asia must be to assist in the development of truly independent, friendly, stable and self-sustaining states in conformity with the purposes and principles of the United Nations Charter. In order to achieve this, we must concurrently oppose the domination of Asia by any single country or coalition. It is conceivable that in the course of time a threat of domination may come from such nations as Japan, China, or India, or from an Asiatic bloc. But now and for the foreseeable future it is the USSR which threatens to dominate Asia through the complementary instruments of communist conspiracy and diplomatic pressure supported by military strength. For the foreseeable future, therefore, our immediate objective must be to contain and where feasible to reduce the power and influence of the USSR in Asia to such a degree that the Soviet Union would encounter serious obstacles should it attempt to threaten the peace, national independence or stability of the Asiatic nations.

The report then turned to specific policy. With respect to Korea it repeated some of the language of NSC 8/2 of the previous March 23, in which it was agreed that in pursuit of the national interest the United States should aid the Republic of Korea in consolidating "significant gains" thus far made "in terms both of the welfare and aspirations of the Korean people through continued grants of political support and economic, technical, military and other assistance." The principal objective of America's Korean policy was to strengthen the Seoul government to the point where it could "(1) successfully contain the threat of expanding Communist influence arising out of control over North Korea, and (2) serve as a nucleus for the eventual peaceful reunification of the entire country under a democratic basis.''

National policy toward Formosa was inevitably less clear and precise. The government had been bedeviled by members of the China lobby since the decision had been made by the administration the previous spring not to grant further credits to the Chinese Nationalists. Styles Bridges claimed Acheson was out to ''sabotage . . . the valiant attempt of the Chinese Nationalists to keep at least a part of China free,'' while Senator Pat McCarran charged that the State Department's Bureau of Far Eastern Affairs was responsible for ''losing'' China because its staff was ''definitely soft to Communist Russia.'' Acheson realized the situation was getting out of hand. The administration needed every vote it could muster in Congress for its still controversial European aid policies. Should the China lobbyists increase their influence, the economic and social reconstruction of Europe might well be jeopardized and Communism might well engulf the entire continent. During the summer of 1949 Acheson began meeting privately with various senatorial opponents. He told H. Alexander Smith of New Jersey in early July that ''we certainly would continue the recognition of the present National government . . . possibly as long as any vestige of strength remained in it. . . .'' Acheson added, however, that he believed ''Chiang Kai-shek had collapsed entirely, and whatever prestige he had was gone.'' The Secretary also told Smith, ''we would definitely withhold any recognition of the Communist Chinese government'' because it was not our intention ''in any way, shape, or manner to give any comfort to Communism in China.'' At the end of November the Secretary reiterated this pledge to the senator.

Such equivocation regarding policy toward the two Chinas was subsequently carried over into NSC 48/2. American military occupation of Formosa would lay the United States open to charges of imperialism, the NSC report stated, and would ''seriously affect the moral position of the U.S. before the bar of world opinion, particularly in the Far East.'' Yet it would be impossible to otherwise hold Formosa. ''It is not believed that denial of Formosa to the Chinese communists can be achieved by any method short of actual US military occupation.'' Acceptance of the eventual fall of Formosa to the Chinese Communists was thus inevitable. The report quoted a portion of NSC 37/7 of August 22, 1949, to the effect ''that 'the strategic importance of Formosa does not justify overt military action. . . .' " However, "a modest, well-directed and closely supervised program of military advice and assistance to the anti-Communist government in Formosa would be in the security interest of the United States. . . ."

The report was not wholly negative toward the new Communist regime in China. It stated that while "The USSR is the primary target of those U.S. economic policies designed to contain or turn back Soviet-Communist imperialism," China and other Communist nations were not, and therefore it would be "inappropriate" to apply similar forms of economic sanctions and warfare to China as to Russia. Trade with Peking in strategic materials must cease, since it should "be our objective to prevent Chinese Communists from obtaining supplies of goods of direct military utility which might be used to threaten directly the security interests of the western powers in Asia." But trade in nonstrategic goods with China should continue, if for no other reason than to supply the rebuilding Japanese industry with a certain and potentially vast market area.

Nonetheless, in its conclusions the report was characteristically unyielding. "Prevention of power relationships in Asia which would enable any other nation or alliance to threaten the security of the United States from that area, or the peace, national independence and stability of the Asiatic nations" was the supreme policy of the U.S. government vis-à-vis the Far East. This was to be achieved, in the words of NSC 48/2, which in briefer, more bureaucratic form summarized the introductory report, by "Development of the nations and peoples of Asia on a stable and self-sustaining basis in conformity with the purposes and principles of the United Nations Charter." Needless to say, Washington would define stability, security, proper development, and true independence in light of its own values, perspectives, and psychology.[33]

NSC 48/2—and NSC 8/2 and NSC 37/7, insofar as we know of them from the Pentagon papers—thus anticipated the sweeping commitments and strategies which it has been assumed until now were not accepted by the Truman administration until the appearance of NSC 68 in the spring of 1950. But did rhetorical commitment necessarily imply or demand the ultimate application of *military* force? It is impossible to answer this question with certainty. NSC 48/2 is suffused with the notion that eventually Asian "nationalism" and Russian "imperialism" might well prove wholly incompatible. This, of course, was the message which Acheson had cautiously sought to convey in Senate testimony on the China aid bill earlier in 1949. NSC 48/1 clearly implied the hope that in the long term America could have her way in Asia without resorting to violence.

Despite the determined tone of its new Asian policy, the United States possessed little in the way of military power to support its newly assumed commitments. Whether the United States possessed the will and strength to carry out the provisions of NSC 48/1 remained to be seen. Certainly Acheson's celebrated speech of January 1950, which excluded both Formosa and Korea from America's Asian defense perimeter would seem to indicate that despite the administration's current hard line toward Peking, American policy makers publicly recognized and sought to convey the limits of national power in the Far East. Thus when Peking, emboldened by the recently signed pact with Moscow, launched a strong propaganda attack against the American occupation of Japan and ostensible support of Chiang Kai-shek, Washington did nothing. Nor did the Truman administration react with emergency measures when Peking began to express faith in and support of "local wars" and "armed insurrections" throughout Asia. America reacted only with expressions of unease to news in the spring of 1950 that Communist China had massed hundreds of thousands of troops in the coastal provinces opposite Formosa. "Washington gloomily estimated that Chiang's days were numbered. O. Edmund Clubb, the last United States consul general in Peking, felt that the Communist regime would 'coordinate any move in the Formosa Strait with Communist actions planned for other sectors.' No one could say where.''[34] The answer came within weeks—in Korea.

NOTES

1. Walter Millis, ed., *The Forrestal Diaries* (New York: Viking Press, 1951), pp. 284-287, 372.

2. Joyce and Gabriel Kolko, *The Limits of Power: The World and United States Foreign Policy, 1945-1954* (New York: Harper & Row Publishers, 1972), p. 552.

3. See the relevant volumes of U.S. Department of State, *Foreign Relations* series for 1946, 1947, and 1948, and portions of U.S. Department of State, *United States Relations with China with Special Reference to the Period 1944-1949*, reprinted and hereinafter cited as *China White Paper*, 2 vols. (Stanford, Calif.: Stanford University Press, 1967) covering this period, specifically the Chungking

embassy report of 20 September 1947, noting "that the most disheartening feature of the Chinese situation, in economic as well as in other fields, was the overt reliance upon American aid to extricate China from its pressing problems and a corresponding lack of self-reliance and self-help in meeting these problems." *China White Paper*, 1:262. See also Marshall's comment "that the Generalissimo had done about everything he had asked him to, 'but always too late,' " quoted in John Robinson Beal, *Marshall in China* (Garden City, N.Y.: Doubleday & Co., 1970), p. 337. Beal observed in connection with this comment that "Chiang, I felt, had to be the judge of how fast and how far he could move the Chinese government, how sure he could be of getting obedience from his military commanders."

4. Dean Acheson, *Present at the Creation: My Years in the State Department* (New York: W. W. Norton & Co., 1969), p. 304.

5. *Life*, 20 December 1948, p. 26.

6. Ibid.; Acheson, *Present at the Creation*, p. 305; "China's Tragedy," *Life*, 6 December 1948, p. 46.

7. Millis, ed., *Forrestal Diaries*, pp. 533-534.

8. U.S. Department of State, *Foreign Relations of the United States, 1948*, 9 vols. (Washington, D.C.: U.S. Government Printing Office, 1972-), 7:704.

9. Acheson, *Present at the Creation*, pp. 305-306; *China White Paper*, 2:978. Acheson implies that Chiang requested the diversion of supplies to Formosa on the day of his resignation. *China White Paper* gives 6 December 1948 as the date of the request.

10. Russell D. Buhite, *Patrick J. Hurley and American Foreign Policy* (Ithaca, N.Y.: Cornell University Press, 1973), pp. 284-287.

11. Claire L. Chennault, "We Must Help China Now," *Reader's Digest*, April 1948, pp. 121-122.

12. "MacArthur Says Fall of China Imperils U.S.," *Life*, 20 December 1948, p. 25.

13. Thomas E. Dewey, "China Deserves Aid: Political Integrity a Fundamental Part of U.S. Foreign Policy," *Vital Speeches* 14 (15 December 1947):134-137.

14. *John Fitzgerald Kennedy: A Compendium of Speeches, Statements, and Remarks Delivered during his Service in the Congress of the United States* (Washington, D.C.: U.S. Government Printing Office, 1964), pp. 41-42. Kennedy's complementary charge, that the American government had threatened to withhold aid from Chiang unless a coalition with the Communists was formed, seems to be refuted by the record as it has so far appeared in the *China White Paper* and the appropriate volumes of the *Foreign Relations* series.

15. See the brief comment of Kenneth O'Donnell and David F. Powers on this incident in *"Johnny We Hardly Knew Ye": Memories of John Fitzgerald Kennedy* (New York: Pocket Books, 1973), p. 86.

16. U.S. Congress, Senate, Committee on Foreign Relations, *Economic Assistance to China and Korea, 1949-1950*, 81st Cong., 1st and 2d Sess. (Washington, D.C.: U.S. Government Printing Office, 1974), p. 39.

17. Ibid., pp. 30-34; "NSC-48/2, The Position of the United States with Respect to Asia," 30 December 1949, in U.S. Department of Defense, *United States-Vietnam Relations, 1945-1967)*, 12 vols. (Washington, D.C.: U.S. Government Printing Office, 1971), 8:270 (hereinafter cited as *United States-Vietnam Relations*).

18. Acheson, *Present at the Creation*, pp. 302-303, 306-307.

19. It is impossible at the present time to assess with precision the immediate effect of the Communist triumph in China upon events in both Indonesia and Indochina. However, it is significant that on 27 December 1949, just eight weeks after the formal Communist assumption of power in Peking, Queen Juliana signed at Amsterdam the document "unconditionally and irrevocably" transferring sovereignty over the former Netherlands East Indies to the New Republic of the United States of Indonesia, while earlier that same year the French, after months of protracted negotiations with Bao Dai, granted "independence within the French Union" to the states of Laos, Cambodia, and Vietnam. Zainu' ddin, *A Short History of Indonesia* (New York: Praeger Publishers, 1968), p. 238; Bernard Fall, *The Two Vietnams: A Political and Military Analysis*, 2d ed. rev. (New York: Frederick A. Praeger Publishers, 1967), pp. 210-214; Dwight D. Eisenhower, *Mandate for Change* (Garden City, N.Y.: Doubleday & Co., 1963), p. 168. Certainly the strenuous efforts of Bao Dai and Achmed Sukarno were instrumental in gaining independence for their respective nations, but might not the spectre of an incipiently Communist China also have influenced Paris, Amsterdam, and Washington to acquiesce in or encourage the inevitable? Evidence in the case of Indochina is strong, indeed.

20. *China White Paper*, 1:212-218.

21. U.S. Department of State, *Foreign Relations of the United States, 1947*, 8 vols. (Washington, D.C.: U.S. Government Printing Office, 1972-1973), 7:850-851.

22. U.S. Congress, Senate, Committee on Foreign Relations, Staff Study, *The United States and Communist China in 1949 and 1950: The Question of Rapprochement and Recognition*, 92d Cong., 2d Sess. (Washington, D.C.: U.S. Government Printing Office, 1973), pp. 6-15; U.S. Department of State, *Foreign Relations of the United States, 1949*, 9 vols. (Washington, D.C.: U.S. Government Printing Office, 1974-), 9:93-220 passim (hereinafter cited as *FR, 1949*).

23. U.S. Congress, Senate, *United States and Communist China in 1949 and 1950*, p. 17.

24. Ibid., pp. 17-18.

25. Peter Calvocoressi, *Survey of International Affairs, 1949-1950* (London: Royal Institute of International Affairs, 1953), pp. 338-343.

26. Quoted by Reinhard Luthin, *American Demagogues* (Boston: Beacon Press, 1954), reprinted in Earl Latham, ed., *The Meaning of McCarthyism* (Boston: D.C. Heath and Company, 1965), p. 5.

27. "Toward an Explanation of McCarthyism," *Political Studies*, October 1960, reprinted in ibid., p. 106.

28. See, for example, the essays of Daniel Bell, Richard Hofstadter, and others in Daniel Bell, ed., *The Radical Right* (Garden City, N.Y.: Doubleday & Co., 1963).

29. Richard Rovere, *Senator Joe McCarthy* (New York: Harcourt, Brace & World, 1959).

30. Richard Freeland and Athan Theoharis, "The Rhetoric of Politics: Foreign Policy, Internal Security, and Domestic Politics in the Truman Era, 1945-1950," in Barton J. Bernstein, ed., *Politics and Policies of the Truman Administration* (Chicago: Quadrangle Books, 1970), pp. 196-235; Richard Freeland, *The Truman Doctrine and the Origins of McCarthyism* (New York: Alfred A. Knopf, 1972).

31. William Shirer, *Midcentury Journey: The Western World through its Years of Conflict* (New York: Farrar, Straus and Young, 1952), pp. 275-276.

32. "While Hurley never actually joined the McCarthy camp in the strict sense nor condoned some of the Senator's actions, he did his part in setting the national mood. . . ." Buhite, *Hurley*, p. 285.

33. NSC 48/2 and its accompanying report are printed in *United States-Vietnam Relations*, 8:225-272. The comments by Bridges and McCarran are from the *New York Times*, 16, 17 April 1949; and the *Congressional Record*, 81st Cong., 1st Sess., pp. 4862-4863; and Acheson's July interview with Smith is from the H. Alexander Smith Papers, Box 98, Princeton University Library, all cited in Richard F. Grimmett, "The Politics of Containment: The President, the Senate, and American Foreign Policy, 1947-1956" (Ph.D. dissertation, Kent State University, 1973), p. 81. Acheson's renewed pledge to Smith on nonrecognition in November is in *FR, 1949*, 9:207.

34. Marvin Kalb and Elie Abel, *Roots of Involvement: The U.S. in Asia, 1784-1971* (New York: W. W. Norton & Co., 1971), p. 61.

chapter 8

Climax to Cold War: The Korean Conflict

The Korean War began in the rainy summer dawn of June 25, 1950, when a 110,000-man North Korean army spilled across the thirty-eighth parallel from sea to sea, brushed aside what Republic of Korea forces stood in the way, and raced a strong armored force down the hilly Uijongbu corridor toward Seoul. But were the North Koreans lured into conflict either by Washington or by Syngman Rhee? There are some who think so. I. F. Stone and Stephen Ambrose have argued that Harry Truman needed a war that torrid summer in order to bludgeon the American public into accepting a vast rearmament program deemed essential by Washington officialdom in light of recent cold war history, including Soviet detonation of an atomic bomb the previous year. According to Stone and Ambrose,

> The Americans in Tokyo, like those in Washington, had a good general idea of what was coming and had their countermeasures prepared. Intelligence reports on North Korean intentions had been specific enough to allow the State Department, days before the attack, to prepare a resolution to submit to the Security Council condemning North Korea for aggression. . . . Truman, too, was ready with his countermeasures. Within hours of the attack he ordered MacArthur to dispatch supplies to the South Koreans, then ordered the U.S. Seventh Fleet to sail between China and Formosa to prevent an invasion.

Stone has further suggested that the South Korean forces, far from being defensive in attitude or deployment, might have launched the initial thrust, which was repulsed and then followed up by the irrepressible soldiers from the North.[1]

Joyce and Gabriel Kolko have recently argued that Rhee was the catalyst of war, with the enthusiastic support of MacArthur, who believed Asia to be America's "great frontier" against Communism and himself the man of destiny who would rule and shape that frontier. According to the Kolkos, Rhee's very weakness at home—a weakness compounded of domestic turmoil against his American-imposed rule which led to frequent riots, plus a weak but rapidly strengthening army, plus continued economic chaos— led him at once to seek firm military support from MacArthur and equally firm political support from junketing American public figures such as John Foster Dulles. When the North Koreans launched their attack in response to increasingly strident calls from the South for unification by any means, and when the Republic of Korea forces found themselves overwhelmed, Rhee—and possibly MacArthur—was secretly pleased because now American military might would have to be projected onto the peninsula, sanctifying Rhee's rule and opening the possibility that it could be used as an instrument to attain Rhee's most cherished goal, forcible unification of the two Koreas under his aegis.[2]

The last days of the Korean peace and the early hours of the Korean War were sufficiently disturbed and confusing as to lend superficial credence to any hypothesis; it is ever so when conflict is precipitated by surprise attack. We might care to remember that the aggressor always seeks to mask his violence in rectitude: Hitler told the world in 1939 that the Poles had attacked him first, and he tried to lend credence to the charge by dressing up German convicts in Polish uniforms and then shooting them down inside the borders of the Reich. The Kolkos' charge seems most readily refutable because of its own doubtful internal logic. From their own evidence, based solidly on available data, South Korea in the eighteen months after the establishment of the republic in August 1948 was in chaos. The econony was a shambles, the army, while numerically larger, perhaps, than has been previously acknowledged, was purely defensive in nature as it contained neither armored forces nor tactical aircraft, those basic weapons of modern war, as the Kolkos later admit in a brief passage on the earliest phases of the conflict. Moreover, the ROK army had been constantly harassed and distracted during its brief period of training by the need to quell domestic disturbances, root out guerrilla bands infiltrated from the North, and defend the parallel against constant probes from the North which the Kolkos also admit and which ended only in April 1950—at just about the time it would be expected that a North Korean general staff bent on invasion would begin husbanding all resources. Possibly Rhee was foodhardy enough to believe that he could send an ill-trained and ill-equipped army northward, or could use it as a sacrificial pawn to draw American power to his side. Possibly he was able to manipulate MacArthur and Dulles and Omar Bradley and other Americans with whom he came in contact to the view that whatever he did or said, however provocative his actions, America must rescue him from the consequences of his own folly. After all, he had before him the example of Chiang. But, of course, that lesson cut both ways. Eventually, Washington had abandoned the Kuomintang in the face of insupportable demands for aid. Ultimately the Kolkos' argument, and that of Stone and Ambrose as well, fall before a number of basic facts. First, MacArthur himself as early as March 1949 had defined South Korea as being beyond the bounds of direct American military responsibility, and Acheson had done no more than ratify this definition the following January.[3] Second, there can be little serious question that the Korean War was begun by the forces of the North attacking suddenly along a very broad front with both air and armored forces, as all three critics admit. Third, there is also little question from available evidence that Rhee *had* been successful in convincing American military and political leaders that while his country was outside the pale of U.S. military responsibility, he could successfully ward off an attack from the North without outside aid. This fact seems scarcely credible now, but there is strong evidence from a variety of sources that it was widely accepted in both Washington and Tokyo at the time. Perhaps this was so because of a fourth fact which was, simply, that an attack on South Korea from the North was not really expected in 1949 or 1950.

There seems little doubt that the Korean War was precipitated by a brutal act of aggression from the North. This does not mean that Seoul or Tokyo or Washington were as dumbfounded by the invasion as David Rees has argued, Douglas MacArthur has asserted, and Dean Acheson has implied.[4] According to the official army history of the war, a "United States intelligence agency," presumably the CIA, had information as early as June 19 "pointing to North Korean preparation for an offensive," but it was not used as an official estimate of the situation. "The American officers did not think an attack was imminent. If one did come, they expected the South Koreans to repel it."[5] These two sentences seem to summarize cogently the attitudes in both Washington and the Far East. To be sure, there were indications all over the Far East during the spring and summer of 1950 that the forces of some Communist country might be preparing an offensive. China could thrust south into Indochina; the North Koreans could cross the parallel. Perhaps the Soviets might risk World War III with a massive blow against Japan. But what seemed most likely at the time was an assault by the Communist Chinese across the Formosa Strait to obliterate Chiang once and for all.[6]

The possibility of an invasion of South Korea by North Korea seems to have been widely discounted. In mid-July of 1949 Major General W. E. Todd, then director of the Joint Intelligence Group, Joint Chiefs of Staff, told a Senate committee that "action on the part of the North Korean People's Army we think would be improbable, because the forces numerically of North and South Korea are almost equal." The North Koreans were at that stage better armed, Todd admitted, but the American military advisory group that had been left behind in the South once the occupation forces had been withdrawn "will improve the efficiency of the South Korean Army, and they [the South Koreans] do have good equipment." Later in his testimony Todd added: "We feel that if the Soviets attach any priority to areas in which they would like to move by means of armed aggression, Korea would be at the bottom in that list of priorities." Then followed this exchange:

Senator [Henry Cabot] Lodge. Do you think, General, that all of the other places where Soviet aggression might take place would be more attractive to them and the prizes to be gained more lucrative?

General Todd. I think so. They would improve their strategic position very little in the Far East by occupying South Korea.

Senator Lodge. It doesn't help them? It is just a projection and doesn't help them in establishing their ascendancy in China?

General Todd. No, sir.[7]

Acheson's subsequent "exclusion" of South Korea as an area of vital strategic interest to the United States in his famous January 1950 National Press Club speech deserves to be interpreted from this perspective.

There was thus a haunting similarity to the days just before Pearl Harbor, a connection which some Western leaders in 1950 instantly perceived once the North Koreans launched their attack.[8] Once again there was the dread of an attack; once again there was profound concern over where it might come, matched only by an equally profound ignorance of the potential enemy's true intentions. As Roberta Wohlstetter has convincingly demonstrated, there was ample warning of the impending Pearl Harbor attack available to Washington officialdom in November and December 1941.[9] In the late spring of 1950, "A senior American officer in KMAG [Korean Military Advisory Group], Colonel John E. Baird, also sounded a lonely warning. He informed our newly appointed ambassador to Korea, John Muccio, that the type and quality of material available to the ROK army was not sufficient to maintain existing borders. He reported that the outnumbered ROKs were thoroughly outgunned by the NKPA [North Korean People's Army]. . . . And he urged that the ROKs be given some means of defense against air attack, recommending that we supply them with F-51 aircraft. His urging went unheeded."[10] But as Wohlstetter has also shown, the rich evidence of Japanese intentions in 1941 was buried in a mass of what proved to be irrelevant and incorrect information. The warning was surrounded by an enormous amount of "static," and only *after* the attack could investigators, knowing exactly what to look for, conclude that the evidence of Japanese intentions had been there all along. The pattern seems to have been the same nine years later in Korea. Washington has always been a one-crisis town, its planners riveting their gaze on one potential danger area. In 1941 it appeared that Japan would enter World War II by attacking south toward Malaya and the Philippines. In 1950 it appeared that the next great imbalance in the global status quo would come in the Formosa Strait, where Mao would seek to cap his incredible mainland victory with a massive invasion of Chiang's island bastion.

So there was little real thought during the spring of 1950 of an imminent attack by the North Korean People's Army. There was also a widespread feeling—and this was a crucial factor in official American thinking—that if such an attack should materialize, the South Koreans could handle it alone. In light of what transpired in June and July 1950 such an assessment quickly took on the dimensions of high folly, but it was rather widely accepted in Tokyo and Washington before the invasion. "Uncertainty about the nature and weight of the attack and optimism about the ability of the South Korean Army to repel it characterized the reactions" of many officials in Korea to the first reports of fighting along the parallel.[11] John

Foster Dulles, then in Japan as Acheson's consultant on the possibility of negotiating a Japanese peace treaty, wired the State Department on the morning of June 25 that it was "possible that the South Koreans may themselves contain and repulse the attack and, if so, this is the best way."[12] Dulles based his cautious optimism on MacArthur's first reaction that the North Korean attack was nothing more than a reconnaissance in force, which "I can handle with one arm tied behind my back."[13] Indeed, John Allison, who was serving under Dulles at the time, has recalled that not until the morning of June 27, forty-eight hours after the invasion had begun, had the news from the peninsula become so worrisome as to shatter MacArthur's *insouciance.*[14] By this time, too, Washington and "the nations of the Western world" had become "intensely" anxious over the survival of Rhee's Korean republic. Rhee himself had cried that the initial air and naval aid extended by the United States on the twenty-fifth had been " 'too little and too late.' " The UN Security Council, in the fortuitous absence of the Russians, had issued its first resolution calling on North Korea to withdraw, but obviously it had little effect.[15] On June 29 MacArthur flew to the battlefront for a personal evaluation and witnessed the rout of the South Koreans below the Han. Seoul was already gone. The entire peninsula seemed defenseless. The moment for decision was at hand. MacArthur recommended the commitment of American troops, and half a dozen UN members, including Britain, the Netherlands, and three of the Commonwealth countries, backed their pledge of support for the UN resolution against North Korea with promises of troop commitments of their own.[16]

There can be little doubt as to who began the Korean War, nor, in the context of that anxiety-ridden time could the Western response have been anything else than it was. It had not been the West which had put military pressure on Turkey and Iran in 1946 or on Berlin in 1948. To the Munich generation no other reaction but swift and firm retaliation against aggression in Korea could have been possible.[17] And yet one question does remain unanswered: Was the Soviet Union behind the North Korean thrust? It has long been an article of faith in the West that this was so. Charles Bohlen, for example, has labeled as "childish nonsense" any suggestion that North Korea acted independently in 1950. "How could an army, trained in every respect by the Soviet Union, with Soviet advisers at every level, and utterly dependent on Moscow for supplies, move without Soviet authorization?"[18] Available evidence remains inconclusive, and the *Pueblo* incident, to take but one example among many, ought to stimulate some rethinking as to the extent to which great powers can control or restrain those smaller states that supposedly are so tightly within their orbit. The North Korean People's Army in 1950 was well trained and well equipped—with Soviet weapons and advisers, it is true—and the North Korean generals must surely have been receptive to the idea that they could sweep down the peninsula so swiftly that no adequate response could be mounted by the Americans or the Western world at large. Nonetheless, the most detailed account to date of the Communist movement in Korea does strongly assert Soviet instigation. After a year of "ominous" speeches from North Korea advocating and demanding unification of the peninsula, Stalin ordered the attacks in early 1950 and so informed Mao and the Chinese. Mao gave his assent, and, as is well documented, some forty thousand veteran North Korean soldiers returned home from Manchuria in April, accompanied by a flood of materiel including Yak fighter planes and the fearsome T-34 tanks. Actual planning for the strike was hurriedly undertaken and completed between June 10 and June 25 and was restricted to those "at the uppermost rungs" of the North Korean hierarchy.[19]

Those who argue that the U.S. government was not averse to having a war thrust upon it in mid-1950 might recall how close Truman and MacArthur came to total disaster that June and July. America had, save for its nuclear bomber fleet, almost completely demobilized since 1945, and "The Defense Department did not even have a contingency plan for American intervention in Korea in the event of a Communist invasion." A lone, undermanned aircraft carrier steamed the broad western Pacific. In Japan MacArthur could initially dispatch only two regimental combat teams to the embattled peninsula. The Far Eastern air force was small and wholly oriented toward tactical bombing. These puny units almost suffered an American Dunkirk at Pusan before the situation could be stabilized.[20] The first American forces to arrive drove up to meet the oncoming North Koreans only to find themselves so outmanned and outgunned that their flanks were easily turned, the North Korean People's Army simply flowing around them, and they were forced to withdraw and retreat time after time. Not until mid-July, with the frantic rush of arms and some reinforcements from elsewhere in the world, were MacArthur and his generals able to stabilize a very thinly held ROK-American line along the Naktong River but fifty miles above Korea's southernmost tip.

And while this thin line repelled the North Korean thrusts with incredible tenacity the United States began a feverish mobilization. Less than five years after the end of the most terrible of world wars the veterans of that holocaust were recalled to service from all over the United States; there was no time to wait while their younger brothers and sons trained as raw recruits. In frequent anger and despair the older men, who had spent their youth fighting across North Africa or Europe or the Pacific, left the comfortable houses and promising jobs, the pleasant summer towns or hot cities, of home and returned to soldiering. They collected in suddenly bustling camps with familiar names—Dix, Pendleton, Lewis—then traveled through well-remembered portals to war—Seattle, San Diego, San Francisco. Meanwhile the armament and aircraft factories cranked up once more, while the mothballs began coming off warships in navy yards from Boston to San Pedro and government bureaucrats began planning for a comparatively modest system of domestic controls. Across the Pacific, however, an impatient MacArthur refused to wait for his country's contributions. He was determined to launch a bold counterstroke with slender available resources. The initial phase of the war was nearing its end.

It closed with the remarkable success of the Inchon landing on September 15. Inchon was an incredible—many would say foolhardy—gamble. The attractions of landing there were many. Just twenty-five miles east of this port town, where Americans had first come ashore in 1945, lay Seoul, where many of the peninsula's main roads and rail lines converged. Thus a force landing at Inchon would have to fight inland only a very short distance to cut off North Korean supply lines to the Naktong battlefront in the South. Moreover, a successful landing over a hundred miles to the enemy's rear, particularly if it could be synchronized, as it was, with an allied offensive north from the Naktong line, would catch the entire North Korean People's Army in an enormous vise, forcing it to either fight for freedom or splinter into hundreds of small, ineffective battle groups seeking retreat along the hills and ridge lines. Swayed by the enormous possibilities of the situation, MacArthur managed to scrape together a two-division assault force even while feeding reinforcements piecemeal into the Naktong lines.

But Inchon also posed terrible risks, risks which the navy and MacArthur's superiors in Washington considered for a time to be prohibitive. First there were the extreme Yellow Sea tides, ranging as much as thirty feet, which might literally strand any invasion fleet in the mud if the assault timetable were thrown off to any extent by determined enemy resistance. And such resistance, it was argued, could be almost guaranteed since the landings would be made in the middle of a built-up supply area. Then, too, there were high sea walls girdling much of the port, which the assault forces would have to scale in the face of major enemy resistance. And, finally, MacArthur was deliberately choosing to commit the last of his available reserves to the operation at a time when no more were to be forthcoming from the United States for some weeks. "Four National Guard divisions had been federalized on September 1, but none of these was yet ready for combat duty; and, while the draft and call-ups of members of the Organized Reserve Corps were substantially increasing the size of the Army, they offered MacArthur no prospect of immediate reinforcement."[21] But MacArthur was determined to have his way. Late in August, while the Naktong line held tenuously, two members of the Joint Chiefs of Staff, General Collins and Admiral Sherman, were dispatched to Tokyo to try to make MacArthur see reason. Instead he won them over with a passionate defense of his plan. The prestige of the entire Western world hung in the balance, he told his mesmerized listeners. " 'I can almost hear the ticking of the second hand of destiny,' " he intoned. " 'We must act now or we will die.' " Inchon would succeed. One hundred thousand lives would be saved. " 'We shall land at Inchon and I shall crush them, . . .' he ended, his voice sinking to a whisper." " 'I wish,' " Sherman sighed after some later, futile expostulation, " 'I had that man's confidence.' "[22]

The sources of MacArthur's arrogance lay in a political and even military primitivism that approached outright warmongering. If Stone, Ambrose, and the Kolkos have been unable to adduce anything beyond speculation about the responsibility of Seoul or Tokyo—to say nothing of Washington—for the outbreak of the Korean War, it is nevertheless an incontestable fact that MacArthur had been spoiling for a fight with the *Chinese* Communists since at least the late summer of 1949. The general at once encouraged—and was himself encouraged by—those elements in and out of the U.S. Congress who devoutly hoped to see Chiang Kai-shek and his exhausted regime returned to power on the mainland. In a briefing of the Huber congressional committee that was visiting Tokyo, MacArthur said on September 5, 1949: "Relatively little effort will be required now to turn the tide in China but the longer we wait we will find difficulties mounting in geometric rather than arithmetic proportions. The communist forces are grossly overrated. Evidence of their weakness are slowness of their advances, the administrative and logistic difficulties which are inherent in their situation." Chiang was surrounded by corrupt officials, MacArthur admitted, and furthermore the Generalissimo, while highly intelligent, knew nothing of war. "The Generalissimo has, however, a driving determination and strength of character which makes him a natural leader.'' If four things could be done, MacArthur continued, the tide could be turned against communism in China even at this late date. They were:

a. Make a ringing declaration that the United States will support any and every one who is opposed to communism.

b. Place 500 fighter planes in the hands of some ''war horse'' similar to General Chennault.

c. Give volunteers the right to join such a fighting force without penalty.

d. Assign surplus ships to the Chinese Navy sufficient to blockade and destroy China coastal cities.

In closing MacArthur reiterated his firm belief that there could be no Korean war. ''South Korea is in no danger of being overrun by North Korea,'' he told his congressional listeners. ''The Kremlin has South Korea outflanked and knows that eventually it must go the way the continent of Asia goes. As long as South Korea is not a threat to North Korea no action will be taken by the Kremlin to absorb it as there would be nothing to gain by taking it over.'' Then MacArthur added a stunning observation: ''However, if South Korea tries to take over North Korea retaliatory measures could certainly be expected. If the United States by default fails to support South Korea the consequences will be most devastating to United States interests.''[23]

Was MacArthur here implying what the Kolkos have subsequently asserted, namely the distinct possibility of a South Korean strike northward tacitly supported and encouraged by the U.S. government, or at least that portion of it domiciled in Tokyo? The implication cannot be dismissed. However, the weight of available evidence must be kept in mind. That evidence indicates almost beyond question the determination of the North Koreans to unify the peninsula by a quick act of power and the general astonishment in Seoul, Tokyo, and Washington in June 1950 that the North had chosen to act as it did. Moreover, both South Korea and the United States possessed little conventional military power in 1949 and early 1950, and thus the chances of a successful push to the Yalu by Syngman Rhee were slim at the very best, given the widely known fact of North Korean military power. Finally, the thrust of MacArthur's September 1949 briefing to the Huber committee was clearly that there would be no Korean war, and, indeed, given the realities of the current American military posture in the Far East, no China war either. The talk of ''ringing declarations'' against communism and the placing of five hundred war planes in the hands of some old "war horse" was, given the existing military reality, just talk and no more. America did not possess five hundred planes—nor even a hundred planes—to put in the hands of any "war horse," and both MacArthur and his congressional listeners knew it. Neither MacArthur nor his country were in a position to wage another Asian war in 1949 or early 1950. What his remarks did reflect was a simple, unsophisticated abhorrence of Asian communism in general and Chinese communism in particular.

But, of course, once a war did come, once conflict was thrust upon America and its Korean client, all of the general's fiery hatred of and contempt for Asian communism would burst forth to dictate policy and strategy. Once the *other* side had struck, wish became fulfillment, and unlimited retaliation in a righteous cause was not only proper but mandatory. "The ticking of the second hand of destiny" demanded it. So MacArthur was willing to gamble all at Inchon—and beyond. And this time he would carry his government and, indeed, almost the entire United Nations with him.

Inchon did succeed, of course, beyond the wildest expectations of anyone in Washington or the Western world at large. The enemy was caught napping; resistance was light. Within a few days Seoul had been recaptured, the Naktong offensive had begun, the North Korean army was completely and utterly routed. Hubris had been rewarded. It was to be the last time.

Now the question became whether to end the war in limited triumph, which had, after all, been the mandate voted by the United Nations on June 25, or to try to win it all as had been implied in a subsequent resolution by the General Assembly on June 27—to capture the entire peninsula for the United Nations and the Western world. In their decision to go north in October 1950 the United States and the United Nations did more than choose to cross a parallel; they crossed a rubicon.

As early as July Kennan and Bohlen, then the State Department's top resident Soviet experts, had begun receiving strong indications that American authorities and especially right-wing opinion in the Republican party might not countenance a halt at the thirty-eighth parallel and restoration of the status quo in Korea. Kennan was concerned, Bohlen slightly appalled. When rumors circulated during the second week in the month that the Chinese had accepted an Indian proposal to terminate the Korean conflict on the basis of status quo ante, "our government . . . was quite unwilling to entertain this suggestion, considering that this would leave South Korea defenseless in the face of the possibility of a renewed North Korean attack."[24] But there were other reasons as well. No less a figure than Dean Acheson was turning increasingly hawkish as a result of righteous indignation over the North Korean attack, and the possibility, however remote at this stage, of turning the tide against an aggressive Communist state was irresistibly attractive. "While fundamentally cautious and calculating in his diplomacy toward the Communists, it was not in Acheson's nature to pass up an opportunity to enhance the strength and stability of the non-Communist world." Nor did Acheson stand alone within the executive branch of government. The Joint Chiefs of Staff and the Secretary of Defense contemplated extending the war into North Korea over a week before MacArthur launched his bold gamble at Inchon, and their recommendations were swiftly forwarded to the National Security Council, which just as swiftly gave its approval.[25] Both Kennan and Bohlen spoke at length of their concern that UN forces not drive so far up the peninsula as to get "into an area where mass could be used against us" by a properly provoked China or Russia. "We warned that Communist countries would react strongly if hostile forces approached their borders," Bohlen recalled. "We had both China and the Soviet Union in mind, of course. Basic to our thinking was our conviction that the main objective of the leaders of Communist countries is preservation of the system. American troops on the Chinese border at the Yalu River, only a short distance from Vladivostok, would certainly be viewed as a threat. It was folly, Kennan and I argued, to take the chance of prodding China and/or the Soviet Union into a war."[26]

Sound advice. But the triumph at Inchon after such initial apprehension over its feasibility induced a fatal overconfidence in Washington *and* among the Western members of the United Nations. It was at this moment, apparently, that Acheson, if not Truman, came to repose that fatally blind trust in MacArthur's military judgment that was to lead to such tragedy along the Chongchon River three months later.[27] Less than three weeks after the brilliant storming of the sea walls, MacArthur's armies stood poised along the thirty-eighth parallel. But at this point fortune began to abandon the general and his troops. For the North Korean army had not been obliterated. It had been defeated, it had been routed, but it had not surrendered or disappeared. MacArthur had hoped to obtain unconditional victory south of the parallel and had not. Four days before the Americans went ashore at Inchon Truman had initialed a National Security Council paper, which directed MacArthur to conduct military operations either to force the North Koreans behind the parallel or to destroy their armies south of it. If there was no indication of an entry by Soviet and/or Chinese forces, then MacArthur "was to extend his operations north of the parallel and to make plans for the occupation of North Korea. . . ." This directive reached MacArthur on D-Day at Inchon, and a week later it was clear that despite the brilliant coup a significant proportion of the North Korean army would reach haven north of the parallel. One senator (William Knowland) then bespoke the consensus of Washington and the opinion of much of the country when he stated that to leave this force intact would be tantamount to appeasement. At a time when Senator McCarthy was riding high no official could afford to ignore completely such a warning. "The border, at the parallel, had proved its insufficiency as a defense line. To break off when it was reached was to invite a new attack across it, when and as the North Koreans chose. Short of pursuing and destroying their field forces, there seemed no effective way to meet that threat. . . . Within a week of Inchon all Truman's advisers were agreed upon pursuit if nothing else turned up to simplify (or complicate) the problem militarily." The UN partners needed little urging. After nearly five years of a cold war which seemed defined by Communist expansion and probes and with a devout sense of shame for the earlier appeasements of Hitler, the sudden sense of victory and purpose was overpowering.[28] So on October 7, 1950, the General Assembly of the United Nations, "recalling that the essential objective was the establishment of a unified independent and democratic Korea," recommended that all appropriate steps be taken to assure stability throughout the peninsula. What had been impossible to achieve through diplomacy and negotiation in 1946-1948 would now be attempted by force of arms.[29]

But already the dreaded prospect of possible Chinese intervention began to loom on the Korean horizon. Peking, in fact, had already taken profound offense at an American action which at the time had seemed an almost casual afterthought. When Truman on June 27 had ordered the navy and air force to give all-out support to Syngman Rhee's beleaguered forces, he had also ordered Seventh Fleet units into the Formosa Strait for the express purpose of preventing both Peking and Taiwan from assuming hostilities then or in the future.[30] From Washington's perspective this was a wise precautionary move to insure that the burgeoning war in Korea did not spread to engulf China and Formosa as well. But the Chinese Communists interpreted it far differently. Chou told Edgar Snow in 1960, "After war broke out in Korea in June, 1950, Truman changed the [American] policy [of disengagement from Chinese affairs] and adopted a policy of aggression toward China. While sending troops to Korea the United States at the same time dispatched the Seventh Fleet to the Taiwan Straits and exercised military control over Taiwan. *Beginning from that time the United States started new aggression against China.*"[31]

The first overt sign that Peking might shift from its formerly quiescent posture did not come until August 20. The change seems to have been in response to three developments. First, Soviet delegate Jacob Malik had returned to the UN Security Council on August 1 to take his normal turn as president and had sought to end what he called the "civil war" between Seoul and Pyongyang. American delegate Warren Austin, with the support of the Western powers, brushed this initiative aside. "This is not a battle for any fragment of the population; it is for the right of the Korean people to choose their own future," Austin cried, thereby reflecting the growing mood in Washington that a thrust north of the thirty-eighth parallel was politically as well as militarily mandatory. Second, it was clear by mid-August that the North Koreans had lost their desperate bid to sweep over the South before effective UN reinforcements could appear. The Naktong line was holding, and it was quite obvious from the Western press that thousands more UN soldiers were on their way to the peninsula. Austin's remarks could only be interpreted by prudent men in Peking as threatening a UN sweep right to the Yalu. And third, the Western press in July and August had reported increasingly bellicose remarks attributed to both Washington and Tokyo officialdom regarding American and/or UN intentions, not only toward Korea, but also toward renewed support for Chiang Kai-shek. It was at this time that the first serious suggestions that Chiang might be "unleashed" against the mainland began to appear in American newspapers and news magazines. It was obviously time for a warning. On the twentieth, therefore, Chou En-lai cabled UN headquarters at Lake Success endorsing Malik's peace initiative and demanding representation for Peking at any and all discussions of Korea's future.[32]

But, of course, nothing came of Peking's demand except the implicit UN answer at Inchon three weeks later. Now Peking became seriously alarmed. How far did UN intentions run? A week after Inchon Peking officially admitted to an earlier charge by MacArthur that it had given substantial military assistance to Pyongyang before the June invasion by the transfer of ethnic Korean troops to the North Korean army. Three days later, on September 25, Chinese officials warned Indian Ambassador

Panikkar that the People's Republic would not "sit back with folded hands and let the Americans come to the border." On the thirtieth Chou En-lai publicly reiterated this warning.[33] Such somber signals induced a faint and temporary sense of caution in the Western camp. On September 27 MacArthur was issued new instructions. Destruction of the North Korean army remained the major goal, and military operations north of the thirty-eighth parallel were now specifically authorized, provided that "at the time of such operation there had been no entry into North Korea by major Soviet or Chinese Communist forces, no announcement of an intended entry, and no threat by Russian or Chinese Communists to counter our operations militarily in North Korea." And under no circumstances should any allied forces cross into Manchuria or the Soviet borders of Korea. Then came a curious postscript. "In the event of the open or covert employment of major Chinese Communist units south of the 38th parallel, you should continue the action as long as action by your forces offers a reasonable chance of successful resistance."[34] Were Truman and the Joint Chiefs aware of how fearsomely they had provoked Peking? The answer is unclear. But the answer to another question which naturally arises is not: Why, with victory in their grasp, did the United States and United Nations move north anyway? The North Koreans had been frightfully drubbed, and as Richard Neustadt has remarked, at no time had the forceful unification of the peninsula "been Truman's dearest objective" or even a major objective at all. Once the Chinese did intervene, both Washington and the UN dropped this objective quickly and silently. Why, then, the act of hubris?

Years later Neustadt asked Truman "if he had not grown concerned while UN troops, dividing as they went, moved toward their fatal 'end-the-war' offensive" north of the parallel. "What we should have done," Truman replied, "is stop at the neck of Korea [presumably on a line from Pyongyang to Wonsan, some 150 to 200 miles south of the Yalu]. . . . That's what the British wanted. . . . We knew the Chinese had close to a million men on the border and all that . . . but (MacArthur) was commander in the field. You pick your man, you've got to back him up. That's the only way a military organization can work. I got the best advice I could and the man on the spot said this was the thing to do. . . . So I agreed. That was my decision—no matter what hindsight shows."[35] MacArthur said that the war could only be won by a sweep to the Yalu. To millions of Americans he was the military hero par excellence, defender of Bataan and architect of victory in the Pacific, who apparently, to use one of his own phrases in another context, had "lost none of his old punch," as Inchon had just revealed. Conversely, the President's hold on public opinion was always questionable at best; the image of a cocky, but often fumbling and incompetent bantam was never far from popular consciousness. When the attitude of the allies in and out of the UN was also taken into consideration, there seemed little to argue about. The offensive would go on.

The first American troops crossed the parallel on the same day that the UN unification resolution was passed. Twelve days later Pyongyang fell to the advancing UN columns. But now the brute facts of modern war and Korean geography began to work a baleful influence on the UN forces. The UN army—which at this early stage of the war was comprised almost exclusively of American and South Korean units—was comparatively small, probably no more than 250,000 to 300,000 men, a little less than half of whom were American. Lack of numbers had been compensated by tremendous mobility and devastating fire power. But precisely because the army was small and mechanized, it could not move along the interior hill lines, but was forced to use the main valley roads that generally ran along both coasts. Thus after leaving the Pyongyang-Wonsan area, the UN forces divided, the Eighth Army driving toward the Yalu along the west coast, the Tenth Corps, comprised of both army and marine units, driving up the east coast from Wonsan through Hungnam toward the Changjin Reservoir and the Yalu line beyond. And as the UN forces moved north into the heavily mountainous areas that comprised the roof of Korea, two momentous meetings took place, one in mid-Pacific, and, if Khrushchev is to be believed, one at the Caucasian seaside resort town of Sochi.

The Truman-MacArthur meeting at Wake Island on October 15 and the entire Truman-MacArthur controversy has been the subject of considerable study and conjecture.[36] But from the perspective of a quarter of a century the controversy seems to have lost much of its force. MacArthur's ideas now seem so sadly unsophisticated, his insubordination so marked, as to foreclose the need for another extended discussion of his contest with the President. But the Wake Island meeting was a critical turning point in the war, because Truman did accept MacArthur's renewed assurances of early triumph. The two men probably got along as badly as has been often stated. According to a recently published account the President and the general were so concerned with their respective dignities that they circled the island while each tried to get the other to land first. Then, after MacArthur had been forced to make the initial arrival, he sulked in a tent near the airstrip for some time before deigning to come out to greet his infuriated Commander-in-Chief, who sat fuming in the plane.[37] Possibly, as Cabell Phillips suggests, Truman "took MacArthur to the woodshed" over his insolence, but once the discussions got down to substantive matters; the President could only have been appeased. In a conference lasting only an hour and thirty-six minutes MacArthur said the fighting should be substantially over by Thanksgiving and the Eighth Army back in Japan by Christmas. There seemed "very little prospect" of a Chinese or Soviet intervention. To be sure, intelligence reported large Chinese formations lurking near the Yalu, but if they should try to cross the river, allied air dominance would blast their bridges behind them, cutting off their supply routes and forcing them to scavenge off a devastated country. Ultimately "there would be the greatest slaughter" of such military innocents. Apparently the idea that the Chinese might cross at night and then hide themselves with perfect camouflage in the Korean mountains by day until time to strike the oncoming UN columns never entered anyone's mind, military or civilian.[38] With these assurances ringing in his ears, Truman flew back to San Francisco and Washington, while MacArthur returned to Tokyo to prosecute the final, victorious stage of the war.

At roughly the same time a far more obscure meeting was taking place halfway around the world. Chou, apparently at Mao's instigation, visited Stalin at Sochi to ask if Chinese troops might now be moved into North Korea. At first the two men agreed such a move would be folly, but Mao seems to have pressed for intervention, and after reconsideration Stalin and Chou "agreed that China should give active support to North Korea. Chinese troops were already stationed along the border. Stalin and Chou believed these troops could manage the situation completely. They would beat back the American and South Korean troops and save the situation from disaster." Soon after China intervened General P'eng Te-huai, according to Khrushchev, was boasting to Mao that the UN forces would not only be defeated but obliterated by a series of mass flanking movements.[39] In Korea everyone figured to come up winners.

And it seemed in the gloomy days of December 1950 and the first months of 1951 that the Chinese might indeed pull off a stunning coup. Their first units crossed the Yalu on October 16, made fleeting but bloody contact with advancing UN forces, then withdrew—a plain warning to come no further. Thereafter it seems that the Chinese high command extended its warning by placing "volunteers" with the remnants of the North Korean army and allowing their capture and interrogation by increasingly concerned UN intelligence officers. By mid-November, with the Eighth Army taking positions along the Chongchon River, only forty to fifty miles below the Yalu, and with the Tenth Corps on the east coast moving up on Changjin Reservoir, senior officials in Korea were most worried about what lay ahead of them. What they could not know was that the Chinese were not so much ahead of them as beside them, above them, lurking in the cold mountains and hills on the flanks of the valley-bound UN units.[40] A few UN troops did reach the Yalu during the third week in November, and one even brought back a bottle of the river's water for Syngman Rhee. But these were probes in front of the main advance, and on their way back to the Chongchon line some of the lonely patrols were set upon and mauled by a mysterious enemy. By Thanksgiving 1950 everything pointed to disaster for UN forces in Korea. Nonetheless that was the day chosen for the final advance from the Chongchon to the Yalu; that was also the day chosen by the Chinese for their opening offensive, and the Chinese struck first.

The rest is well known. For a time ignorant armies clashed by day and night in the hills and valleys of upper Korea. In the east the snow had already come; in the west it soon fell heavily, and after standing as long as they could, the outflanked and outmanned UN forces began that most melancholy of military maneuvers, retreat in winter. For a time it seemed that retreat would become rout. What were they doing here, anyway, many American troops asked? "Bug out, bug right out, I say," one man cried, and soon the retreat became known as the "Big Bug Out." Constantly harassed by Chinese attacks from above, increasingly low on supplies, usually caught on narrow mountain or valley roads where maneuver was difficult, the Eighth Army and Tenth Corps fought their way hour by hour, day by day, week by week, out of the awful trap and back down across the parallel into South Korea. Possibly it was only the appearance of Matthew Ridgway that at last rallied the shaken and battered UN forces, that and the fact that by February the Chinese had outrun their supply lines and had to break off their advance. This gave the UN forces time to regroup and retrench in a jagged line roughly thirty to fifty miles south of the parallel. The Chinese resumed the offensive in the spring, but this time well-entrenched and prepared UN forces beat them back.

So in the spring of 1951 the war settled into a ruthless stalemate, a brutal slugging match between allied firepower and Chinese mass along a reasonably fixed line. In a way it was World War I all over again. For the next two years in summer heat and winter snows a Punchbowl or a Heartbreak Ridge or a Pork Chop Hill would be taken or held or captured and lost and recaptured again; a line would be "straightened out" from time to time. At odd intervals the Chinese would mount nocturnal human wave assaults, their bugles and star shells adding a surrealist terror to the inevitable slaughter by American artillery and small arms fire on the hill tops, and in the mornings there were the rows of crumpled corpses, sneakered feet sticking out of quilt-clad bodies, or perhaps there was nothing there at all if the Communists had managed to drag away their dead. For two long years it went on without letup while the truce makers met in futile ritual in the tents of Kaesong and Panmunjom. The air force jets leaped off their runways south of the Han or in Japan to go hunting at supersonic speed for the silver enemy in the high blue skies of Mig Alley thirty thousand feet above the ancient Chongchon battlefield. The great, grey, often storm-beaten line of warships prowled offshore, sending forth an occasional vessel and a constant swarm of planes to blast away at the supply and transportation lines of a patiently rebuilding foe until after a time the pilots and sailors, weary of dodging death day after day, came to wonder at the meaning and purpose of an essentially mad existence. Each American, if he lived, only stayed for a year at most; each only flew or shot or fired or froze or sweltered or feared or grew bored for twelve months before returning to the increasingly affluent and uncaring towns and friends of home. But that was long enough.

And in the interim was respite. South Korea and large areas of Japan were turned into vast oriental rest camps for physically and emotionally depleted occidentals. It was a casual imperialism. In fact it was rather reminiscent of that British life style in the Southeast Asia Command that had so infuriated idealistic young Americans a decade before. The groundwork had been laid by the fathers and brothers who had preceded the young men of Korea to Asia. Scattered throughout the accounts by Lauterbach and Isaacs of the American presence in early postwar China, India, and Korea are countless tales of the contempt with which many GIs viewed the oriental in the wake of World War II. The natives were dismissed as "slopeys" or "chinks" or "gooks" or even, on occasion, "niggers." It is hardly surprising that in the midst of yet another war their successors would carry on in the same fashion. Nor is it surprising that such behavior would in turn earn the scorn and contempt of those who were so callously exploited and corrupted.

One of the many wartime boom towns which dotted the peninsula and the islands a quarter century ago was Sasebo, a major staging area and port of embarkation on the west coast of Kyushu across the Korean Straits from Pusan and only a few miles from Nagasaki. The city squatted on a hill at the end of a long bay whose terraced arms and deep water provided ample shelter for the entire Seventh Fleet. On either end of the town sat the shacks and shops of the Japanese, but the center belonged to the Americans. Above the port area loomed a luxurious three-story enlisted men's club, which commanded a wide sweep of blue-watered, green-hilled bay. I don't know where the officers went. Stretching away down the hill to the left was Black Market Alley, where thousands of soldiers and sailors came to live better than they ever had before or, for some, ever would again. Everything was cheap in Black Market Alley, the steaks and the bourbon and the vodka and the women—especially the women. If you were there long enough, you could rent a room or two behind one of the shops or bars and a girl to go with it. For half a month's pay it was possible to enjoy all the comforts of home, wife, and mother with none of the inconveniences and entangling alliances—unless, of course, you counted those many young women who believed with touching sincerity in the facile promises of their men that soon they would be taken to America. The authorities were accommodating too. They practiced in loco parentis with impressive fidelity, and every Thursday morning you could glimpse a large portion of Sasebo's female population patiently trudging up the muddy hill to the dispensary. And when you had to work, there were always swarms of eager, docile Japanese dock hands—often dressed in the tattered remnants of their seedy wartime uniforms—ready to relieve you of the filthiest chores for a pittance. Cleaning up a ship's mess decks in exchange for the contents of the garbage can or for permission to search the urinals for cigarette butts became routine transactions. Such was one aspect of the war against communism.

Another in 1951 and 1952 was the abrupt expansion of American military and economic commitments to worldwide proportions. It was in these years that the U.S. government and people plunged into true globalism. Bohlen is right: "It was the Korean war and not World War II that made us a world military-political power."[41] Washington had assumed from the beginning that the North Korean attack was much more than an isolated incident, possibly quite separate from the European-oriented cold war between Russia and the West. The Korean conflict was perceived rather as part and parcel of a ruthless Communist drive for world domination that must be blunted at any cost. George Kennan found to his dismay that this assumption was frighteningly pervasive that first Korean summer.

Somehow or other, the North Korean attack came soon to appear to a great many people in Washington as merely the first move in some "grand design," as the phrase then went, on the part of the Soviet leaders to extend their power to other parts of the world by the use of force. The unexpectedness of this attack—the fact that we had had no forewarning of it—only stimulated the already existent preference of the military planners for drawing their conclusions only from the assessed *capabilities* of the adversary, dismissing his *intentions*, which could be safely assumed to be hostile. All this tended to heighten the militarization of thinking about the cold war generally, and to press us into attitudes where any discriminate estimate of Soviet intentions was unwelcome and unacceptable.[42]

But it would be a mistake to assume that only Washington felt this way. Edward R. Murrow, the single most influential journalist of that time and a man whose humanely liberal credentials were simply beyond dispute, said of the Korean intervention in July of 1950: "this new policy commits us to much more than the defense of the southern half of the Korean peninsula. We have commitments quite as binding, obligations quite as great, to Indo-China, Iran and Turkey, as we have to Korea. We have drawn a line, not across the peninsula but across the world. We have concluded that communism has passed beyond the use of subversion to conquer independent nations, and will now use armed invasion and war. And we for our part have demonstrated that we are prepared to calculate the risks and face the prospect of war, rather than let that happen."[43]

Murrow was certainly not speaking for himself alone; in the wake of the North Korean assault a number of organizations suddenly appeared, such as the Committee on the Present Danger, with which Murrow dallied for a time. Usually they were composed of business and professional people, and their declared purpose was to alert the public to the need for rearmament and global defense. The Committee on the Present Danger, for example, included on its rolls not only Murrow himself but also J. Robert Oppenheimer, Judge Samuel Rosenman, and as chairman, James Conant of Harvard, and its avowed goal was to assure the defense of Europe through the strengthening of NATO, though "it regarded the

Korean War as part of a world-wide communist threat."[44] There developed then in these years a rough consensus in the country as to the global threat of Communism and the necessity of meeting it with resolution. Long before John Kennedy put the idea into words Americans seemed willing to pay any price, bear any burden, support any friend, oppose any foe, to assure the triumph of freedom—as they defined it—in the world. No one stated the case for reactive globalism in the face of "Communist aggression" more forcefully or eloquently than Harry Truman. In his Special Message to Congress on the Mutual Security Program of May 24, 1951, he wrote:

> . . . the Soviet threat is total, it affects every form of human endeavor. Communist attack may come in the form of armies marching across frontiers; or it may come in the form of internal subversion. Economic warfare, psychological warfare, political infiltration, sabotage, the marching of armies—these are interchangeable aggressive weapons which the Soviet rulers use singly or together according to shifting calculations of greatest advantage. That is why the free world must concentrate on building not only military strength, but also economic, political and moral strength. . . . The communist aggression in Korea dispelled any lingering doubts that the Kremlin is willing to threaten the peace of the world.[45]

Bohlen is caustic: "The government concluded that godless Communism had conspired to take over the world and that the United States was the knight in shining armor who would fight it everywhere." Before Korea the only commitment of a political or military nature outside the Western Hemisphere had been the North Atlantic Treaty, which at that time was merely a defensive alliance. The bases in Germany and Japan were considered temporary and would be surrendered at the end of the occupation. As a "hangover" from World War II we had retained bases in the Philippines, "but there was no pledge on their use"; in England we had transit privileges, in Saudi Arabia an air base. That was all. "As a result of our overinterpretation of Communism's goal, we had by 1955 about 450 bases in thirty-six countries, and we were linked by political and military pacts with some twenty countries outside Latin America." NATO had been "militarized" as much at European behest as by our own inclination, and by that act we had become the military leader of Western Europe.[46] Bohlen might have added, though he did not, that during this period NATO itself was extended to the fringes of the Middle East, and the former German enemy was eventually enlisted in its ranks; that a futile effort was made to establish a Middle East command embracing the area and nations stretching from the eastern Mediterranean to India; that Japan was prodded into a modest defense program of its own, even as it became America's chief military base and workshop in Asia; that America's entire foreign aid program was transformed from one of economic and social reconstruction to outright military buildup through the aptly named Mutual Security Act of 1951; and, finally, that by mid-1951 American military aid to the French in Indochina amounted to half a billion dollars a year, "more than Indochina could absorb."[47]

In many ways Korea did for the cold war what Pearl Harbor had done for World War II. For the Second World War in its early stages was essentially a resumption of that intermittent civil conflict between Europe's people that had wracked the continent for centuries. Only with the eruption of Japanese militarism in 1941 did it truly attain global proportions. So with Korea did the cold war become a world conflict. And as the United States expanded its explicit and implicit commitments, the Soviets and Chinese obviously were tempted, given the built-in dynamics of the contest, to probe and push—or give the appearance of probing and pushing—in many "soft spots" around the planet. What all this led to, of course, was an instinctive American commitment to local non-Communist power structures all across the "free world" in the name and for the sake of "stability" and a corresponding suspicion of any social or political unrest as "Communist inspired." Thus the assumption of an impossible emotional and political burden of power.

Korea's importance as the catalyst to cold war on a global scale should not obscure the existence of a firm universalism in American diplomatic thought and strategy well before 1950. In his famous message to Congress in March 1947 on aid to Greece and Turkey President Truman had said, "At the present moment in world history nearly every nation must choose between alternative ways of life. . . . I believe that we must assist free peoples to work out their own destinies in their own ways."[48] Commenting on Truman's remarks some ten days later "after an inquiry" around Washington, the astute Arthur Krock correctly labeled the "Truman Doctrine" a "global anti-Communist policy which the President asked Congress to inaugurate with loans and grants to Greece and Turkey . . . ."[49] Four months later Kennan published in *Foreign Affairs* his celebrated "Mr. X" article on the sources of Soviet conduct, arguing "that the Soviet pressure against the free institutions of the Western world is something that can be contained by the adroit and vigilant application of counterforce at a series of constantly shifting geographical and political points, corresponding to the shifts and maneuvers of Soviet policy. . . ."[50] Walter Lippmann swiftly perceived the global dimensions of Kennan's containment policy. "How, for example, under the Constitution of the United States is Mr. X going to work out an arrangement by which the Department of State has the money and the military power always available in sufficient amounts to apply 'counter-force' at constantly shifting points all over the world? Is he," Lippmann continued, "going to ask Congress for a blank check on the Treasury and for a blank authorization to use the armed forces?" In light of Lyndon Johnson's later request for just such power in the Tonkin Gulf Resolution, Lippmann's response to his own question was striking indeed: "Not if the American constitutional system is to be maintained."[51]

Globalism was thus a clearly implied—if not firmly entrenched—ingredient of American foreign policy long before the North Korean army rushed across the thirty-eighth parallel in the summer of 1950. But the fact remains that "containment"—"anti-Communism"—remained largely confined within its initial European setting throughout the late forties. Moreover, containment was conceived almost wholly in economic terms as the Truman Doctrine, the Marshall Plan, and even the Berlin airlift clearly revealed. Even economic containment had its definite limits. Recurrent fears of a future depression and persistent congressional unwillingness to spend unlimited sums for either military defense, aid, or economic assistance and social reconstruction practically inhibited universalist-minded policy makers from applying their doctrines and programs on a global scale. Bohlen summarized their predicament and conclusions in a single sentence at the end of August 1947. "In the present state of economic emergency in Europe which has been highlighted by the continuing British crisis, it is inadvisable for this Government to continue to press for long-range objectives, however desirable in themselves, which do not immediately and directly bear upon the solution of Western European problems."[52] Throughout 1947 and into 1948 and 1949 America's primary interest, attention, and programs were riveted upon the defense of Western Europe against feared Soviet ideological and, possibly, military penetration.

The Korean War changed all this. Korea seemed to confirm and fulfill those dire predictions of eventual Soviet aggression against a "free world" which was believed to stretch from Seoul to Berlin, from Saigon to Lima, from Buenos Aires to Athens and Ankara. What had been projected and anticipated from 1947 to 1949 had at last apparently come true in 1950. An eager, basically unquestioning American government rushed to pick up the gauntlet that the Kremlin had apparently thrown before it. In practical terms containment prior to 1950 had meant drawing a line through the center of Europe. After 1950, as Ed Murrow had noted, America's government—and apparently a majority of its people as well—were willing to draw a line across the world.

But the United States that embarked on unabashed globalism after 1950 was an unhappy and frustrated land. Consensus on the existence of an international Communist threat did not extend to agreement on the best means of combatting it. Every foreign policy initiative after 1950 produced some form of partisan bitterness, induced a sense of frustration and betrayal in some American hearts, fostered a steadily developing sense of national division that eventually not even Dwight Eisenhower himself could evade or restrain. Korea itself proved a stalemate of such anxiety-producing proportions as to stimulate its own vibrant recriminations. Even as China crossed the Yalu, MacArthur touched off a long, acrimonious debate over the very nature of America's global mission. In war there was to be no substitute for victory, and he called both before and after his dismissal for the kind of military and political commitment in Korea that would rescue triumph out of the jaws of stalemate. Once the Chinese were held in the spring of 1951, there were renewed calls for a decisive offensive that would sweep them out of Korea once and for all, and if this meant bombing the Yalu bridges, denying Manchuria as a sanctuary, and possibly provoking a Soviet response, then, said many, let it be done. The so-called MacArthur hearings that summer fueled the fires of debate as proponents of both limited and unlimited war had their say. The triumph of the limited war advocates, at least to the end of the Truman administration in January 1953, was profoundly frustrating to millions of Americans in whose memories the unconditional victory of a short half-decade before remained fresh.

The limited war globalists experienced their own frustrations in Korea, which centered around the stubborn figure of Syngman Rhee, that reluctantly created client of the earliest cold war years. China's intervention had abruptly shattered the old man's dream of a unified Korea under his sway, and for the next two and one-half years "His bitter advocacy of reunification by force greatly increased the difficulties the administration met with during the protracted discussions between the truce teams.'' Matthew Ridgway, who presided over UN fortunes on the embattled peninsula after MacArthur's departure, developed a reluctant admiration for the fierce old autocrat. He was, after all, in his own way a patriot. "Yet we who had to deal with the military realities often found him a hair shirt.'' By suddenly releasing thousands of Communist prisoners in the spring of 1953, Rhee jeopardized the delicate prisoner-of-war negotiations that had kept the conflict raging for an entire year after resolution of all other outstanding issues, and a reading of the best history of the Korean conflict to date leaves the impression that the war might have terminated some months, if not years, earlier had not Rhee influenced events by his baleful presence and pronouncements.[53]

The end of fighting in July 1953 brought further horrors as it was revealed that possibly hundreds, perhaps thousands, of allied prisoners-of-war had been unable to withstand "the cauldron of rebirth" in the Chinese and Korean prison camps along the Chongchon and Yalu. It was a shock to see in the newsreels and on the television sets that were just coming widely into use pictures of the defiant "twenty-one who stayed" with their Communist captors. The situation in Asia had changed drastically since those simple days of 1943 and 1944 when Asians could be imagined either as bloodthirsty brutes beyond the pale of civilization or as polite little men in Western business suits mouthing democratic platitudes.

Then, too, some Americans were uneasily aware even then of the possible price of globalism. We are not, despite the barbarities of some among us, a barbaric people; but war is invariably hell. When time came to transform commitment from rhetoric to practice, would Americans be willing to pay the emotional and moral price? Ed Murrow was one who pondered this question. Returning to Tokyo from Korea in mid-August 1950, he spoke in characteristically somber voice and tone.

So far as this reporter is concerned, he doesn't see where or when this conflict will end. For this is not an isolated war, except in the purely geographic sense. It is isolated only for the men who are fighting it . . . when we start moving up through dead valleys, through villages through which we have put the torch by retreating, what then of the people who live there? They have lived on the knife-edge of despair and disaster for centuries. Their pitiful possessions have been consumed in the flames of war. Will our reoccupation of that flea-bitten land lessen, or increase, the attraction of communism?

It was symbolic of the time that Murrow's words were never to be heard. Recorded in New York for that evening's news broadcast, they were suppressed by corporation executives, who decided that they challenged MacArthur's directive barring criticism of command decisions.[54]

So it all flowed together two decades ago: the war, the stalemate, the ignorance, the recriminations, the domestic anxieties amounting nearly to hysteria, the commitment to an often dangerously simplistic—and dangerously enjoyable—globalism. Whether America's strenuous efforts to shape the course of world affairs during the 1950s and 1960s were ultimately beneficial or pernicious to the human race is not really for those of this generation to say with finality—at least not now. For such an evaluation involves not only what happened, but all that might have happened had not the United States chosen to play the role and assume the burdens that it did. Time persistently refuses to freeze for the observer's convenience, and our view of the recent past is repeatedly confounded by the thrust of the present. We can only continue to see and hear and learn and try to understand and preserve something of ourselves, our experiences, and our knowledge for a more distant time when the judgment of these years can be made without passion. But it *is* certain that what the Americans did and did not do in Asia between 1945 and 1953 laid the roots for what everyone— each in his own way—would now accept as the tragedy of Indochina.

Centuries ago Thomas Jefferson remarked that the price of liberty is eternal vigilance. We may now add to that proposition another derived from the ordeal of our own time: the price of power is eternal understanding. No nation, no individual, can meet this superhuman test. But the greatness or baseness of nations and men can be calibrated with fair consistency by the scale and frequency of their failure. By this standard the government and people of the United States must be judged to have woefully discharged the responsibilities of power which they assumed in Asia between 1945 and 1953. To plumb the depths of America's tragedy in early postwar Asia it is necessary to go beyond the realm of pure ideology, which has informed all too much of our recent historiography on the contemporary age, and to look at men. For in the final analysis ideas do not succeed or fail, men do. Abstractions are nothing without the individuals to accept or reject, manipulate or debase, formulate or implement them. When we examine the policy makers who shaped or attempted to shape America's early postwar Far Eastern programs, we find that those who understood or responded to the complex realities and tensions of their own society knew little about Asia, while those who understood something of

Asian realities were ignorant of the history and dynamics of the country which they represented. Too many American policy makers in those years forgot, if indeed they ever knew, that the first task of international politics and diplomacy is to master reality, not define it. The world must constantly be seen as it is in all its diversity and disorder and not merely as an arena within which a single, all-encompassing power struggle is played out.

By the end of 1950, however, American opinion had embraced the proposition that Asia, like Europe, had become a great battlefield of democracy and Communism. Six months after the end of fighting in Korea, Assistant Secretary of State Walter Robertson left no doubt what this country's Asia policy would be from that time forward. During a House appropriations hearing, Representative Frederic R. Goudert asked, "Did I correctly understand you to say that the heart of the present policy toward China and Formosa is that there is to be kept alive a constant threat of military action vis-à-vis Red China in the hope that at some point there will be an internal breakdown?" Robertson responded that this was indeed "my conception." "Fundamentally does that not mean that the United States is undertaking to maintain for an indefinite period of years American dominance in the Far East," Goudert continued. "Yes. Exactly," Robertson replied.[55]

But in the midst of their cold war crusade Americans refused to realize that millions of Asians had not so much rejected democracy in favor of "international Communism" as that they had chosen to reject a historically oppressive Westernism in all its guises. The Kremlin in its turn would soon discover that truth. Beneath the ostensible rhetoric and practice of a kind of Asian Marxism burned the steady, hot flame of nationalism.[56] Some words of the sensitive and perceptive Edgar Snow, written in 1961, are worth pondering:

> What is probably not comprehensible from abroad is the extent to which even anti-Communist Chinese support Peking on any *nationalistic* issue. The fact that the United States has for a decade followed a policy of armed intervention in China's affairs, that this policy has served to discredit influential Chinese on the mainland once friendly to America and has added great force to Peking's ideological attacks on imperialism—which might otherwise seem as obsolete to Chinese intellectuals as they do to Mr. Nehru—is little understood by those Americans most anxious to bring about the downfall of the Communists.[57]

By deciding between 1945 and 1953 to set its face resolutely against Asia's more radical and successful anti-Western revolutionaries and to meet the great revolt with condescension at best (as in Indonesia) and outright hostility at worst (as in China and Indochina), America seemed ready to assume the exhausted and irrelevant burden of the white man's rule which the old European colonial powers had been so recently forced to lay down. The United States appeared literally to be flying in the face of history. That this is not really what most Americans wished is the greatest tragedy of all. But it was an inevitable tragedy given America's own cast of mind. A country which in 1953 still denied its own black citizens their basic rights could not be expected to view the peoples of Asia—however repellent their current leadership—as potential equals in a worldwide search for lasting peace. A country which in 1953 continued to make racism sufficiently respectable as to cause decent men and women to assume a shamed silence whenever it appeared could not be expected to look with understanding or sympathy upon the groping but determined efforts of millions of orientals to shape their own destinies.

The leaders of the great revolt do not deserve to be romanticized; they were not gentle men. Many were brutal, callous, and contemptuous of any way to freedom from Western dominance but their own. They could exterminate without pity, remorse, or question—and often did. Their social philosophy, distinct from their political and military tactics, was crude in the extreme. Parables and precepts in the service of force are always repugnant. But in their profoundly unfree fashion they bespoke a kind of freedom to those they led. This, however, was a paradox which an unsophisticated American nation was not prepared to accept.

In 1953, as in 1943 and 1903, Americans persisted in forcing their own designs, their own hopes, and their own anxieties upon an Asia that stubbornly and rightly insisted on going its own way. James Michener summed it up in a passage from the best-selling novel of the Korean War. "I believe without question," the wise old admiral tells the bitter, doomed, retread carrier pilot, "that some morning a bunch of communist generals and commissars will be holding a meeting to discuss the future of the war. And a messenger will run in with the news that the Americans have knocked out even the bridges at Toko-ri. And that little thing will convince the Reds that we'll never stop . . . never give in . . . never weaken in our purpose."[58] A kind of political physics thus came into being, and in the tense struggle between the irresistible American force and the immovable Asian object was sparked the fires of a new calamity.

Perhaps the statesmen and generals of those far off Korean years failed to sense the shape of things to come. But the soldiers fairly guessed. Swinging down the frozen road to Hungnam that dark December of 1950, the marines who had so magnificently held back the night of disaster at the Changjin Reservoir and had brought out their guns and their vehicles and their dead in a kind of triumph, broke into defiant parody of an old British India Army song that had gained some notoriety in another, mightier war just past:

> Bless 'em all, bless 'em all,
> The Commies, the U.N. and all:
> Those slant-eyed Chink soldiers
> Struck Hagaru-ri
> And now know the meaning of U.S.M.C.
> But we're, saying goodbye to them all,
> We're Harry's police force on call.
> So put back your pack on,
> The next step is Saigon,
> Cheer up, me lads, bless 'em all![59]

NOTES

1. Stephen E. Ambrose, *Rise to Globalism: American Foreign Policy since 1938* (Baltimore: Penguin Books, 1971), pp. 192-195; I. F. Stone, *The Hidden History of the Korean War* (New York: Monthly Review Press, 1952), pp. 1-75. It should be noted that, having accepted the Stone thesis, Ambrose backs away some pages later (194-195), claiming that while circumstantial evidence is strong, "these charges go too far." Indeed, the evidence of a strong, well-coordinated North Korean offensive is so great as to command an excellent military historian to stifle his revisionist impulses.

2. Joyce and Gabriel Kolko, *The Limits of Power: The World and United States Foreign Policy, 1945-1954* (New York: Harper & Row Publishers, 1972), pp. 565-584.

3. Walter LaFeber, "Crossing the 38th: The Cold War in Microcosm," in Lynn H. Miller and Ronald W. Pruessen, eds., *Reflections on the Cold War: A Quarter Century of American Foreign Policy* (Philadelphia: Temple University Press, 1974), pp. 75-76.

4. David Rees, *Korea: The Limited War* (New York: St. Martin's Press, 1964), p. 4; Douglas MacArthur, *Reminiscences* (New York: McGraw-Hill Book

Company, 1964), p. 327; Dean Acheson, *Present at the Creation: My Years in the State Department* (New York: W. W. Norton & Co., 1969), pp. 402-404.

5. Roy E. Appleman, *South to the Naktong, North to the Yalu: United States Army in the Korean War* (Washington, D.C.: Office of the Chief of Military History, Department of the Army, 1961), p. 20.

6. Stone, *Hidden History*, pp. 40-41; Ambrose, *Rise to Globalism*, p. 192.

7. U.S. Congress, Senate, Committee on Foreign Relations, *Economic Assistance to China and Korea, 1949-1950*, 81st Cong., 1st and 2d Sess. (Washington, D.C.: U.S. Government Printing Office, 1974), pp. 175-177.

8. MacArthur, *Reminiscences*, p. 327; T. R. Fehrenbach, *This Kind of War: A Study in Unpreparedness* (New York: Giant Books, 1964), pp. 65-66.

9. *Pearl Harbor: Warning and Decision* (Stanford, Calif.: Stanford University Press, 1962).

10. Matthew B. Ridgway, *The Korean War* (Garden City, N.Y.: Doubleday & Co., 1967), p. 16.

11. Glenn D. Paige, *The Korean Decision, June 24-30, 1950* (New York: Free Press, 1968), p. 85.

12. Quoted in John M. Allison, *Ambassador from the Prairie* (Boston: Houghton Mifflin Company, 1973), p. 131.

13. Ibid.

14. Ibid., p. 137.

15. Paige, *Korean Decision*, pp. 105-161 passim.

16. Ibid., pp. 253-268; Martin Lichterman, "To the Yalu and Back," in Harold Stein, ed., *American Civil and Military Decisions: A Book of Case Studies* (Birmingham, Ala.: University of Alabama Press, 1963), p. 581. MacArthur on his own initiative ordered immediate attacks by the air force on targets in North as well as South Korea, thereby initiating a pattern of insubordination that was eventually to bring his downfall.

17. George Kennan summed up Washington's Korean consensus some years later. "It was clear to me from the start that we would have to react with all necessary force to repel this attack and to expel the North Korean forces from the southern half of the peninsula. I took this position unequivocally on that first day and in all discussions that followed over the ensuing days and weeks. I also took occasion to emphasize, that first occasion and on a number of others, that we would now have to take prompt steps to assure that Formosa, too, did not fall into Communist hands; for two such reverses coming one on the heels of the other, could easily prove disastrous to our prestige and to our entire position in the Far East." *Memoirs, 1925-1950* (New York: Bantam Books, 1969), pp. 512-513. The President was characteristically blunt about the matter. "He would not, said Mr. Truman to persons within hearing, let the United States and its President be pushed around. And he would not let the United Nations be pushed around."

Arthur Krock column of 1 July 1950, reprinted in Krock, *In the Nation, 1932-1966* (New York: Paperback Library, 1969), p. 200.

18. Charles E. Bohlen, *Witness to History, 1929-1969* (New York: W. W. Norton & Co., 1973), p. 294.

19. Robert A. Scalapino and Chong-Sik Lee, *Communism in Korea*, 2 parts (Berkeley: University of California Press, 1972), part 1, pp. 394-395. Khrushchev has written that at the end of 1949 Kim Il-sung went to Moscow and told Stalin that the North Koreans wanted to "prod South Korea with the point of a bayonet." The first poke would touch off internal revolt in the South, Kim maintained. "Naturally Stalin couldn't oppose this idea. It appealed to his convictions as a Communist all the more because the struggle would be an internal matter which the Koreans would be settling among themselves." Nonetheless Stalin was sufficiently cautious as to urge Kim to "think it over" and return to Moscow with a concrete plan. When Kim returned to Russia, "He told Stalin he was absolutely certain of success." Stalin continued to entertain doubts and worried about a possible American intervention. But "we were inclined to think that if the war were fought swiftly—and Kim Il-sung was sure that it could be won swiftly—then intervention by the USA could be avoided." *Khrushchev Remembers* (New York: Bantam Books, 1971), pp. 400-401. Khrushchev's remarks suggest that at the very least the North Koreans put enormous pressure on an always reluctant Stalin to let them have their way.

20. Scalapino and Lee, *Communism in Korea*, part 1, p. 394; Paige, *Korean Decision*, p. 129. Among the histories of the Korean War are: Rees, *Korea: The Limited War*; Fehrenbach, *This Kind of War*; Walter Karig, *Battle Report: The War in Korea* (New York: Rinehart and Co., 1952); Appleman, *South to the Naktong, North to the Yalu*; Walter G. Hermes, *Truce Tent and Fighting Front* (Washington, D.C.: Department of the Army, 1966); James F. Schnabel, *Policy and Direction: The First Year* (Washington, D.C.: Department of the Army, 1972); Ridgway, *The Korean War*; and, for the period until his relief, MacArthur, *Reminiscences*.

21. Maurice Matloff, ed., *American Military History*, Army Historical Series (Washington, D.C.: Office of the Chief of Military History, 1969), pp. 553-555.

22. Quoted in Rees, *Korea: The Limited War*, p. 83.

23. The MacArthur briefing of the Huber congressional committee is printed in U.S. Department of State, *Foreign Relations of the United States, 1949*, 9 vols. (Washington, D.C.: U.S. Government Printing Office, 1974-), 9:544-546.

24. Kennan, *Memoirs*, pp. 515-516.

25. David S. McLellan, "Dean Acheson and the Korean War," *Political Science Quarterly* 83 (March 1968): 17; Lichterman, "To the Yalu and Back," p. 584. Walter LaFeber, in a recent essay, argues: "One of the most striking aspects of the decision" to extend the war beyond the thirty-eighth parallel "was that it was made during July and August, when the military situation in South Korea was

exceedingly grim for the United Nations forces.'' LaFeber points to the vagueness of language embodied in the UN resolution of 27 June requesting members to help repel North Korean aggression so that peace and security could be restored "to the area,'' the "area'' in question being not confined as it had been to the region south of the thirty-eighth parallel in the earlier resolution of 25 June. LaFeber then adduces further, circumstantial evidence regarding American policy toward Formosa, Indochina, Western Europe, and the atomic bomb to support his contention that Acheson and Truman used the war as an instrument and an excuse to expand American power and commitments to global proportions during the summer and autumn of 1950. If one admits the sense of sincere outrage on the part of leading American officials over the unprovoked attack by North Korea and their concern that it could presage a global pattern of limited war against the "free world,'' the argument has merit. LaFeber, "Crossing the 38th,'' pp. 75-82.

26. Kennan, *Memoirs*, pp. 515-516; Bohlen, *Witness to History*, pp. 292-293.

27. McLellan, "Dean Acheson and the Korean War,'' pp. 22-30.

28. Bohlen writes that when he informed French Foreign Minister Robert Schuman of Truman's initial decision to intervene in Korea, "Schuman's eyes filled with tears. 'Thank God,' he said, 'this will not be a repetition of the past.' He was thinking of the French and British failures to stop Hitler before World War II.'' *Witness to History*, pp. 291-292.

29. Richard Neustadt, *Presidential Power: The Politics of Leadership* (New York: Signet Books, 1960), pp. 120-130; Harry S. Truman, *Memoirs*, 2 vols. (New York: Signet Books, 1965), vol. 2: *Years of Trial and Hope, 1946-1952*, p. 410; Lichterman, "To the Yalu and Back,'' pp. 586, 594-595. The vote in the General Assembly was forty-seven to five, the five negative votes coming from the Soviet bloc. France and the other Western nations "took a strong stand that the 38th parallel should not serve as a barrier to protect the North Korean aggressors and that the opportunity had now come to implement the UN's political goals in Korea by armed force.''

30. Acheson, *Present at the Creation*, pp. 407-408.

31. Edgar Snow, *The Other Side of the River: Red China Today* (New York: Random House, 1962), p. 88 (italics his).

32. Allen S. Whiting, *China Crosses the Yalu: The Decision to Enter the Korean War*, The RAND Corporation, 1960 (Stanford, Calif.: Stanford University Press, 1968), pp. 68-90.

33. Quoted in ibid., p. 93.

34. Quoted in Truman, *Years of Trial and Hope*, p. 411.

35. Quoted in Neustadt, *Presidential Power*, pp. 124-125. David McLellan's study, "Dean Acheson and the Korean War,'' fully substantiates Truman's assertion that Washington deferred fully and foolishly to MacArthur's repeated assurances and stands condemned, along with the general, of underestimating Chinese

power and intent while relying upon a military solution to a political problem in the unification of Korea.

36. See especially John W. Spanier, *The Truman-MacArthur Controversy and the Korean War* (Cambridge: Harvard University Press, 1959) and the excellent discussion in Rees, *Korea: The Limited War*, pp. 115-229 passim.

37. Merle Miller, *Plain Speaking: An Oral Biography of Harry S. Truman* (New York: Berkley Publishing Co., 1974), pp. 294-295. Cabell Phillips had earlier recounted this incident: *The Truman Presidency: The History of a Triumphant Succession* (Baltimore: Penguin Books, 1969), pp. 319-320. John P. Roche, on the basis of conversations with both Truman and Richard Neustadt, claims that there was no quibbling over landing rights, nor did MacArthur keep Truman waiting, but that the general's appearance and demeanor were so slovenly as to offend the chief executive beyond recall. John Roche, review of *Plain Speaking*, in *Saturday Review—World*, 23 February 1974, p. 21. MacArthur makes no mention of any conflict whatsoever in his *Reminiscences*.

38. Phillips, *Truman Presidency*, pp. 320-321; MacArthur, *Reminiscences*, pp. 360-364; Truman, *Years of Trial and Hope*, pp. 414-425.

39. *Khrushchev Remembers*, pp. 405-406.

40. A superb account of this period and of the Eighth Army's subsequent ordeal is S. L. A. Marshall, *The River and the Gauntlet: The Defeat of the Eighth Army in the Battle of the Chongchon, November-December, 1950* (New York: William Morrow & Co., 1953).

41. *Witness to History*, p. 303.

42. *Memoirs*, p. 524 (italics his).

43. Quoted in Alexander Kendrick, *Prime Time: The Life of Edward R. Murrow* (New York: Avon Books, 1970), p. 367.

44. Ibid., p. 376.

45. *Public Papers of the Presidents: Harry S. Truman, January 1 to December 31, 1951* (Washington, D.C.: U.S. Government Printing Office, 1965), p. 303.

46. Bohlen, *Witness to History*, pp. 303-304.

47. Acheson, *Present at the Creation*, pp. 562-568, 674. Doubtless Bohlen was unaware of the fact that by early 1952, although the British and the French recoiled from the idea, the Joint Chiefs of Staff had advocated unilateral intervention with air and naval forces in Indochina should Peking decide to assault that unhappy neck of land. "NSC Staff Study on United States Objectives and Courses of Action with Respect to Communist Aggression in Southeast Asia [NSC 124]," in U.S. Department of Defense, *United States-Vietnam Relations, 1945-1967*, 12 vols. (Washington, D.C.: U.S. Government Printing Office, 1971), 8:468-493, especially p. 488.

48. This document has been reprinted many times; I have used the text published in the U.S. Department of State *Bulletin* 16 (23 March 1947):536-537.

49. Arthur Krock, "A New Foreign Policy," *New York Times*, 22 March 1947, reprinted in Krock, *In the Nation*, p. 191.

50. Kennan republished "Mr. X" in *American Diplomacy, 1900-1950* (New York: Mentor Books, 1952), pp. 89-106; the above quotation is on p. 101.

51. Walter Lippmann, *The Cold War: A Study in U.S. Foreign Policy* (New York: Harper & Brothers Publishers, 1947), p. 15.

52. "Memorandum by the Consular [*sic*] of the Department of State (Bohlen), August 30, 1947," in U.S. Department of State, *Foreign Relations of the United States, 1947*, 8 vols. (Washington, D.C.: U.S. Government Printing Office, 1972-1973), 1:763-765.

53. Ridgway, *Korean War*, p. 156; Rees, *Korea: The Limited War*, pp. 284, 416-429. Recently declassified documents indicate that on at least two occasions in 1952 and 1953 the Joint Chiefs of Staff and the State Department seriously considered removing Rhee by means of a coup because of Rhee's intolerable domestic political repressions. *New York Times*, 4 August 1975, p. 1.

54. Kendrick, *Prime Time*, pp. 370-371.

55. Quoted in Snow, *Other Side of the River*, p. 631.

56. See Richard H. Solomon's remarkable study, *Mao's Revolution and the Chinese Political Culture* (Berkeley: University of California Press, 1971).

57. Snow, *Other Side of the River*, pp. 86-87 (italics his).

58. James A. Michener, *The Bridges at Toko-ri* (New York: Bantam Books, 1955), p. 28.

59. Quoted in Fehrenbach, *This Kind of War*, p. 394.

A Note on Sources

As I have suggested in the preface, this work is an exploratory essay on a vast topic, not an exhaustive, finished inquiry. I have therefore relied heavily, though far from exclusively, on published primary and secondary sources.

Primary materials, particularly for the post-1946 period, came largely from the rich documentation found in the relevant volumes of the *Foreign Relations* series, 1945-1949, compiled by the Historical Office, U.S. Department of State; *United States Relations with China with Special Reference to the Period 1944-1949*, issued by the State Department in 1949 and reprinted as *China White Paper*, 2 vols. (Stanford, Calif.: Stanford University Press, 1967); and the twelve-volume study issued by the U.S. Department of Defense in 1971, entitled *United States-Vietnam Relations, 1945-1967*, the so-called "Pentagon Papers" in their most complete form. In addition, there has been a veritable flood of studies and testimonies issued by the U.S. Congress, particularly in recent years, dealing with the multitude of problems faced and finessed by the Truman administration and Congress during the late 1940s and early 1950s. Among the most useful and pertinent of these congressional studies and hearings are: U.S. Congress, Senate, *United States-China Relations: Hearings before the Committee on Foreign Relations*, 92d Cong., 1st Sess. (1971); U.S. Congress, Senate, *China and the United States Today and Yesterday: Hearings before the Committee on Foreign Relations*, 92d Cong., 2d Sess. (1972); U.S. Congress, Senate, *United States Relations with the People's Republic of China: Hearings before the Committee on Foreign Relations*, 92d Cong., 1st Sess. (1972); U.S. Congress, Senate, *Military Situation in the Far East, August 1951: Hearings before the Committee on Armed Services and the Committee on Foreign Relations*, 82d Cong., 1st Sess. (1951); U.S. Congress, Senate, *Causes, Origins, and Lessons of the Vietnam War: Hearings before the Committee on Foreign Relations*, 92d Cong., 2d Sess. (1973); U.S. Congress, House, *Background Information on Korea: Report of the Committee on Foreign Affairs Pursuant to H. Res. 206*, 81st Cong., 2d Sess. (1950); U.S. Congress, Senate, Committee on the Judiciary, *The Amerasia Papers: A Clue to the Catastrophe of China*, 91st Cong., 2d Sess., 2 vols. (1970); U.S. Congress, Senate, Committee on Foreign Relations, *Economic Assistance to China and Korea, 1949-1950*, 81st Cong., 1st and 2d Sess. (1974); and U.S. Congress, Senate, Committee on Foreign Relations Staff Study, *The United States and Communist China in 1949 and 1950: The Question of Rapprochement and Recognition*, 92d Cong., 2d Sess. (1973).

Finally, the monthly series, *Summation* [of] *United States Army Military Government Activities in Korea*, published by General Headquarters, Commander-in-Chief, United States Army Forces, Pacific, from October 1945 through July 1948, provides an invaluable report and narrative of political, economic, and social developments in southern Korea throughout the occupation era.

Among the manuscript collections used in this study, two proved to be indispensable: Records of the Department of State, Lot 54 D 109, Philippine and Southeast Asian Affairs Files, 1943-1948, and Lot 53 D 246, French-Iberian Affairs Files, Operating Records of the French Desk, 1940-1946, both housed at time of examination in the "Main State" Building, U.S. Department of State, Washington, D.C. Other State Department manuscript files consulted include Record Group 84, 710 Series, Foreign Service Post File (Chungking) for 1945, and central files 893.00, the basic China file, and 740.00119 PW, which includes telegraphic traffic and documentation from various American posts in the Soviet Union, both for the period of the 1946 Marshall mission, all in the National Archives, Washington, D.C. Supplementary manuscript material was culled from the Harry S. Truman Official File and the Samuel I. Rosenman Papers, both for 1945-1946, at the Harry S. Truman Library, Independence, Missouri, and from the William D. Leahy and Tom Connally Papers, Library of Congress.

The most useful of the several hundred memoirs and secondary sources consulted in the preparation of this study are cited at least several times throughout the footnotes, attesting to their importance and to the need not to be cited again.

Index